T0266966

MIRACLE MOMENTS
IN
NOTRE DAME
FIGHTING IRISH
FOOTBALL HISTORY

BEST PLAYS, GAMES, AND RECORDS

Michael R. Steele

SPORTS
PUBLISHING

Sports Publishing books may be purchased in bulk at special discounts for sales promotion, corporate gifts, fund-raising, or educational purposes. Special editions can also be created to specifications. For details, contact the Special Sales Department, Sports Publishing, 307 West 36th Street, 11th Floor, New York, NY 10018 or sportspubbooks@skyhorsepublishing.com.

Sports Publishing® is a registered trademark of Skyhorse Publishing, Inc.®, a Delaware corporation.

Visit our website at www.sportspubbooks.com.

10 9 8 7 6 5 4

Library of Congress Cataloging-in-Publication Data is available on file.

Cover design by Tom Lau
Cover photo credit: Associated Press

All interior photos courtesy of University of Notre Dame archives, unless otherwise noted

ISBN: 978-1-68358-437-7
Ebook ISBN: 978-1-68358-187-1

Printed in China

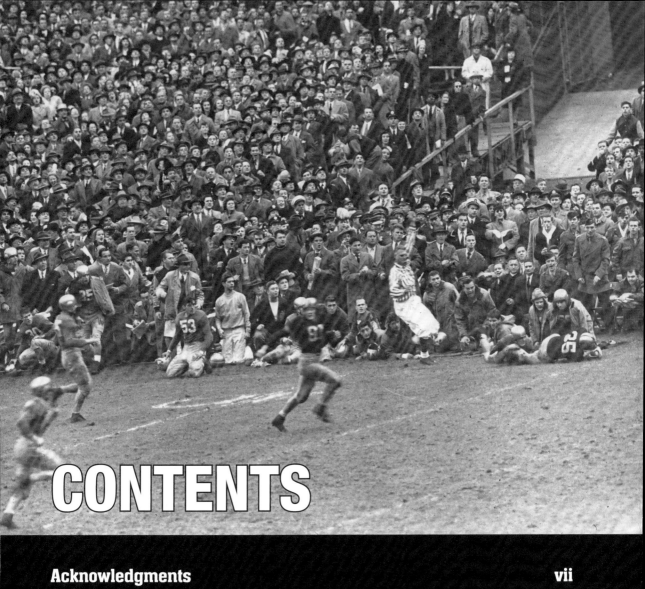

CONTENTS

ACKNOWLEDGMENTS

While the act of writing is typically a very lonesome task, no book comes into the world from one hand alone. In the final analysis, books are the products of team play, very much like the touchdown scored on a long run or pass. The player scoring the touchdown gets the glory, but behind that scintillating play are the coaches, hours and hours of practices, strength conditioning, watching game films, and the sheer beauty of the intricate teamwork by eleven players needed for a given play to result in the score.

So it is here. My wonderful life partner, Gerianne, has somehow put up with my addiction to Notre Dame and its football teams for more than thirty years. She makes sure that the televised games are recorded for later viewing and analysis, that obscure stats emerge from the labyrinth of the Internet, assists with the minutiae of writing, and soothes my wounded ego when the Irish don't win an important game. She hails from Louisiana and roots for the LSU Tigers, except when they play the Irish! The 2018 Citrus Bowl matchup between Notre Dame and LSU was no problem for her. She was not torn, and we both rejoiced when the Irish scored the winning TD.

Ken Samelson, senior editor for Skyhorse Publishing, has been a thoughtful, insightful, and solid supporter of this project from the day that he proposed it to me. He is a skillful editor who avoids putting speed bumps in the way of the writers with whom he works. I am very thankful to have the opportunity to work with him.

Fellow Domer Cappy Gagnon, whose entire adult life has been deeply intertwined with the university we love, has been a very helpful source of information and connections that I had not been able to develop, lacking his decades of experience under the Dome. Thank you, Cappy, and I wish you all the best as you continue your research into some of the past figures lost to today's generation of Irish fans.

Another Notre Dame figure, Charles Lamb, who serves as the Senior Archivist for Photograph and Audio-Visual Collections at Notre Dame's Hesburgh Library, has been an invaluable source of information in my work over the years. He is a talented author in his own right, having done considerable work on a fascinating book he coauthored—*Notre Dame at 175: A Visual History*. Someone in my position simply could not have a better source of information than Charles on the many facets of the Notre Dame story. I am deeply obliged to him for his patience and unbelievably keen ability to find even the most obscure item regarding the university.

Keith Buckley, the head football coach at Pacific University and a close friend for several years, was instrumental in providing his expertise in analyzing film footage of several key plays in Notre Dame's illustrious football history. Keith has always been willing to share information on play execution and tactics. He is an outstanding educator and mentor for his players. I have followed his program's success very carefully and can affirm that Coach Buckley fields players who are mature, thoughtful classroom leaders. Our university is a much better place because of Coach Buckley and the young men he leads.

Notre Dame's head coach, Brian Kelly, very kindly put me in touch with key figures involved in a 2015 miracle play against Wake Forest. His thoughtful gesture resulted in a level of authenticity from those involved that is rare in such projects. Thank you, Coach Kelly.

From the Fighting Irish Athletics Communications office, I must mention Carol Copley. Carol is the senior staff assistant for one of the busiest sports information operations in the world. She has helped me with this and other projects over the years. She is always cheerful and accommodating. Carol has surely contributed to the work of countless writers who deal with the intricacies of the sports scene at Notre Dame. I look forward to a continued professional relationship with her. Thank you, Carol!

Finally, I must mention my children—Erica, Jared, Matt, and Sean. They have had to put up with my addiction/love/commitment to Notre Dame … including frightening Sean when he was not quite two years old when I jumped up and cheered an Irish TD while he was napping nearby. Sorry, Sean. I think you have recovered from the trauma. They are great children, all with families of their own now. I am very proud of them and love them with all of my Irish heart!

Go Irish!

INTRODUCTION

For over 125 years, young men have donned football gear and uniforms in order to play the game of football while representing the University of Notre Dame. The beginnings of Irish football were modest, to say the least, but the brilliant endeavors of the players and coaches eventually captured and held the attention of the whole nation as the Fighting Irish took on all comers, ultimately playing the first coast-to-coast schedule (1926), and in the process becoming the first college football team to be a *nationally* recognized power. The rest is history.

The University of Notre Dame, founded in 1842 by a visionary French priest of the Congregation of the Holy Cross, Father Edward Sorin, is dedicated to the Holy Mother, Mary. Perhaps its very existence as an institution of higher learning is a bit of a miracle in itself. There was little but hope and dreams in the cold of North Central Indiana when Sorin took the incredible risk of declaring a humble log cabin to be the site of a university. The fledgling institution hung on, however, and even overcame the loss of its main building to a devastating fire in 1879, merely eight years before the school fielded its first football team. The replacement building still stands and is universally recognized as "The Golden Dome." (Irish alumni call themselves "Domers.") Given its rich Catholic roots, one should not be surprised that the school's fervent students and fans look to the skies in the "Notre Dame Victory March":

Cheer, cheer for old Notre Dame,
Wake up the echoes cheering her name,
Send a volley cheer on high,
Shake down the thunder from the sky.
What though the odds be great or small
Old Notre Dame will win over all,
While her loyal sons are marching
Onward to victory!

And many an opponent has wondered about those skies, what with all the prayers that apparently ascend to the heavens from countless nuns, priests, Catholic high schoolers, "subway alumni," Irish students, and the players and coaches. Surely, now and then a prayer is heard and a seemingly divine intervention changes the course of a given Notre Dame play, or a game, even a season (see the Irish win in the 2018 Citrus Bowl against LSU, for example).

The school's rise to prominence in football signaled a definite shift away from the dominance of the eastern colleges that had characterized the first six decades of intercollegiate football. The Irish also used changes in the rules of football after 1906 to help popularize that baffling new tactic—the forward pass. With a balding, twenty-five-year-old Norwegian immigrant as team captain, the Irish defeated a heavily favored Army team in 1913 by a convincing 35–13 score. That immigrant, Knute Rockne, would go on to become the most famous coach in the annals of intercollegiate football, amassing a stunning record of 105 wins, 12 losses, and five ties from 1918 to 1930, a winning percentage of .881 that still ranks at the top of the list three quarters of a century after his tragic death at age forty-three. (For comparative purposes, Rockne nudges out Notre Dame's fiery Frank Leahy, who knocked off opponents at an impressive .855 clip. Of today's top coaches, Urban Meyer comes close with a winning percentage of .851. The immortal Bear Bryant's winning percentage, .780, was a full 100 points lower than Rockne's. Alabama's Nick Saban wins at a .781 rate. As you can see, trying to match Rockne's record is not for the faint of heart.)

There have been countless miracles involving the Fighting Irish. Notre Dame has had twenty-three undefeated seasons, eleven national championships, and seven Heisman winners. As of 2017, the school's football team has produced more than 250 players honored as All-Americans 297 times, 85 consensus All-Americans 101 times, and more than 500 players on active rosters of professional teams. Four players have won the Walter Camp Award and three the Outland Trophy. Seven have won the Maxwell Award. Six coaches have been inducted into the College Hall of Fame as have forty-six Irish players. The Irish have pulled off major upsets, and they have suffered them as well. Their players who have been season leaders in rushing, passing, receiving, and other categories constitute a Who's Who of college football players. The following chapters will flesh out the stories, but here are some previews of what's to follow:

1887: The first team to give it a try for old Notre Dame.

1903: The first Irish team to play a full schedule, undefeated and unscored upon.

1918–20: The George Gipp years—winning 21, losing one, tying two under Rockne.

1922–24: The Four Horsemen years—winning 27, losing two, tying one.

1929–30: Rockne's last two teams, undefeated at 19–0.

1931: Rockne's tragic death.

1943: Undefeated national champs; Angelo Bertelli wins Heisman.

1946: The famous 0–0 tie against Army.

1947: Undefeated national champs; Johnny Lujack wins Heisman.

1948: Undefeated season.

1949: Undefeated national champs; Leon Hart wins Heisman.

1953: Leahy's last team; undefeated season; John Lattner wins Heisman.

1956: Paul Hornung wins Heisman despite Irish's terrible 2–8 season.

1964: Ara Parseghian's first year; John Huarte wins Heisman.

1966: Undefeated national champs.

1973: Undefeated national champs highlighted by Eric Penick's 85-yard TD run vs. USC and Tom Clements's game-saving pass to Robin Weber to beat Alabama.

1977: National champs.

1979: All-time comeback—down 34–12 to Houston with six minutes left in the Cotton Bowl, they win, 35–34, led by Joe Montana.

1987: Tim Brown wins Heisman.

1988: National champs.

2006: Jeff Samardzija's game-winning catch vs. UCLA.

Miraculous plays by Eric Penick, Rocket Ismail, Tim Brown, Josh Adams, and Miles Boykin.

Miracles are a hard thing to prove. They essentially mean that the normal order of the known universe is temporarily suspended, revealing a different reality for one sparkling moment. Can such be the case for an entire season? For those who pay close attention to the tendencies and history, a full season of miracles might be asking too much. Such, however, might have been the case when the Irish hired a new coach in late 1963, Northwestern's Ara Parseghian, following an utterly dismal 2–7 1963 season. Parseghian worked motivational magic on the team, making the players believe in themselves, moved some players around to different positions, and inserted a large group of promising sophomores to bring the Irish to the brink of the 1964 national championship. Was it a miracle? Or sheer hard work and a much better use of the talent on hand? Or perhaps the miracle operated on a micro level, a block sustained here to nullify a defensive player for a split second, a fingertip catch there, a runner juking a defender at precisely the right moment to create a long gain. Such small, barely noticeable miracles can add up, or they can be packaged into a frenetic, unbelievable six minutes of a game such as the 1979 Cotton Bowl, with Notre Dame trailing Houston, 34–12. Enter Joe Montana. The rest is history. Yes, miracles *can* happen!

PART I

EARLY MIRACLES

John Farley's Miraculous Record

We have all heard that records are made to be broken. Having said that, there are some records that will be very, very difficult to break: Joe DiMaggio's hitting streak, Wilt Chamberlain's 100 points in an NBA game, Cy Young's 511 career wins in major league baseball, and Knute Rockne's career winning percentage. And some records reside in total obscurity, for various reasons. Irish football player John Farley, who competed for Notre Dame from 1897 to 1900, most likely holds a record for his school that may never be broken, but it is also totally obscure.

The science of keeping accurate records in sports did not reach maturity until well into the twentieth century, and is still evolving, as anyone who follows major league baseball knows. In collegiate football, uniform and accurate records were not guaranteed until the 1940s. For this reason, John Farley's heroics on the gridiron will never be officially recognized. His feats were reported, yes, but sports journalists in the late nineteenth century were not trained statisticians. Nevertheless, even allowing for a touch of hyperbole, John Farley did something spectacular that ought to be recognized.

Hailing from Paterson, New Jersey, Farley enrolled at Notre Dame in 1897. He played end for the Irish in the era of mass play. Not blessed with a large frame, at 5-foot-9 and 160 pounds, he would have to use guile and toughness to stay competitive. But he had another qualification that made him stand out—blazing speed. In the ninth season that Notre Dame fielded a football team, this freshman would use that speed in the third game of the season, on October 28, against Chicago Dental Surgeons. (Obviously, Notre Dame was then nowhere close to the nationally known football power that it became

John Farley's 1897 single-game rushing record may never be broken.

two decades later. Most of the thirty games played to date were either at home or within a 250-mile radius of the campus.)

Perhaps the would-be dentists were sleepy from their studies because they seem to have overlooked the speedy freshman left end, who romped through them for 184 yards in the first half alone. In the second half, Farley turned on the jets for 280 more yards, including TD bursts of 25 and 50 yards, to go with an 85-yard frolic on a "backward pass" play. His rushing yardage for this one game reached a stunning total of 464 yards.

Keep in mind that this yardage was compiled by a freshman playing left end. Coach Frank Hering apparently knew well how to take advantage of a player's skill set. There were no legal forward passes in those days, so Farley's forays into and through the hapless dentists had to be executed as reverses, inside fakes and the like. Mass play lent itself to losing track of a player with Farley's speed.

John Farley, like another end who played a few years later under the Dome, never left Notre Dame. He played three more seasons and was on the 1900 team that Red Salmon played for as a freshman. After he graduated, Farley studied to be a priest, joining the Congregation of the Holy Cross in 1907. He served the school's students as a dorm rector and helped coach interhall football, teaming up with Knute Rockne to coach the Corby Hall intramural team in 1910. He became rector in other halls as well and came to be known as "Pop" by the students. After suffering a stroke in 1937, he lost a leg and spent his remaining years in the Holy Cross infirmary. How ironic that a man who holds the unofficial single-game rushing record for the Fighting Irish would become an amputee.

His heartbreaking final days, however, do nothing to remove the luster from his amazing feat running with the football accomplished some forty years earlier.

Red Salmon and the 1903 Season

Louis J. "Red" Salmon, by today's standards, was an undersized fullback for Notre Dame. He stood 5-foot-10 and weighed 175 pounds for his senior season in 1903. Although there had been some fairly large players for the Irish in prior seasons, the 1903 squad had only one starter who weighed more than 200 pounds.

Salmon was in his fourth season for the Irish that year. He started as the left halfback in 1900 but switched to fullback for his final three campaigns. From all accounts, he was an utterly fearless player, totally committed to "bucking" the line when called upon to do so. Bucking the line was simple … basically, it was a fullback dive play. The runner had to have total confidence that his linemen would neutralize the defenders, opening something that resembled a hole in the line to blast through. Failing that, there was always Plan B: the fullback would have to make his own hole—through, under, or over the defenders. The faint of heart need not apply.

Prior to the 1903 season, Notre Dame had fielded fourteen teams, starting with 1887 and their very first game, a losing effort against Michigan. In those fourteen campaigns the Irish had compiled a respectable, if modest, .689 winning percentage with 51 wins, 21 losses, and seven ties. In that span, the team played a mixture of recognizable teams that are still with us but quite a few outfits that have gone to their greater reward, at least in terms of intercollegiate football. Nevertheless, as the 1903 season loomed the Irish could boast of four previous wins against Michigan State (then MAC—Michigan Agricultural College), three victories over Indiana, two wins against Northwestern, and a single win against Purdue. The best full season the Irish enjoyed to that point was Salmon's sophomore campaign, 1901, during which the team posted an impressive 8–1–1 record, including back-to-back wins against in-state rivals Indiana and Purdue.

This was football at the end of its initial incarnation, not distinctively different from the game played in 1874 between Canada's McGill University and Harvard (Princeton and Rutgers had played in 1869, but that game was more like soccer). It was a brutal game being played with pitifully ineffective equipment, emphasizing "mass play," which is exactly what the phrase described—piles and scrums of players, virtually indistinguishable from each other, with some poor guy "running" with the ball exclusively. For the spectators, it must have been a visually unappealing spectacle, unless the runner somehow managed to bust out of the scrum and break loose for a long gainer. The prevailing tactics, combined with primitive equipment, almost guaranteed that injury rates would be high. A few seasons after Salmon's senior year, President Theodore Roosevelt, alarmed by some well-publicized deaths caused by the violent tactics of the day, forced collegiate authorities to come up with a safer version of the game. Under this pressure from the president, a rules change that allowed for the forward pass came into effect in 1906, but few coaches or teams fully integrated the newfangled idea into their game plans.

This is all to say that Red Salmon, the captain of both the 1902 and 1903 Irish squads, was still playing the version of the game inherited from the 1880s and 1890s. His flaming red hair matched the flair with which he played the game. He was a fiery leader, exhorting his teammates to play at their very best; he simply never took off a play. His intensity led him to be the scoring leader for Notre Dame for more than three quarters of a century (and his TDs counted for fewer points than today). In 1903, Salmon scored 105 points—a mark that held until 1984. His 36 career TDs and 250 career points scored stayed as Irish records until 1984 and 1985 respectively.

His individual heroics took the Irish to the school's first undefeated season. On top of that, no team scored on them. Nine games, nine shutouts—a record that will certainly stand for perpetuity. Notre Dame amassed 291 points to zilch. Only Northwestern marred the season, escaping with a 0–0 tie in a game played in Chicago at the site of the White Stockings' baseball games, South Side Park. Charles Comiskey had built this park a few years before the 1903 football game; it seated 15,000 in wooden stands … a sign that collegiate football was becoming more prominent.

As captain and coach, Red Salmon led an undefeated 1903 Irish squad.

Of course, this was one-platoon football, so Salmon was playing two ways. In this 0–0 tie, the Irish punting game twice went badly awry, with punts that gave the ball to the Wildcats at the Notre Dame 2-yard line and the 5-yard line. The Irish defense, with Salmon's fierce play leading the way, stuffed Northwestern's scoring efforts to avoid a loss.

For his stellar senior season, Red Salmon became Notre Dame's first All-American, in the considered opinion of Walter Camp, who bestowed upon him third-team status—Notre Dame's first miracle player.

Many more were to follow.

The Greatest: George Gipp

This book is being written one hundred years after a man named George Gipp first suited up in the fall of 1917 to represent the University of Notre Dame in an inter-collegiate football game. His coach that first year was the estimable Jesse Harper, in his last season as the school's head football coach and athletic director. After Harper left Notre Dame, his replacement was Knute Rockne, the tough little Norwegian immigrant who starred in the 1913 upset of mighty Army.

The passage of a century can make the brightest star in the firmament lose some of its luster. In the curious case of George Gipp, there is the statistical record of his achievements, many of which are still to be found in the Irish record books. These are facts. There is another dimension, however, to the case of Gipp, arguably the best football player ever to play for Notre Dame. There are the facts, yes, and then there are the myths. The George Gipp we have come to know is a curious amalgamation of the facts and the mythology that has sprung up around his memory, some of which may be attributed to Rockne's fertile imagination. There are several sources for the myths: (1) Rockne himself, (2) Hollywood's cinematic treatment of his memory, and (3) the needs of the American consuming public … the culture itself.

A strong case can be made that Knute Rockne and George Gipp were the original odd couple. Only seven years older than Gipp and only recently graduated from Notre Dame a few years earlier before Gipp enrolled, Rockne was a driven man, driven to succeed academically but also in a difficult sport for someone not blessed with amazing physical skills like those possessed by Gipp. Rockne was fast, yes, but that was about it physically. He was undersized and came to take pride in creating and coaching undersized teams—as seen in the average weight of the nearly unbeatable Four Horsemen (158 pounds) or an All-American guard in 1930 named Bert Metzger—all 152 pounds of him. It was Rockne against the football world, driven to succeed on the field and in the classroom, then driven to succeed as a head coach. His mark is still to be found on the sport of football, and it is the mark of his brilliant mind as he contemplated how to create tactical advantages for his team—play by play, game by game, season by season, from 1918 until 1930. It was said that he coached in inches and his record would seem to support the contention. No detail was too small to be ignored—and he was doing this long before all of the technological advantages that coaching staffs enjoy today.

George Gipp's sparkling star illuminated the sports world's firmament for only four years. He never lived long enough to have a pro career in any of the emerging professional sports (he had hoped to go into pro baseball), dying at age twenty-five in December 1920 shortly after his final game for the Irish. His reputation was immense at the time, but because the facts were relatively limited in terms of chronology, he is more or less trapped in the amber of culture … fixed in ways over the ensuing years that he could not have imagined—or liked.

If Rockne was the epitome of the man driven to succeed, paying attention to the smallest details, his younger counterpart was almost totally indifferent, curiously diffident about the scene around him. Gipp certainly had a main compulsion: competition, using his wit and physical skills to win on the field, in the pool hall, in a card game. He liked the challenge of the process more so than the end product, the actual matchup between scheming minds and physical talents. Former Irish Athletic Director Moose Krause once told me of a story he had heard from Gipp's teammates from a decade or more before Moose arrived in South Bend as a freshman. The team was on a long train ride to an away game and some card sharks had wiped out the novice Notre Dame players that were dumb enough to dive into games of chance. The captain went looking for Gipp and found him asleep in another car. He woke him up, told him of the situation, and Gipp went to the defense of his teammates. He found the card sharks and took them on by himself, winning back all the lost money in short order and returning it to his thankful Irish buddies. Beyond the field of honor and the smoky pool halls, he did not seem to have a plan for his life. He must have been a serious challenge for Rockne, who saw Gipp's many gifts and promptly set about making him the centerpiece of a dominating Irish football team. But there was a trade-off for the neophyte coach: he would also have to devote far more attention to his player off the field than on it. Gipp was clearly *the* Notre Dame star, especially from 1918 to 1920 (a broken leg curtailed his freshman action in 1917), the latter two seasons undefeated, but he must have been a very high maintenance star for the young coach. There are credible tales from eyewitnesses who saw Rockne prowling the streets of South Bend looking for his wayward star, finding him in some less-than-desirable place, then shepherding him to the campus, away from the bad influences of the gamblers and pool sharks who lurked in the downtown shadows. Gipp seems to have kept his own practice schedule, showing up three weeks later than his teammates one season. It is not to be discounted that this amazing talent was never elected captain by the players he led on the field. They knew they could absolutely count on him in a crisis within a game of football, but they probably could not count on him in the other areas where team discipline is a priority. They knew their man.

Rockne never relied on one superstar again. One was enough.

On the other hand, there can be no doubt that Gipp was perfectly capable of leaving an indelible mark on an opposing team. In 1920, for example, Gipp annihilated Army with 480 all-purpose yards—rushing, passing, and returning kicks. Charlie Daly, the Army head coach, not so affectionately said of him, "He's no football player. He's a runaway sonofabitch." It is not an overstatement to say that Gipp could do it all. He could run, pass, punt, kick, snag interceptions, tackle with ruthless efficiency, return punts, and handle kickoff returns. The closest comparison to his overall mastery of the game is that of Paul Hornung's 1956 Heisman campaign nearly fifty years later, except that Gipp basically did it for three full seasons from 1918 to '20—leading the team in rushing *and* passing each year. His handiwork reached impressive totals: 2,341 yards rushing and 1,769 yards passing (with a football shaped more like the ball used in rugby). Adding in his interception yardage, punt returns, and kickoff returns, Gipp wrecked opposing defenses to the tune of 4,833 total all-purpose yards, not to mention the 3,690 yards of punts that helped put the other teams in dire straits. Basically, every time Gipp stepped on the field of play, he could be counted on to rack up about 180 yards of total production on both sides of the ball.

The brilliant promise of George Gipp to showcase his many talents at the professional level never came to pass as he died on December 14, 1920, of a strep infection. He had been in failing health in the latter part of the season, made a brief appearance in the Northwestern game in late November in Chicago, and, before that game, had put on a football clinic for a friend in the frigid Chicago weather. It was too much for his weakened system.

Rockne made sure that Gipp would be immortal when he told the 1928 team, at halftime of the game against Army at Yankee Stadium, of Gipp's alleged deathbed request, to "Win one for the Gipper." This was Rockne's worst season; he *had* to beat Army, and he used Gipp to do it, bringing the All-American hero back from the grave to inspire a Notre Dame team that might otherwise have thrown in the towel against a very tough Army team. But rather than just chucking it, the team came out of the tunnel in Yankee Stadium for the second half and clinched the much-needed win, apparently spurred on by the ghost of Gipp. Hollywood made sure that Gipp's dying request was immortalized in the 1940 Warner Bros. film that celebrated the late Rockne.

I've written two books on Rockne, and he is absolutely central to any understanding of the Notre Dame mystique. In 1979–1980, believe it or not, half of the 1920 Irish backfield, quarterback Chet Grant and fullback Paul Castner, was still alive, and I was able to interview them. Both men were dubious about Rockne's claim. Castner told me quite specifically that "Gipp never called himself 'The Gipper.'" Of course, they were not in the hospital room with Gipp and Rockne, but the famous line is typical of the way that Rockne romanticized situations to make them more appealing and memorable to the masses. He was, of course, the master of the *bon mot*. We can perhaps pardon him for putting the words in the dying

Gipp's mouth. Frankly, knowing Rockne, it was too good to let go. His teams following Gipp's death, before the subpar 5–4 season of 1928, had never needed this kind of motivational ploy. They were typically in total control of their games and never came close to losing more games than they would win. But 1928 was not at all like that, and Rockne knew it in his bones. He had said that Gipp was nature's pet, but she made him pay for it. If so, his appeal to his team in the Army game showed that Rockne could even manipulate the dictates of nature.

Miracles imply that the usual patterns in life are suspended for a moment. Can a miracle sustain itself for three years or more, as in the case of George Gipp? It would certainly seem to be the case. We might also say that Gipp's shining star in the pantheon of American culture heroes is still burning brightly, that the miracle has thus remained with us almost a century after his tragically brief life ended.

The immortal George Gipp follows his fullback in a 1920 win over Nebraska.

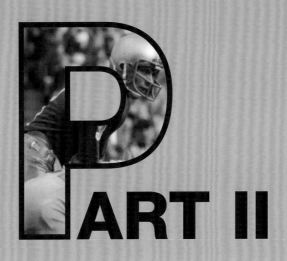

PART II

NATIONAL CHAMPIONSHIP
SEASONS

1919

With the successful but truncated and traumatic 1918 season over and done with, Rockne could look forward to a talented, veteran team featuring the more or less untamed George Gipp at left halfback, the premier position at the time in the Notre Dame box formation. This was not yet a truly national schedule, although there were several teams that had already reached heavyweight status: Nebraska, Purdue, Army, Indiana, and MAC (later Michigan State). The others were good enough for the day but either wouldn't survive the collegiate game's evolution or accepted second-tier status.

Four returners gave Rockne a great core for the line, including both ends, Bernie Kirk and Eddie Anderson. Then there was the tough as nails left guard, Heartley (Hunk) Anderson, either the heart or the soul of this team, eventually to become the head coach following Rockne's tragic death in 1931. Pete Bahan moved from his right halfback position in 1918 to the quarterback spot for 1919. Gipp returned as the left halfback, of course, for his third Irish football campaign. Dutch Bergman took Bahan's spot at right halfback. Fritz Slackford won the fullback spot, left vacant by a man with different hopes for his football career—Curly Lambeau of Green Bay.

The Irish opened with Kalamazoo, winning 14–0, although the score should have been higher. Gipp had two long TD runs called back on penalties—80 and 68 yard bursts for naught. Ever the cut-up, he told the refs to use one whistle to stop a play, two to tell him to keep going. Even without those two big plays, he gained 149 yards. Bergman scored on yet another long jaunt, a 55-yard burner.

College football in Ohio had not yet settled on Ohio State as the crown jewel. For their second contest, Notre Dame played the reigning state champs, Mt. Union, and decimated the Purple Raiders to the tune of 60–7. Somehow, the first quarter ended in a 7–7 tie. Gipp started the Irish scoring avalanche after that with twin TD runs of 30 yards, adding another 168 yards passing, rushing, and returning kicks. Seven other Notre Dame players joined in the scoring as Rockne spread the wealth.

Nebraska made a careful note of Gipp's gridiron repertoire, but he still had an ace up his sleeve when the Irish met the Cornhuskers in Lincoln, Nebraska. The first Notre Dame possession showcased another Gipp talent—the lateral pass. It worked for a nifty 90-yard touchdown run by Dutch Bergman. To round out his efforts, Gipp completed five of eight passes for 124 very wet yards. Later in the game, after

Rockne's first undefeated team—the 1919 champs.

Nebraska had tallied a TD, Rockne opened up Gipp's entire portfolio—passes, runs, a criss-cross play—as they mounted two long drives. The Huskers blunted the first one, but Gipp was adamant, coming right back with all his tricks to lead to Pete Bahan's 1-yard dive for the winning score as the defense allowed a later field goal in a 14–9 Irish win.

Western Normal (now Western Michigan) folded easily, 53–0. The Irish blasted in for three scores in the first quarter, the first by Gipp's sub, Grover Malone, then the others by Gipp. Two more subs added TDs in the second quarter—quarterback Joe Brandy and right halfback Norm Barry. Rockne plumbed the depth chart for two more TDs, but Bergman tallied the final TD for the regulars.

Rockne knew that he had something good with this team; he now faced some difficult decisions as Army loomed. Should he rest his starters against Indiana? Or use them full-tilt and live with the consequences? He decided to do a little of each as Gipp played enough to carry the ball 18 times for 82 yards, gaining another 57 yards on pass receptions, and scoring a field goal with a nifty dropkick. Dutch Bergman scored two TDs before hurting his knee as Notre Dame prevailed, 16–3.

Rockne's concern about Army seemed to be on target. After the long trip east, the game turned into a real slugfest. Without Bergman, Rockne used the very reliable Norm Barry. But it was Gipp who carried the load by rushing for 70 hard-fought yards and passing for 115 more on seven completions. The Irish defense stopped Army several times deep in their own territory, escaping with a 12–9 win. As always, Rockne watched the game intensively. Little did he know that the Army squad's third-team All-American end, Earl "Red" Blaik, would become a chief nemesis of the Irish in a few years while serving his long, distinguished career as the Army head coach. Rockne's eagle eye also noted a loss of $603.83 for the team's trip expenses, as reported by Irish researcher Jason Kelly.

A hefty MAC team (renamed Michigan State University starting in 1955, its centennial year) came southwest from East Lansing for the next game. Some two hundred "Aggies" fans came for the ride, as well as fifty-piece marching band, early harbingers of the popularity, intensity, and colorful entertainment that these two teams would foster throughout the series. Gipp played well in all phases of the game, but the MAC team was rugged and determined. Rockne actually had to use a trick play for the first score, a tackle-eligible play. Gipp fired a pass to left end Bernie Kirk for the final touchdown and the 13–0 win.

Purdue came out of the gates to establish an early lead on their home field and then Gipp cut loose with two TD passes. The Irish defense scored two more with interceptions by guard Hunk Anderson and starting center George Trafton, good indications that Purdue was using short passes, knowing that Gipp was deep (he still snagged two errant Purdue passes anyway) as Notre Dame prevailed in good fashion, 33–13. Rockne claimed that not one pass was ever completed in Gipp's vicinity during his entire career to go with the five passes he intercepted for Notre Dame.

The team completed its undefeated season with a trip to Sioux City, Iowa, to play the Maroon Chiefs of Morningside College. It was Thanksgiving weekend, but there wasn't much to give thanks for regarding the weather: 10 degrees and snowing. Perhaps the conditions contributed to the Chiefs' first score after Gipp mishandled a punt on his 11-yard line. As usual, Gipp would atone for his error by conducting a long drive in the third quarter, punctuated by his 3-yard TD burst. In the third quarter it was Morningside's turn to fumble a punt, with the Irish capturing the ball at the 10-yard line. Gipp probed the left side for a yard, liked what he saw, and ran the same play for a 9-yard TD, the winning score in a 14–7 ice bowl. Later, he played keep-away with the ball with a long run and an interception, saving the undefeated season. Both the National Championship Foundation and football historian Parke H. Davis retroactively assigned national championship status to Rockne's 1919 team, the first of many for the little Catholic school in North Central Indiana that had started with a modest log cabin for its first building.

1920

For the 1920 campaign, Rockne had a solid, largely veteran group that would feature one of the all-time Notre Dame greats in left halfback George Gipp. Both ends returned as did the left tackle and left guard, Frank Coughlin and Hunk Anderson. Experienced players from the second unit moved up to fill the other vacancies. This was also true for Gipp's backfield mates, quarterback Joe Brandy, right halfback Norm Barry, and fullback Chet Wynne. They were all familiar with the system that Rockne had refined from the Jesse Harper years, and they were an excellent blend of size, quickness, and sheer speed to complement Gipp's many talents. Rockne had devoted considerable time and energy to "managing" his talented left halfback through various issues; in some ways, the mythology about their relationship had already begun. And that mythology would only become more intriguing, as events would prove.

The Wolverines of Kalamazoo were the first victims for this Irish team. Gipp literally ran wild—183 yards on 16 carries. Wynne rumbled in for the first score, then Gipp broke loose for a 30-yard second quarter scoring strike. In the third quarter, Gipp repeated his 30-yard run, followed it with a 28-yard pass to left end Roger Kiley, setting up Barry's TD run. Sub fullback Paul Castner intercepted a Kalamazoo pass to give Brandy an easy TD opportunity. Another reserve, Cy Kasper, recovered a fumble and scooted 35 yards with it. He also got the call for a short TD run a few plays later. Gipp's sub, John Mohardt, blasted in for the final tally in Notre Dame's 39–0 opening victory.

A late summer heat wave descended on South Bend just in time for the Western Normal contest. That meteorological condition did little to hamper Rockne's team, as they poured it on their visitors to the tune of 41–0. Gipp maintained his torrid pace as a runner with 123 yards gained on 14 carries, good for two TDs to go with three PAT kicks. Mohardt added a TD run, and third team fullback Bob Phelan scored with the best run of the day, a sparkling 55-yard effort. Another fullback, Paul Castner, powered in for a score from 35 yards away, and Joe Brandy rounded out the scoring with a punt return for a TD. This game was yet another example of Rockne's philosophy and strategy of being able to score from anywhere with any opportunity—his so-called "perfect play."

The Irish played their next game in Lincoln, Nebraska. The Huskers had almost played too coy the week before in a 7–0 squeaker over Colorado State, with coach Henry Schulte risking a loss by resting his regulars. His decision paid off for Nebraska against the Irish as the Huskers dominated the statistics for the game. A veteran of Fielding Yost's "Point-a-Minute" Michigan teams (1903–05), Schulte's Nebraska squad nevertheless fell far short of that historical precedent, losing to Notre Dame, 16–7. The teams traded punts on several early possessions, with the Irish emphasizing the passing game. Eventually, Rockne's stalwarts reached the Huskers' 2 foot line but could not push it in. Nebraska took over on downs. Rather than risk a cheap Irish TD, they elected to punt from that spot on the next play, but the punter bobbled the ball, and a teammate recovered in the end zone for a safety. Even with that adversity, Nebraska put together a good drive in the second quarter to take a 7–2 lead. The Huskers stopped two drives in the third quarter, but Gipp was beginning to take their measure. He hit right end Eddie Anderson with two passes that covered 60 yards, once again getting inside the 1-yard line. This time, Brandy plunged in for the first Irish TD. Gipp scored on a trick play especially saved for this game, but it was nullified by a holding penalty. Undaunted, Gipp finally punched through a tackle for the final score of the game. Nebraska held Gipp to mortal figures—70 yards rushing on 15 tough carries, but he chipped in with 117 yards on six pass completions. He added 30 yards on three punt or kick returns and made both PATs. Even in this tough, physical game, with Nebraska totally focused on stopping the Irish one-man show, Gipp still picked up a total of 217 all-purpose yards.

Nearby Valparaiso visited South Bend and took advantage of Rockne's shock troops to snag an early 3–0 lead. Whenever Rockne used his reserves to start a game, he made sure that they had a good punter with Gipp not being in the lineup. This duty fell to sophomore fullback Paul Castner whose towering punts kept the Irish out of trouble. Having seen enough—and knowing that Army was up next—Rockne sent in his starting unit, and the visitors watched helplessly as their brief lead turned into a 28–3 defeat. Gipp started hitting passes, including a 38-yard beauty with Kiley as his target, but his next pass was intercepted. In the third quarter, Wynne scored "over the top" after a short drive to take the lead. Then Gipp tallied a quick score, followed by another Irish TD. Rockne pulled out a tackle-eligible play that earned Coughlin a 32-yard reception from Gipp, but the drive stalled. Reserve right end Dave Hayes intercepted a pass, and John Mohardt gathered the scoring honors for the final tally.

An undefeated Army team was next. Played in late October, harsh winter conditions had not yet set in, but they would soon—and prove to be a factor in ending the football career and life of George Gipp. The previous summer, his physician had advised him to have his infected tonsils removed, but Gipp chose to play baseball, then football season came along—yet another potential health factor in the events that would transpire in the next few weeks. As expected, the Army game would be a very physical affair. A devastating hit on Wynne caused a fumble, and Army took advantage of that turnover for an early lead. On their drive, they earned two first downs which proved to be half of their total of four for the entire game. On a later possession, the Irish came together on a beautiful drive with a Gipp pass to Kiley, then a Gipp burst off tackle, followed by a streaking Gipp going wide around end before Mohardt scored to tie the game. The Irish forced an Army punt, and Kiley scored on a 35-yard TD pass. Army was also opportunistic with a 60-yard punt return for a TD followed by a poor Notre Dame punt that gave them an easy field goal and a 17–14 halftime lead. Rockne was growing antsy in the third quarter as Army held on to the lead, but in the final frame, Gipp kept up the pressure well enough to lead to a Mohardt TD and an Irish lead, then he rumbled for a 50-yard gain to set up Wynne's 20-yard dash down the sideline for the final score. If anyone in the country had any doubts about Gipp, his production in this game was unbelievable: he rushed for 150 yards, returned kicks for 207 yards, and passed for 123 yards for a total of 480 all-purpose yards, to go with three punts and one interception. After the game, Cadet players saw Gipp in the showers and noted that he looked somewhat emaciated.

For the Irish homecoming game against in-state rival Purdue, Gipp somehow kept up his torrid pace: 129 yards gained on only 10 runs, 128 yards with four completed passes, one punt return for 35 yards, and scored one TD and 3 PATS in a convincing 28–0 victory. The shock troops started the game, and diminutive quarterback Chet Grant, who had served in the military in World War I, scampered 50 yards to pay dirt with a pass. Gipp played only part of the game as Rockne noticed some fatigue, yet he pulled off one of his patented dashes for a 35-yard TD run. A long Irish drive seemed stopped when Norm Barry dropped the ball but Buck Shaw fell on it for a TD. Purdue did not give up, but their final drive ended when Mohardt snagged an interception. And so it went for Purdue that day as the Irish hadn't lost an in-state game since 1906.

That streak was seriously threatened the following week by Indiana as the Hoosiers roared to an early 10–0 lead. Gipp was not at his best, with only 52 yards gained on 16 rushing attempts and only 26 yards gained on three pass receptions.

In punting, however, he was a busy man, with eight punts for 359 yards. He scored one TD, piling in from short range—with a dislocated shoulder no less—and added one PAT. The Hoosiers were primed to stop Gipp, so they stacked their line as a Notre Dame drive neared the end zone, fully committed to denying Gipp. As they took care of Gipp, however, Joe Brandy scampered past the melee for the winning TD. Hunk Anderson played the dramatic contest with a cracked rib. It was that kind of game.

Two more road games concluded the season. First up was Northwestern in Chicago. Anyone who had followed the Irish that season would have recognized immediately that Rockne was not using Gipp as he had in prior games. He was still nursing a bad shoulder, so the great Irish back never carried the ball as a runner. Rockne knew his star was sick, so he was trying to protect him. The fans were calling for Gipp all through the game; in the fourth quarter, Rockne relented and inserted him. Right out of a movie script, it seems, Gipp completed his first two passes—35 yards and 70 yards—for touchdowns. Gipp went on to complete five of six passes for 157 yards and those two TDs and fielded one punt for no return yards. The story goes that the Northwestern players knew Gipp was suffering, and they gently brought him down as he hauled in the punt. That was most likely the last play George Gipp made on a football gridiron.

After the Indiana game, Gipp had kept a promise to a former teammate to do a kicking clinic for his friend's high school team in Chicago, even though the weather was miserable. The conditions didn't improve by the time of the Northwestern game. He then stood on the sidelines of that game for three quarters, bad shoulder and all, with his chronically infected tonsils, on a typically blustery Chicago day with the temperature in the 20-degree range.

A team banquet was held in mid-week following the Northwestern game. Gipp was in attendance but had to leave the event due to his nagging illness. He checked into a South Bend hospital for treatment, but the state of the medical arts at the time was not going to be able to save him. He did not go easily, however. Gipp clung to life for another three weeks. Death eventually claimed him, but he didn't go without a fight.

While he was languishing in a hospital bed, his somewhat distracted teammates went to East Lansing for the final game of the season against the MAC Aggies. Putting their concerns about Gipp aside for the moment, the team executed brilliantly on the game's first play as running back Danny Coughlin took the opening kickoff 95 yards for a TD. Castner blasted into the Aggies' end zone twice in the third quarter, and Eddie Anderson completed the scoring when he scampered 25 yards with a blocked punt in the fourth quarter, making the final score 25–0.

With that victory, Notre Dame had battled to 18 consecutive wins over the past two seasons. In his first three seasons as the Irish head coach, Rockne's record was almost unbelievable: 21–1–2 (a .917 winning percentage). Counting the earlier, shorter campaigns following the founding of the team in 1887, it was the tenth undefeated season for Notre Dame.

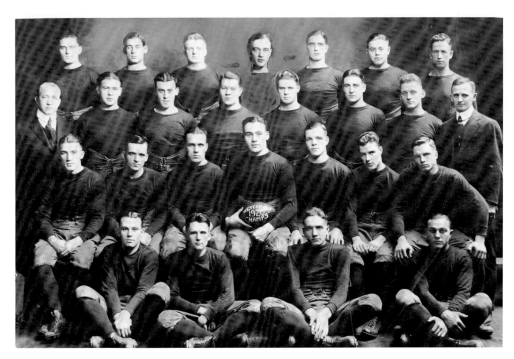

The 1920 national champs, with Gipp's 1919 photo added to top row, middle.

While there was a time to celebrate their gridiron accomplishments, the Christmas season that year for Notre Dame's players was one of grim awareness that their star was in a far more serious situation than any game they had played. Gipp died on December 14, 1920, having achieved first-team All-American status. Both Parke H. Davis and the Billingsley Report retroactively declared this team to be national champions.

The campus was, of course, grief-stricken, as were all Irish followers.

Playing a sport is a performance art. One's physical efforts are here and gone, unless recorded by modern technology. Gipp's day gave us a few photographs, the athlete captured at a split second, much like a Greek statue … perfection frozen in time. In death, the famous athlete is linked to past heroics, to tales of superhuman feats, to the gods themselves. The full life and victories that might have been will forever remain unknown, unknowable.

In the case of Notre Dame, at the height of its early fame, the school and its team was brought to a shocking contemplation of human mortality. In little more than ten years, the school and its team would go through the same trauma once again.

Even as the student body, coaches, and alumni mourned the loss of Gipp, it was announced that he and end Roger Kiley had been honored as All-Americans for 1920.

1924

If ever there was a Notre Dame team that epitomized Rockne's penchant for scoring from anywhere at any time, the 1924 unit is that team. Not yet having suffered harsh rules changes to thwart Rockne's tactics, this was also the team that best displayed his preference for small, light, extremely agile, speedy, and intelligent football players who were experts at detecting the slightest weakness in an opponent, who knew how to use angles, leverage, and an opponent's momentum against him. His players could outthink and outmaneuver any team they faced, and they could score almost at will from any spot on the field. He had contempt for the vestiges of nineteenth-century mass play—bulky players, plodding tactics, uninspired "bovine" football. Rockne was all about looking to the future of the sport, dragging it into the twentieth century one emphatic victory at a time. He sensed that the growing, enthusiastic crowds wanted to see a flashy, colorful, wide-open game. He was perfectly content to let his ball handlers use sleight of hand to fool defenders, but he also brought the game's tactics out into the open, out of the indiscriminate scrums—masses of writhing bodies—in which no one could see the ball or detect the exquisite pattern of blocking, running, and passing that Rockne taught and promoted.

For the sake of perspective, here are the weights of the 1924 starters from left end to right end: 177, 186, 165, 187, 165, 180, and 172. Here are the weights of the front seven for the 2017 Irish, wide receiver and left tackle to tight end: 224, 312, 329, 305, 320, 313, and 256. The 1924 line averaged 176 pounds, with the heaviest man, center Adam Walsh, tipping the scales at 187 pounds. The 2017 Irish offensive line averaged 294 pounds, 118 pounds heavier. More specifically, the biggest player for Rockne, Walsh, would be giving away 142 pounds to the largest 2017 starter. This provides a dramatic insight into the changing nature of the game. Given modern strength and conditioning regimens, specific to individual players, the 1924 Irish line would have a hard time moving the linemen of today.

But they played one-platoon football, with stringent substitution rules. The figures mentioned are for the seven line players for the two teams. Keep the 1924 squad on the field and have them look at the 2017 Irish defense: the four linemen came in at 281, 308, 284, and 255 pounds, averaging 282. The linebackers show up as 240, 238, and 230 pounds, averaging 236. Not until we see the size of the contemporary defensive backs do we find anyone remotely close to the size of the 1924 team: 175, 187, 208, and 190 pounds, an average of 190. Captain Adam Walsh, the starting center and biggest player in 1924, would be larger than only one man on the 2017 team—a cornerback. A further contrast is found in the 1924 backfield: they averaged 158.75 pounds, with the heaviest man, Jim Crowley, the left halfback (the glamor position for many teams of that era), at 162 pounds.

This does not mean that Coach Rockne would be disgusted with modern football. He placed an absolute premium on speed, agility, and maneuverability. The modern football player, even given the size proportions, has these in abundance. In a way, Rockne wins the case.

The 1924 season was not quite the model for the campaigns that Rockne sought to set up. It was not yet a national campaign, although the trip to Pasadena for the 1925 Rose Bowl against Pop Warner's Stanford team would show Rockne that he could handle the logistics for transporting a team, his staff, and the necessary equipment across country by train. Indeed, this trip led directly to Notre Dame successfully seeking out USC for a series, thereby creating the first planned and executed cross-country intercollegiate football schedule—the 1926 Irish campaign—and, not so coincidentally, the greatest intersectional rivalry to be found in college football. Every time these two teams lace up their spikes and the fans either fill the respective stadiums or tune in a national broadcast, they should be sure to thank the memory of Knute Rockne for having the vision of how to enhance the game, embedding it in our culture, and getting it done in the first place.

Notre Dame and Rockne were ambitious with regards to upgrading the quality of the team's opponents. The Irish had opened their seasons seven times with Kalamazoo, with several opening contests in the seasons just prior to 1924. Kalamazoo never scored on the Irish in those seven games while Notre Dame averaged more than 45 points per game. They dropped Kalamazoo without finding a replacement, making Lombard the opening game. A Unitarian college in the Chicago area, Lombard also failed to score a point in the 1924 game, succumbing 40–0 (and then closed down as an institution in 1930). A Chicago paper called it a "listless" game, but Rockne did not coach his players to be listless. He did start his "shock troops" to start the game, and Lombard held them to a draw of sorts. In the middle of the second quarter a shock trooper tackled the Lombard quarterback, breaking his collarbone. The deluge followed. Halfback Don Miller scored a TD to end a drive, then subs ran wild on jaunts of 50 and 57 yards. The final score was reached with TD runs by Crowley, fullback Bill Cerney, and Miller again. Cerney took home the effort award for the day with his TD as he was hit just feet away from the goal line but somersaulted for the score. He was not listless.

In-state competitor Wabash was next up, another holdover from a different era of Irish football, as the first game between the schools was in 1894, long before Notre Dame had any pretensions about national recognition. Rockne played his subs for most of the game, well aware that the next game was against a powerful Army team. Crowley did manage one of his classic long jaunts around end for a TD, so the blocking scheme was doing its job as designed (there are photographs from the Rockne years in which every man from the other team has been blocked out of the play or is about to be blocked—the so-called "perfect play" that Rockne's players aspired to execute on each play). Ward Connell, a senior playing right half-

The 1924 Four Horsemen posed in honor of Grantland Rice's famous depiction of their football prowess.

back, apparently did not need any blockers when he scored a TD after a long run, carrying five Wabash players with him into the end zone as part of Notre Dame's 34–0 victory.

When we consider the enormous physical differences between players of the Four Horsemen era and players today, toughness is one thing that cannot be reduced to numbers. Notre Dame's captain, Adam Walsh, the starting center for Rockne (remember, this is one-platoon football) played the entire 1924 Army game at New York's Polo Grounds with two broken bones in his hands, while also intercepting a pass and leading the team in tackles. Playing center in those days, under Rockne's system, also meant that the center snap could go to any one of the running backs and the targeted back might be in motion, meaning that the snapper had to lead the runner, snapping the ball with the right timing and angle so that it arrived at the pre-arranged spot on time for the back to haul it in and commence the rest of the play. He was the key to starting the famous Notre Dame shift with perfect timing and an accurate center snap.

Try doing that sometime with two broken hands and see how it goes.

This thrilling game took on greater cultural significance because of an account of the game penned by the famous sportswriter, Grantland Rice, published on October 18, 1924, in the *New York Herald Tribune*:

> "Outlined against a blue-gray October sky, the Four Horsemen rode again. In dramatic lore they are known as Famine, Pestilence, Destruction and Death. These are only aliases. Their real names are Stuhldreher, Miller, Crowley and Layden."

Rice's brilliant lede became immortal and forever fixed the Notre Dame backfield, and Rockne himself, in the minds of Irish fans across the country. Even today, his brilliant insight is well-known. But Rice could do more than verbal pyrotechnics; he was also a keen observer of the game, as seen in his account of the game:

> "The Army brought a fine football team into action, but it was beaten by a faster and smoother team. Rockne's supposedly light, green line was about as heavy as Army's and every whit as aggressive. What is even more important, it was faster on its feet, faster in getting around.
>
> "It was Western speed and perfect interference that once more brought the Army doom. The Army line couldn't get through fast enough to break up the attacking plays; and once started, the bewildering speed and power of the Western backs slashed along for 8, 10, and 15 yards on play after play. And always in front of these offensive drivers could be found the whirling form of Stuhldreher, taking the first man out of the play as cleanly as though he

had used a hand grenade at close range. This Notre Dame interference was a marvelous thing to look upon."

His insights accurately captured the essence of Rockne's system—speed and devastatingly accurate blocking. After that, everything takes care of itself, as Army learned.

Notre Dame played it safe in the first quarter, as did Army. Both teams probed and tested to see how best to attack. The Irish figured it out first. From their 15-yard line, Crowley burst past the left end for 20 yards … then Miller scooted for 11 more … Harry Stuhldreher passed to Crowley for 12 yards … Miller hauled it outside for 20 more before Layden carried the mail 10 yards for the game's first score. In the third quarter, Layden cropped up again by snagging an Army pass at the 48. Crowley dashed around right end for 15 yards. Miller and Layden made short gains, then Army made a rare stop. But Crowley got loose again around the left end, cut back and scored from the 20-yard line. Army managed a score after that, but the Irish adamantly refused to allow another one and the game ended with a 13–7 Notre Dame victory. The Four Horsemen had trampled through the pride of the east.

Making its case again in the east, the Irish pounded Princeton 12–0, stacking up 23 first downs to Princeton's four, allowing the Tigers to advance no further than the ND 30, while showcasing Crowley's 250 yards rushing and two TDs. Crowley lost one TD on a penalty and another possible score when he fumbled at the 9-yard line. Rockne rubbed it in a bit on Eastern football when he started the second half with a flying wedge formation to return the Princeton kickoff, a final reminder of the kind of football that he was intent upon replacing. This kind of gesture indicated that the former central role of Eastern football was well on its way westward. And just as the Irish were in the process of upgrading their selection of opponents, the Princetons of the football world would become less and less attractive as opponents as their power and influence waned.

Stuhldreher had been hurt in the Princeton game; Red Edwards would replace him against Georgia Tech, then known as the Golden Tornado, in the Irish's homecoming game. Walsh was still nursing his injuries, but Rockne called on him once again when he decided to replace the shock troops to start the second quarter. Georgia Tech had taken a 3–0 lead thanks to some bruising running by their big fullback, Douglas Wycoff. With Edwards at the controls, the regulars in the Irish backfield slashed through Tech's defense—Miller for 35 yards around left end, Crowley over right tackle for 16 yards, Cerney up the middle for seven more. Tech composed itself for a play or two but eventually Crowley found Miller on a fourth-down play for a TD pass from the 11. The Irish now had the lead and had no intentions of giving it up. John Roach scampered for a 45-yard gain past left end later in the second quarter, setting up his own 3-yard blast for a TD. He would score again in the fourth quarter on a pass from quarterback Eddie Scharer. Rockne kept playing subs even late in the game; fullback Bernie Livergood romped for several long runs in the fourth quarter to set up TDs in their 34–3 rout. The surviving members of Notre Dame's first football team—1887—were honored at the game. Notably, the win gave Notre Dame a total of 200 victories since those brave men had donned primitive uniforms (there were only enough to suit up eleven men) in 1887.

Having conquered teams from the East and the South, the Irish turned their attention to the Midwest for the next three games: Wisconsin, then archrival Nebraska, and Northwestern. The Badgers went down, 38–3, gaining most of their yardage against the Irish shock troops in the first quarter. Irish sophomore fullback Harry O'Boyle dropkicked a field goal to give ND the early lead. Wisconsin then had its way with the subs, reaching deep into Irish territory before Rockne decided to put in the first team unit to stifle the threat. They held the Badgers to a tying field goal and then the rout was on. Four TDs later, Rockne relented and the subs played the fourth quarter. The Four Horsemen scored twice (Layden and Miller) in the second quarter and twice again in the third quarter when Crowley broke loose for a 60-yard gain then scored on a short run and later one of his classic gallops around left end, making it 31–3. At that point, Rockne started to make substitutions at every opportunity. John Roach capped the scoring with a TD. Rockne utilized more players than were listed on the Irish roster in the game program. One scribe theorized that Rockne played so many different units that he probably did not even know the names of all of his players.

During the Rockne years, Nebraska, along with Army, were the Irish's main rivals. In his tenure as head coach to this point, he was 3–2–1 against the Cornhuskers. The problem was that the Irish had suffered the two losses in consecutive years—1922 and 1923. So 1924 loomed as a crucial year in Rockne's mind when it came to Nebraska. He had written some novels for juvenile readers and "Aksarben" was the chief foe his gridiron heroes faced. That Rockne had impressed upon his charges the importance of this home game can be seen in the first downs earned by the teams: 24 to 3. The Irish would put on a rushing clinic for the overflow crowd of 22,000 at Cartier Field by racking up 465 yards on the ground, the major chunk of the 566 total yards that day for the home team. They completely stuffed the Huskers, allowing only 56 yards rushing and 20 yards passing. Rockne's backfield completed 8 of 11 passes—three for TDs; his defenders allowed Nebraska only one completed pass all day. Surprisingly, Nebraska scored first, a TD following a Layden fumble. This must have aroused the fight in the Irish as that was all the good news for the Huskers that day. Notre Dame romped from that point for a convincing 34–6 victory. At one point, Layden slipped and was almost in a sitting position, but he threw a pass anyway to Crowley, who maneuvered 65 yards for a touchdown. Stuhldreher and Miller had scored in the second quarter, Miller again in the third, and Layden wrapped up the scoring late in the game. Rockne was not messing around in this contest with kindly substitutions.

To wrap up their three-game stretch against Midwestern opponents, the Irish took a train to Chicago to play Northwestern at Grand Park Stadium. Some 45,000 fans packed the facility—the most ever to see a football game in the Windy City at that point. The Irish seemed to have suffered a post-Nebraska letdown or lack of focus, or perhaps it was a sodden field, as they only managed to pull out a squeaker, 13–6. The Wildcats scored with two early dropkicked field goals by Moon Baker against the shock troops and an alarmed Rockne inserted his starters. Taking command immediately, Stuhldreher did the scoring—his first on 2-yard run after completing a long pass to Crowley and, shortly after that, scoring on a 40-yard pass play to reach the final score. Layden intercepted a pass to stop a drive, and Baker missed a third field goal try. Two Irish drives died at the Northwestern 25- and 5-yard lines, thanks to outstanding defensive efforts. It wasn't pretty, but it was a win.

Notre Dame wrapped up a perfect season with a 40–19 pasting of Carnegie Tech in Pittsburgh. With both teams working hard to overcome snowy conditions, the home team fought valiantly to achieve a 13–13 halftime score, with their first TD coming off a blocked punt and 50-yard return by Benny Kristoff for the score. Their final scores were mirror images: a fake pass and a scoring run by their fullback, Dwight Beede, once in the second quarter and then against subs near the end. The interim, however, pretty much belonged to Rockne's team. Miller scored first for ND on a 40-yard pass from Crowley, then Cerney piled in on a short run to tie the halftime score. Lacking an injured Layden, three of the Horsemen ran and passed at will, with Stuhldreher setting a "world's record" of twelve consecutive pass completions. Two of those passes went for scores in the third quarter, then Stuhldreher and Livergood wrapped it up in the fourth quarter. The three TDs scored by Carnegie Tech proved to be the most points scored on Notre Dame since 1916.

The Irish—Rockne, the administration, and West Coast alumni—had been considering the obvious benefits of adding a West Coast game to the team's schedule.

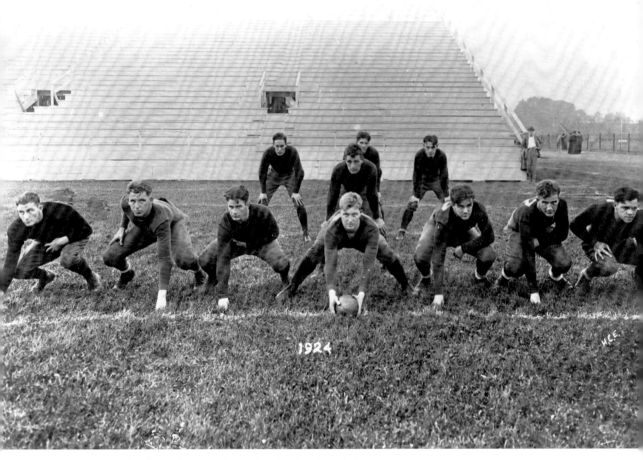

Rockne's third undefeated team, the 1924 national champs.

As the 1924 season unfolded, there were tentative inquiries about the possibility. Stanford, reluctant at first, won the Pacific Coast Conference and a Rose Bowl invitation. There were no binding contracts with other conferences, so Notre Dame was an obvious candidate. The arrangements were settled and Rockne took thirty-three players on a long train ride, the tedium broken up by several pit stops for practices.

Stanford's head coach, Glenn "Pop" Warner, was an advocate for a totally different brand of football than Rockne. Warner liked big players and—somewhat like Woody Hayes's penchant for three yards and a cloud of dust decades later at Ohio State—used them in a powerful wingback formation to grind out first downs, sustain long drives, kill the clock, and win the game. It worked more often than not. Warner so prized the first down that he had suggested a scoring change at one point—a point per first down.

Against Rockne and his brand of quick-strike football, it did work to create a lot of first downs, but the Notre Dame team capitalized on eight Stanford turnovers (five interceptions and three fumbles) as the key to a convincing 27–10 Irish victory in the school's first bowl game as well as its first contest west of Nebraska.

Stanford earned the first score, a field goal surrendered by Rockne's shock troops halfway through the first quarter. The Irish pieced together a 46-yard drive with Layden zipping into the end zone from the 3-yard line early in the second quarter. Rockne, ever the perfectionist, had made a slight adjustment in Layden's defensive alignment; he had noticed a slight "tell" in Stanford's passing game. If Warner's All-American fullback Ernie Nevers was going to throw from a running formation, he would swing out a little wider as he neared the line of scrimmage. Rockne had Layden widen out from his normal position so he could see this slight change better. Sure enough, halfway into the second quarter, that's what he saw. Nevers threw across the field and Layden was sitting on it, and he returned the interception 78 yards for a TD and Stanford never saw the lead again. Late in the third quarter, Stanford fumbled a Layden punt on their 20, and Ed Hunsinger recovered it and ran it in for another TD. Stanford got that back with a long drive and a TD pass, but the Irish held them in check the rest of the way, including a stop at their 8 inch line. With time running out Layden saw another opportunity, a Stanford pass floating across the middle. He jumped it and roared 70 yards for the game's final TD.

It looked like a statistical mismatch. Stanford had 17 first downs to ND's 7, and piled up 316 total yards to ND's 186—except the Irish had 139 yards gained by their defense. Stanford had its opportunities but did not capitalize on them the way Rockne's players did.

Three of the Horsemen were declared to be All-Americans: Stuhldreher, Layden, and Crowley. Center Adam Walsh was also recognized. Rockne had been at Notre Dame six seasons, and his 1924 national champs gave him his third perfect season. Notre Dame football was taking on miraculous dimensions in the mind of the public.

1929

The Irish suffered their worst season in many years in 1928 with losses to Wisconsin, Georgia Tech, Carnegie Tech, and USC. The Carnegie Tech loss was the first loss for Notre Dame at Cartier Field since the 1905 season. Cartier had been the Irish's home field since 1900, but once the team had reached the heights of popularity and public demand under the leadership of Rockne, its seating limitations became manifestly obvious. For example, they had played Army at the Polo Grounds and in Yankee Stadium in previous seasons and knew what it was like to perform in front of 65,000 spectators. Rockne also had a keen eye for the revenues that such crowds could bring in. Bursting at the seams, Cartier Field could handle less than half of the spectators than Yankee Stadium. He pleaded with the school's administration to try to improve Notre Dame's home game accommodations and, allegedly, submitted his resignation for added pressure. In any case, the administration relented and set into motion the complex planning needed to create a state of the art stadium, using Michigan's recent stadium construction as a model.

While Rockne got what he wanted—the new stadium would have a seating capacity of 50,000 or more (59,075 once a regular head count was established, but now seating nearly 81,000 after expansion in the 1990s)—he would also have to use an entire season for nothing but road games. That turned out to be the 1929 season. Coming on the heels of the wretched 1928 season, this was a major risk, but Rockne knew he had to do it. Three "home" games were scheduled for Chicago's cavernous Soldier Field (the game held there against Navy in 1929 recorded an attendance of 120,000, a figure that has not been exceeded in college football in the intervening eighty-eight years). Only two scheduled games would require rather long trips—Georgia Tech and Army in Yankee Stadium. All the others were more or less in Notre Dame's neighborhood. It was by no means a cupcake schedule, and other complications would set in early in the campaign, but at the start, Rockne was confident that he had the playing personnel to handle the difficult task facing them.

The 1929 team inherited three returning starters on the line, the others moved up from the subs. The backfield was composed of all new starters, but it would prove to be explosive, some of the best and speediest players Rockne would coach. The quarterback was sparkplug Frank Carideo, a heady, tough player, perfectly suited to Rockne's system. Jack Elder and Marty Brill handled the halfback spots, with Moon Mullins at fullback, Joe Savoldi the sub. Elder was reportedly the fastest man on earth in a 75-yard dash, a talent he would display several times in the season on both sides of the ball. In the wings was yet another very good back, Marchmont Schwartz. This backfield group had as much talent, size, and speed as any group fielded at Notre Dame in Rockne's tenure. Rule changes had chipped away somewhat at the Notre Dame shift as exploited by the Four Horsemen, so it's not a perfect comparison. Formerly, the small backs would use the shift to over-whelm defenders at the point of attack, often with seven men on one side of the center. Now his backs were more or less on their own to exploit openings made by the linemen. The old days with the entire backfield in motion at the snap was gone, but Rockne was in the process of fine-tuning the Irish machine.

The undefeated 1929 Irish, who never played a home game that season.

Indiana provided the opening competition. To the surprise of Irish fans who were still traumatized by the four losses in 1928, Rockne started his shock troops rather than just pound the Hoosiers with the first team. The subs did not score but did put together three good drives before Rockne called in the cavalry. A nifty Elder pass to Mullins set up Elder's 20-yard TD burst around right end early in the second quarter. Carideo showed some first-game jitters with a fumble that ended a drive, but he did snag a Hoosier pass later in the game, hauling it 60 yards before fumbling again at the Hoosiers' 8-yard line. Elder struck again in the third quarter with a 60-yard TD jaunt off left tackle with a sharp cutback to his right. He scored untouched. The Irish amassed 351 yards on the ground against the Hoosiers, who did not seem inclined to stop them on a regular basis.

As if having no home games were not enough adversity, this game provided even more for the Irish to have to deal with—in the first quarter, with Indiana in possession of the ball, aggressive Irish pursuit resulted in a sideline pileup in which a gaggle of three players slammed into Rockne, damaging his legs enough that phlebitis would eventually set in, severely curtailing his physical activity for the rest of the season. His assistant coaches would handle the heavy lifting—primarily Tom Lieb but also Jack Chevigny. Having been physically involved in his coaching all through his career, Rockne must have been beside himself. The McGann funeral home in South Bend retrofitted one of their hearses so that Rockne could be wedged into the vehicle while confined to a wheelchair, enabling him to attend some practices, covered in blankets, under constant medical supervision. With his family's home not far from the campus, he arranged for his players to visit him in position groups and face rapid-fire questions about plays, formations, and tactics. If he was unable to physically attend a game, he would listen to telephone reports from the press box. All in all, he was miserable not being able to do his work the way he had since 1914 when he worked as an assistant under Jesse Harper.

Unable to travel to Baltimore, Rockne had to be tormented to learn that Navy had scored in the first quarter against the scrubs. The starters, however, had not lost any faith and took off on a drive of their own, with a TD coming early in the second quarter—a slant pass from Carideo (from a kneeling position, with only one usable leg after nearly dodging a Navy hit) to Elder. Two fumbles and penalties kept the score tied until well into the second half. The opportunistic Carideo intercepted a Navy pass and hauled it back to the Middies' 32. From there, Brill romped for 17 yards, then seven more, setting up Mullins's 1-yard plunge for the final score of 14–7.

Rockne was forced to stay home for the second game in a row while his team went to Soldier Field in Chicago to meet the Wisconsin Badgers. Moon Mullins was hurt, so the fullback duties fell to Joe Savoldi, a powerful but speedy runner, and he made the most of his opportunity, scoring on long-haul runs of 40 yards in the first quarter and 71 in the third quarter. The Badgers did reach the Irish 3-yard line in the first quarter against the second team, but the drive fizzled right there. Against the starters the Badgers were stymied, never putting together more than three consecutive first downs (they had a total of seven for the whole game). Jack Elder flashed his brilliant speed in between Savoldi's scores with a 43-yard TD run.

Part Two

Notre Dame held Wisconsin pretty much in their end of the field once the starters entered the game. With this 19–0 shutout, the 90,000 fans at the game came away convinced that the 1929 Notre Dame team was going to be very difficult to beat.

The 19–0 score against Wisconsin had ominous echoes for many of the 1928 players because their next opponent, Carnegie Tech, had beaten the 1926 Notre Dame team by that very score, a game that Rockne had not attended so he could do some personal scouting at the Army-Navy game in Chicago. It proved to be a bad choice on his part; the shutout loss was the only blot on the 1926 schedule. In 1928, Rockne's weakest team, Tech had pasted the Irish, 27–7, as their battering ram fullback, 230-pound John Karcis, pretty much ran at will against an over-matched defense, setting up a very effective passing game. So the '29 team knew this would be a ferocious encounter. They did have Rockne at the game this time, however, as he ignored his doctor's orders to travel with the team. Bundled up in blankets, he was confined to a wheelchair on the sidelines. It was more than a mere gesture. His was a sheer act of will, dangerous though it was, that certainly helped propel Notre Dame past Carnegie Tech by a 7–0 margin. The Notre Dame line-men won the laurels for this game, keeping the dangerous Karcis under control, including the outstanding work of 193-pound guard Jack Cannon—the last Irish player to suit up without wearing a helmet of any sort. Cannon was a whirling der-vish throughout the game, including a decisive tackle of Karcis, causing a 2-yard loss late in the game. The only score came in the third quarter following a Carideo punt return to the 50. From there, Elder dashed 33 yards to the Tech 17. Brill powered to the 8-yard line. Then it fell to Savoldi from that point … four straight carries, with the last one launching him high over the pileup in the middle of the line of scrimmage for the game's only score.

A week later the Irish met Georgia Tech, the defending 1928 national champs in Atlanta. Tech took a 6–0 lead midway into the second quarter following a Mul-lins fumble at the Irish 19. Brill took the kickoff to the 40. After Mullins slammed off tackle for 6 yards, Elder turned on the jets for a 53-yard TD run. Later in the quarter, Cannon appeared to have blocked a Tech punt with his head, giving the Irish the ball at the Tech 31. Carideo hit right end Tom Conley with a 25-yard pass and Mullins blasted in from the 2-yard line as the Irish took a 13–6 halftime lead. In the third quarter, Carideo broke loose with a 75-yard TD punt return. The last score came in the fourth quarter when Marchie Schwartz showcased his quickness and determination with a TD burst from the Tech 8-yard line, wrapping up the 26–6 Irish win.

The Drake Bulldogs proved to be just that when they took advantage of an Al Howard fumble to march through Rockne's subs for a 7–0 lead, Chuck Van Koten slamming in from the Irish 2. Howard made amends by sparking a replying drive with a 35-yard jaunt deep into Drake's end of the field. Notre Dame kept hammering at the Bulldogs line and after a series of runs, Howard took the scoring honors from the Drake 3, but the PAT was missed. Drake held on to that score doggedly until well into the third quarter. With the game being played at Soldier Field, Rockne was able to be in attendance and he let the subs do what they could to rectify the situation, but a stalemate ensued until late in the third quarter when Elder spun loose for a 17-yard TD run. Late in the game, Mullins exploded for a 23-yard scoring run that put the game out of reach for Drake at 19–7.

The Irish returned to Soldier Field a week later to test themselves against USC, a team leading the nation in scoring including a 76–0 obliteration of UCLA. This was already an important intersectional rivalry only in its fourth iteration. Rockne again defied medical advice to attend this game. More than 110,000 spectators jammed the venue once again, and they weren't disappointed. Thousands of them had not even taken their seats before the Trojans scored with a long pass, thanks mainly to Irish defender Bucky O'Connor's black eye, injured moments before, and swollen shut to the point that he never saw the receiver or the pass. It may have been the easiest TD the Trojans ever scored on the Irish. All-American quarterback Marshall Duffield heaved the pass to his end, Marger Apsit, on the game's second play for a quick 6–0 lead as they missed the PAT. The score stayed that way until the second quarter when the shifty Conley hauled in a perfect 35-yard pass from Elder and finished off the final 20 yards for an Irish TD and a 6–6 tie. This score held into the second half when Notre Dame's Joe Savoldi blasted in on a short yardage play, with Carideo making good on the PAT. Unbelievably, the Trojans came right back when running back Russ Saunders (who served as a model for the Tommy Trojan statue on the USC campus) blasted past lunging Irish kickoff coverage for a 96-yard tally. The second missed PAT by USC spelled the difference in this crucial Irish victory, 13–12.

For the third week in a row, the Notre Dame football team made the trip to Chicago, this time to play Northwestern, but without Rockne this time, who had used this game as a motivational ploy for his players by reminding them that a win here would be his 100th win since 1917. (Of course, he had been involved in a 100th win much earlier than this 1929 game, so Rockne was cherry-picking to make a point; he wanted an undefeated team, yet another example of the great Notre Dame coach working on the emotions of his players to produce a desired result, as he had in the 1928 Army "Gipper" game.) His players apparently listened carefully to his plea; once the scrubs had handled the first quarter duties, the starters blasted the Wildcats with three scores in the second quarter—Schwartz blitzed for 40 yards to the Northwestern 40, Savoldi going the distance from there on the next play, then Schwartz hitting Brill with a 25-yard pass to the 10, scooting in himself from there around right end. The desperate Wildcats tried a long pass, but Carideo intercepted it and ran it back 85 yards for the final Irish TD of the half. Savoldi scored in the third quarter on a short run, capping a drive that featured his 32-yard run to the 8-yard line. Northwestern's lone score came when an errant center snap to an Irish back went astray, allowing the Wildcats' 254-pound tackle Dal Marvil to fall on it in the end zone to make the final score 26–6.

This left the Army game. Army … again … at yet another crucial point in the Irish schedule. The Cadets were led by their great All-American quarterback, Chris "Red" Cagle, then in his seventh consecutive season of college football, the first four being at Southwestern Louisiana. (Obviously, eligibility rules then were quite different from today, as seen in Army's Elmer Oliphant who played two seasons at Purdue in 1912–13 before playing for Army in 1916–17, helping to defeat the Irish in 1916.) The game was played in Yankee Stadium on a frigid day. With only a few exceptions, Army played even with Notre Dame. The Irish subs managed a few first downs in the early going but were unable to score. In the second quarter a big break gave Army their best chance when a powerful Cadet rush on a punt play pushed Elder into Carideo just as he contacted the ball, causing it to bounce erratically until Army downed it on the Irish 13-yard line. Army tried two runs and gained two yards, then Cagle took the snap and faded to his right, looked to his left, and heaved a high pass to the left corner of the goal line. The pass floated a bit and just as his receiver, Carl Carmark, was going to gather it in, Elder jumped high, intercepting the ball, and then started running at top speed down the right sideline. Three potential tacklers missed him and by the 50-yard line, he had John Law for a blocker trailing near him. Elder crossed the Army goal line untouched after dashing the full 100 yards of the field. Carideo kicked the PAT and the Irish defense held on, grabbing three other Army passes to keep the Cadets scoreless.

And with that 7–0 victory, thanks to Elder's miraculous play, the Irish cinched perhaps the most challenging national championship they would ever achieve—with no home games, Rockne on the sidelines for only three games, and very determined opponents. Three of Rockne's stalwarts were honored as All-Americans: quarterback Frank Carideo, the helmetless guard Jack Cannon, and tackle Ted Twomey.

1930

The house that Rockne built was ready for occupation. Southern Methodist would provide the first house guests at Notre Dame Stadium. There wasn't a bad seat in the entire stadium; viewing lines were outstanding from any angle. (It has been claimed that Rockne somehow envisioned the needs of television when he helped in the design process.)

Tragically, this would be Rockne's last Notre Dame team. His death at age forty-three in a commercial airplane accident in March 1931 would fix his reputation among the immortals of America's sporting pantheon. Of course, no one could have known this as the 1930 season commenced. They would have known, however, that he was returning to his usual frenetic level of activity, minus the hands-on practice approach he had championed for years with his players. He was still under close medical supervision, but the phlebitis in his legs was under control.

In 1918, his first as head coach, he had seven linemen who averaged 176 pounds. His backfield averaged 171 pounds. This 1930 team showed an increase in size of almost ten pounds on the line and five pounds for the backs, and he had some freshmen in 1930 that were considerably larger, such as Ed "Moose" Krause who was pushing 220 pounds. This illustrates a slow evolution in the nature of the game and Rockne's willingness to make adjustments, although the 1930 outfit still featured a classic Rockne-type player in right guard Bert Metzger, all 5-foot-9 and 149 pounds of him.

The first Notre Dame play with the ball the fans saw in the new stadium was Joe Savoldi taking SMU's kickoff up the middle of the field 98 yards for a TD. Quite the initiation! His score tied the game at 7–7, SMU having used its aerial circus to good effect in the first quarter to score on a four-play drive against the Irish reserves. In the second quarter a Mustang punt from the end zone resulted in a good runback by Carideo to the SMU 11-yard line. Two plays later, Schwartz sped off tackle for Notre Dame's second TD. SMU used three long passes after that to make the halftime score 14–14. After the break, Schwartz found Conley with a 48-yard bomb that put the Irish in good shape deep in SMU territory. A pass interference call placed the ball on the 4-yard line, and Schwartz cut back around left end for the score, making it 20–14. In the game's final moments SMU persisted with its passing game but the Irish center, Tommy Yarr, intercepted three passes to end their drives and preserve the win.

Navy was the next opponent, chosen for the formal dedication of the new stadium, but the story of the game can pretty much be told in two words: Joe Savoldi.

"Jumping Joe" ransacked the Middies' defense for three scores on runs of 55, 23, and 8 yards. He carried the ball 11 times for 123 yards. His first score was the 23-yarder in the second quarter, with a lateral pass from Brill off left tackle, duplicated moments later with a 55-yard TD burst. In the third quarter he pounded in from the 8 for his final tally. Sub fullback Fritz Staab bulled his way into the end zone in the fourth quarter for Notre Dame's final score, helped considerably by fellow reserve player Clarence Kaplan's 96 yards rushing, mostly late in the game. Other Irish subs gifted Navy with their two points with an errant snap to the punter, who downed the ball in his end zone for the 26–2 final score.

The last time Carnegie Tech had played under the Dome, it was at Cartier Field in 1928, and they convincingly delivered the first Irish home loss in a generation. Cartier Field was long gone for the 1930 contest, but the old sod had been transferred to the new stadium. Perhaps the sod had memories of that loss; certainly the Irish players and faithful remembered. So it was poetic justice that the terrible 1928 loss was avenged by the 1930 team by a 21–6 score. The Irish defense did a masterful job of keeping the Tech offense bottled up. They only reached Notre Dame's territory once in the whole game, earning their only touchdown. Meanwhile, Rockne pulled out all the stops on his offense using a baffling series of spinners, reverses, and laterals that had the Tech defenders totally confused. For the first Irish score, Schwartz hit end Ed Kosky with a 13-yard TD pass. After swapping interceptions, Schwartz capped a drive by pounding in from the 2-yard line. Tech's Howard "Dutch" Eyth scintillated the crowd with a sterling 72-yard TD run in the third quarter. Schwartz nullified that score later in the game, with a 56-yard TD throw to Conley. As a sign that Rockne *really* wanted this win, the shock troops only saw two minutes of game action; his regulars played 58 minutes.

After three straight home games, the team took a train to meet Pittsburgh, another tough, savvy Pennsylvania team. Pitt received the ball first but couldn't move, so they punted. The Irish took over at their own 40, and Schwartz had the first play—a run past left tackle that found him in the open. With a juke here and a juke there, he ended up in the end zone for the first of five TDs that the starters would register in the first half of the game. Schwartz's play was a microcosm of Rockne's game plan—run the ball, then run some more, as Pitt had worked diligently to repair the deficiencies revealed in their pass defense in earlier games. Effective running enabled the Irish to reach the 1-yard line a few minutes later and Mullins bucked the line for the TD. Savoldi recovered a Pitt fumble and teamed up with Brill to pound the ball to the Pitt 1-yard line again before Savoldi got the honors for the TD plunge. In the second quarter it was Savoldi again … but this time with an interception and a 42-yard TD return. The shock troops pieced together the last Irish scoring drive, highlighted by Bucky O'Connor's end runs of 32 and 45 yards before Mike Koken scored from the 5-yard line. Down 35–0, Pitt managed three scores against Notre Dame's deep reserves in the second half to make the final score 35–19.

Indiana visited Notre Dame next, and the first half was the opposite of the Pitt game's first half. The enthusiastic, hustling Hoosiers held the subs in check for the 20 minutes they were in the game, then did the same thing to the first team until halftime. After the half, though, the real Irish team showed up, with the irrepressible Savoldi romping for a 33-yard TD run, followed shortly thereafter by Schwartz's 26-yard tally. Schwartz grabbed a kick muffed by Mullins and raced 79 yards to set up Brill's first TD of the day, a 9-yard scramble. Brill then capped the scoring with a 23-yard TD burst. With his first two scores of his Notre Dame career (he had transferred from Penn) Brill led the Irish to 432 yards of total offense to Indiana's 76 … and the 27–0 win.

After his Indiana warm-up, Brill was squarely focused on meeting his old team, Penn. When he was a freshman, someone at Penn had told him that he was not good enough to play there. That remark rankled the young man who then made the decision to transfer from Penn and give it a try under the Golden Dome. He sat out the 1928 season but earned the starting right halfback spot on the 1929 team, as well as 1930. He and Irish captain Tom Conley played this game in front of their Philadelphia fans and family members. The outcome was perhaps a foregone conclusion. Rockne once again basically eschewed the forward pass and had his team work almost exclusively on the ground. The Quakers seemed primed as they were coming off a 21–6 upset of undefeated Kansas. Their hopes for another upset were destroyed when the Irish decimated them, 60–20. Indeed, Rockne's starters racked up a 43–0 score against a hapless Penn outfit. The Irish subs gave up the 20 points while they added another 17 for the final score. Brill ran wild, scoring three TDs—scoring enough to beat Penn by himself. On his first carry, he made a point of showing he was good enough by blasting past his former teammates for a 65-yard TD. The starters racked up a 28–0 lead by halftime. Rockne let his subs play for a bit until he realized that Penn was an even match for them, so he got the starters back in to run it up to 43–0. Brill added two more touchdowns on long runs to go with TDs by Carideo, Schwartz, Savoldi, Mullins, and O'Connor. The Quakers never managed a first down against the starters.

Drake was supposed to be a breather the following week, but the visitors had plenty of fight in them. Unfortunately, the Irish had lost Savoldi to marriage (with a divorce pending). His marital status had been kept secret and, when exposed, the school's strict rules of the day required expulsion. Rockne had been keeping an eye on one of the scrubs, Dan Hanley, and promoted him to the second team. The Bulldogs starters played the Irish shock troops to a scoreless tie in the first quarter, then Rockne sent in the first unit. Hanley was with them on one drive and showed his stuff right away with a 32-yard TD scamper. Drake tied it before Schwartz broke loose with their kickoff to all the way down to the 13. Two runs later, the Irish pulled off a trick play from the 3-yard line … the center's snap to Carideo who then faked a pass, then handed off to Brill, who took it in for the go-ahead TD. Mullins slammed in for another TD in the third quarter, thanks to timely passing by Schwartz, who later wrapped up the scoring at 28–7 with a 43-yard run.

The defending national champions next met the Big Ten champs, Northwestern, in Evanston, so something had to give. It looked like it would be Notre Dame in the second quarter as the Wildcats twice reached the Irish 5-yard line only to be denied by furious line play by the Irish defense. Shortly after Northwestern would turn the ball over on these failed drives, Carideo would blast long punts to avert further threats. Schwartz sparked a drive with pinpoint passing to reach the Wildcats 18-yard line. At that point, he pulled out a "delayed half spinner" that rocketed

Rockne's last Notre Dame team, the undefeated 1930 national champs.

him through a hole by the right tackle, following a great block by end Johnny O'Brien, to record the first score of the day. Carideo made the PAT and later put Northwestern in deep trouble with a punt that went out of bounds at their 1-yard line. Northwestern had to try something to turn the tide, so they opted for a hook-and-ladder play but guard Tom Kassis was there and intercepted the lateral on their 27-yard line. Moments later, Schwartz found Carideo with a 13-yard pass to the 1-yard line, with Hanley taking it in from there to make the final score 14–0.

The one major difference in the 1930 matchup against Army was that the game was not played in the East. Instead, this was the first time the Cadets had made the long trek from the Hudson River to an appropriate site for them—Soldier Field in Chicago. At least 110,000 fans showed up for the game, and every one of them, along with the teams, suffered through a frigid, wet, sloppy day. Both teams took a conservative approach to the game in light of the terrible footing and soggy footballs. The crowd wanted a football game, and they got a punting duel, with Carideo handling this chore slightly better than his Army counterpart. With only five minutes left in the game, neither team had scored. Only two passes were completed all day. The Irish were insistent about running off tackle and using spinner and fake spinner plays. Finally, the "Perfect Play" that Rockne preached incessantly happened right there in front of 110,000 people: Schwartz careening off tackle with blockers to spare, and bolting 54 yards for the Irish TD. Carideo made the PAT. The teams exchanged possessions in the time remaining before Army's Dick King surged through the Irish line to block a Carideo punt and fell on it in the end zone for an Army touchdown. Notre Dame, however, returned the favor by blocking Army's PAT attempt, sealing the 7–6 win and maintaining their hard-earned undefeated status.

The 1930 finale was against highly ranked Southern California on their home field. The Irish had survived the Army melee, but Rockne had lost his lone remaining fullback, Mullins, to injury. Of course, Savoldi was a distant memory. The team would take the long train ride out west and look for opportunities to stretch their legs and get in a little practice. The ever-keen Rockne saw an opportunity here. The team had a gaggle of reporters meeting them at every stop, and they were invited to watch the practices and report on them. Little did they know (except for Notre Dame alumnus Francis Wallace, who kept mum about the whole affair) that Rockne was orchestrating his greatest ruse ever right before their eyes. He switched second-string right halfback Bucky O'Connor to the fullback spot. More to the point, he had him suited up as Hanley, the last remaining fullback. Now, O'Connor was several inches taller than Hanley and 15 pounds heavier but he was almost as fast as former star Jack Elder. Rockne carefully choreographed practices in which O'Connor looked like the fullback no one would want—slow, inclined to fumble, broken plays. You name it, Rockne had O'Connor do anything to make himself—as Hanley—look terrible. Of course, the naïve members of the fourth estate took this major scoop in hook, line, and sinker and reported it often enough that the news made it to the Trojans, who feasted their hopes on the details of incompetence. It's pretty fair to say that this charade would never happen today.

Just prior to the game, Rockne had one more trick: In the Coliseum's locker room just before the game was to start, right in front of his team he had the team trainer wrap his ailing legs with the rubber sheathing used to control the phlebitis that had afflicted him since the Indiana game of the prior season. The players all knew full well that Rockne had suffered terribly during the 1929 season, even though he made every effort to be there for his young men. And here he was again, possibly putting his life on the line as the Irish faced the famous Southern Cal juggernaut. The Trojans had suffered one loss early in the season, a surprising 7–6 upset at the hands of Washington State, but under head coach Howard Jones they had simply crushed many of their opponents after that: 65–0, 74–0, 52–0, 32–0.

The Trojans never knew what hit them. Actually, what hit them was Bucky O'Connor. Early in the second quarter, with the Irish leading, 7–0, thanks to a Trojan fumble and a 19-yard TD pass from Schwartz to Carideo, O'Connor was unleashed on an 80-yard TD run. Prepped for a slow fullback, the Trojans didn't have a chance. O'Connor tacked on a 7-yard TD burst later in the game. Hanley, who was supposed to be the fullback, intercepted a Trojan pass later in the game and sub quarterback Nick Lukats then ripped in for the final TD from the Trojans 11-yard line. Notre Dame's dominance in all phases of the game is reflected in the statistics underlying the 27–0 score: 433 yards of total offense to 140 yards, 16 first downs to 8. USC made it to the Irish 33- and 34-yard lines on two occasions; as the game ended they reached the Irish 21 with frantic passes to no avail. The slow fullback O'Connor averaged almost 11 yards per carry.

Four days later, the team was honored with a ticker-tape parade in Chicago, such was the fervor they generated. Notre Dame was declared the undisputed national championship team, and the 1930 season should be remembered forever by all who love the Irish. This illustrious group saw seven men honored as All-Americans: Frank Carideo (for the second time), running backs Marchy Schwartz, Marty Brill (not good enough for Penn), and Joe Savoldi, with guard Bert Metzger, end Tom Conley, and tackle Al Culver rounding out the honors.

Tragically, it would be Knute Rockne's final season as head coach for Notre Dame. He spent twenty years of his life there and is forever wedded to the school's name and reputation. His death in a plane crash in March 1931 would bring the entire nation to a state of shocked grief. The fate of the Fighting Irish football team would be left in the hands of others, who would often find themselves and their coaching results unfairly compared to the little immigrant from Norway.

1943

Barely two years into the decade of the 1940s, for the second time in a generation, America found itself embroiled in a world war. This brutal fact impacted virtually all facets of life in this country, including intercollegiate football. Notre Dame's famous former president, Father Theodore Hesburgh, C.S.C., stated on many occasions that the university owed its continued existence at that time to the US Navy for placing one of six V-12 officer training programs at the school that quickly registered as many as 1,300 officer candidates. There were hundreds of players who were transferred from their home institution to other schools, meeting the demands of the military build-up. Notre Dame, for example, picked up running back Julie Rykovich, among others, from Illinois.

Only two players returned from the 1942 starting team—Angelo Bertelli at quarterback and the last of the Miller clan, Creighton. No less than twenty-three men who had won ND monograms in '42 had graduated. The entire line had to be replaced with former subs; fullback Jim Mello would join Bertelli, Miller, and Rykovich in the backfield. Overall, this was a fairly large group from end to end, tipping the scales at a 200-pound average, while the backfield was immensely talented, with a quarterback who would win the Heisman Trophy and his back-up, Johnny Lujack, who would win the same award a few years down the road. It would prove to be a high-scoring outfit that could put the hammer down on defense.

Pitt, now coached by Clark Shaughnessy, formerly of Stanford, where he drew national attention for his innovations with the T formation, would provide the competition in the first game. His 1940 Stanford team had gone undefeated and he was also instrumental in the Chicago Bears' 73–0 dismantling of the Washington Redskins in the NFL title game. So there was plenty to fret about in the run-up to the game.

As it turned out, there was little reason to worry. Frank Leahy was almost never outcoached, and his 1943 Notre Dame team would make a splash right away by drilling Shaughnessy's Pitt Panthers on their home turf, 41–0. The teams tested each other for most of the first quarter, but a Pitt fumble on their 35 led quickly to Creighton Miller barreling in from the 4-yard line, and the rout was on. Miller wasn't done yet. Moments later, he took off on a 40-yard TD jaunt. Another Pitt fumble, this one on their 2-yard line, led immediately to a Bertelli fumble recovery and TD. Rykovich added two TD runs, and Bob Palladino tacked on the last Irish TD of the day. The Irish ground game was overwhelming; they only used six passes all day, just to keep it interesting. Leahy's defense never let Pitt go further than the Irish 32-yard line, and that advance was courtesy of the Panthers' only pass completion of the day.

They had some old business to take care of in their second contest against Georgia Tech. The Yellow Jackets had upended Notre Dame in South Bend in 1942, 13–6. In beautiful weather, the Domers annihilated Georgia Tech, 55–13, running roughshod over their defenders for 451 yards on the ground, accumulating 24 first downs, and tallying eight TDs. Bertelli threw three TD passes and fullback Jim Mello blasted in for another three scores. Bertelli's scoring targets were Rykovich, Miller, and Ray Kuffel; Irish subs Bob Hanlon and George Sullivan tacked on the final two touchdowns. Georgia Tech had to resort to trick plays, but a Statue of Liberty play was demolished by Notre Dame's 6-foot-7 tackle John "Tree" Adams, causing a fumble and leading to an Irish TD.

There was more business to attend to as the No. 1 ranked Irish took a train to Ann Arbor to meet the Wolverines, the team that introduced the game of football to Notre Dame in 1887 and the winner of nine of the previous ten contests between the schools. The only Irish win had come in 1909. As usual, Michigan was loaded with talent, including their great running back Bill Daley, complemented by the estimable Elroy "Crazy Legs" Hirsch, sent to Michigan from Wisconsin by the military. Past Wolverine wins meant nothing to this group of Irish players, however. Early in the first quarter, Creighton Miller blasted through left guard and then broke to his right, roaring 66 yards for the TD, silencing the 90,000 Michigan fans. The Wolverines' Bill Daley scored shortly after that, but the PAT went wide, and Michigan never came any closer after that. Michigan then kicked off, and the Irish seemed to be assembling a patient drive, but on the fourth play Bertelli found running back Freddie Earley 20 yards downfield on the 50, hit him in mid-stride with a perfect pass, and Earley did the rest for the second Notre Dame TD. Miller did it again shortly after Earley's stellar play, 57 yards this time, but a holding penalty brought the ball back. After driving to the 9, Notre Dame could not score but Michigan was forced to punt, letting Bertelli work his magic again, with a long pass to right end Jack Zilly that set up a TD blast by fullback Jim Mello. In the second half, Rykovich made a great 40-yard punt return deep into Michigan territory, giving Bertelli the privilege of a short plunge for his own TD. Bertelli later wrapped up Notre Dame's scoring with a 16-yard pass to Miller. Michigan kept trying, with the Irish subs stopping them at the 6 inch line at one point, but they managed a consolation score as the clock hit 00:00, making the final score 35–12.

Next came yet another grudge game, this one against Wisconsin. The Badgers, coached by former Four Horseman Harry Stuhldreher, had tied the Irish, 7–7, in 1942. The seven points in their 1942 score would be more than their yards gained rushing for the entire contest in the 1943 game—five yards. The Badgers had basically been stripped of returning starters due to military reassignments. On the other hand, Leahy kept his starters in the game for just a few plays: 22 rushing plays to be precise, and they scored five TDs in that 18-minute span. Subs scored three other TDs for Notre Dame. With Bertelli at the helm, Rykovich slammed in for the first Irish score within three minutes of the first quarter kickoff. Shortly after that, Mello capped a 52-yard drive with a second tally. Miller repeated three minutes later. Nine minutes, three Irish TDs. And so it went; the Badgers reached Notre Dame territory only twice in the entire game.

The Fighting Illini provided the opposition for Bertelli's last home game, as his military call-up was pending. The Illini were also another team that had been depleted by the military ripple effects of the world war. Rykovich was facing his former teammates, and quickly scored the first TD of the game with a 25-yard pass from Bertelli, initiating a TD barrage for Notre Dame: Miller, Lujack, Earley, and Palladino all hammered in TDs as the Irish dominated the game from start to finish, winning, 47–0. In three consecutive games against Big 10 opposition, Leahy's Irish prevailed, 132–12, and would remain at the top of the rankings for the rest of the campaign.

Notre Dame took a train to Cleveland to play Navy in Memorial Stadium, with 80,000 reportedly in attendance, a stadium record for the day. In his Notre Dame career finale, Bertelli fired three TD passes as the Irish swamped Navy, 33–6. The story of the game might have been Notre Dame's pass defense, as Middie quarterback Hal Hamberg had only eight completions in 38 attempts. By contrast, Bertelli had 36 attempts with 25 completions, good for 10 TDs in his six-game 1943 season. Bertelli's first TD against Navy went for 50 yards to Rykovich, who turned on the jets after receiving the throw. Miller turned a short Bertelli pass into a 40-yard wonder for the second TD as he juked and squeezed past flailing Navy would-be tacklers. In the third quarter, ahead by only one TD, Bertelli found 6-foot-4 right end John Yonakor for his third scoring pass of the day. A Mello interception set up a second Miller TD, this time on a 3-yard run. Navy reached the Irish 14, but couldn't score. Sub fullback Vic Kulbitski staggered the Middies with a 71-yard run, prepping the scene for yet another Irish TD, an 8-yard keeper by Bertelli. With the 33–6 score, Bertelli then left the university and joined the active duty Marines. After various postings to stateside Marine facilities, Lieutenant Bertelli saw a different kind of action: Iwo Jima. A Japanese mortar shell almost killed him during that battle, surely a moment that put his glorious football career in a very different perspective.

Keeping the military theme going, the Irish played undefeated Army in Yankee Stadium with a new quarterback, Johnny Lujack. An early Irish drive died at the Army 3-yard line, as the Cadets put up a stout defense, with Irish penalties aiding the Cadet cause as well. Moments later, following an Army punt and return that put the ball on the Army 31, Lujack spotted Yonakor and pitched a perfect pass to him in the corner of the end zone for the opening score. The Irish defense kept Army frustrated; Miller snagged an interception, Bob Kelly grabbed two, and Jim White swiped the ball from the grasp of Glenn Davis to set up the second TD. Lujack took the scoring honors on a short run for the third Irish tally, and Earley slammed in from the Army 3-yard line to round out the 26–0 shutout.

With the academies dispatched, there was an interim game with civilians (Northwestern) before the Irish would run smack into two more units much more closely affiliated with the war effort than any college: the Iowa Pre-Flight Seahawks (ranked No. 2 nationally) and the Great Lakes Navy Bluejackets. But first came Northwestern on their home turf. The Wildcats played the Irish straight up for almost the entire first half, but Lujack had seen enough to find Bob Kelly open for a TD strike. The 6–0 lead held into the third quarter, and Lujack hooked up again with Kelly. Miller and Rykovich tacked on their own TDs for the Irish's total of 25 points. Northwestern scored on a windfall play—a lateral from sub quarterback Frank Dancewicz intended for Miller but the Wildcat end on that side of the play had crashed through the blockers and grabbed the football in midair. Of course, there was no one left to tackle him, and he rumbled into the end zone for their only score.

For the second time in the season, Leahy would be meeting another team coached by one of the key innovators of the game—Don Faurot, who would lead the Missouri Tigers to 101 wins in his two terms as their head coach (separated by his military career). Faurot, a living legend in the Show Me State, had unveiled his split T formation in 1941, taking the Tigers to an 8–2 record. The split T was the forerunner of today's option offenses and created some serious problems for the defenses of the 1940s. Whereas Clark Shaughnessy had a rather weak team at Pitt, Faurot's 1943 Iowa Pre-Flight Seahawks boasted former pro players to go with some good college players on the roster. Leahy's team had their work cut out for them.

The Seahawks kept the Irish from scoring in the first half, while they racked up one TD by Art Guepe (who had last played college football in 1936). Leahy fired his team up at halftime and they showed new intensity in their first possession of the second half, driving 64 yards with Bob Kelly slashing in from the 3 for the tying score. Later in the third quarter, there was a rare Lujack error—a fumble that led to a Dick Todd to Dick Burk TD pass, but the PAT kick ricocheted off the right upright, a costly mistake. The Irish responded with a 55-yard TD march, Miller rumbling in for the tying points from the 6-yard line. The PAT by Fred Earley was good, giving the Irish a 14–13 lead. The Seahawks were unable to capitalize on a subsequent Irish fumble, their frantic passing game in the waning moments of the game going for naught, including a missed field goal. The Irish had taken the Seahawks' best shot and came away victorious by a point. The No. 1 team in the country had successfully defended its ranking against No. 2.

Notre Dame faced one more daunting test—the Great Lakes Navy Bluejackets, possibly a better team than Iowa Pre-Flight, featuring a young running back who had earlier enrolled at Notre Dame before being reassigned by the military—Emil "Six Yards" Sitko. Lujack directed a long, patient drive for the first score, taking the ball himself for the score. Great Lakes drove twice for scores, the first by Sitko (one wonders how painful this was for this great back), the second by Dewey Proctor who got loose for a 50-yard scoring sprint. Notre Dame came right back with another long drive, 80 yards in 18 plays, with fullback Mello cashing in 54 of those difficult yards. Lujack found Miller with a spot-on pass for the go-ahead TD, giving the Irish a 14–12 lead. With less than a minute remaining in the game, and the ball at the Irish 46, Bluejackets quarterback Steve Lach set up to pass, but a strong rush pressured him, with one Notre Dame lineman getting a hand on him just as he threw the ball to Paul Anderson, who made a clean catch and a short run of 5 yards for the game-winning TD.

Even after this bitter 19–14 defeat, this magnificent college football team was awarded the national championship by the Associated Press. Six players earned various All-American honors: Bertelli, halfback Creighton Miller, and almost enough linemen to fill out the front—end John Yonakor, tackle Jim White, guard Pat Filley, and center Herb Coleman.

1946

The Irish could have suffered through two lean years in 1944–45 after having lost a Heisman–winning quarterback and many of the leaders of the 1943 national championship team. Several starting players had entered the war effort, head coach Frank Leahy was in the Navy, Lujack was not running the team, and so forth. Indeed, the team had two head coaches—Ed McKeever in 1944, and Hugh Devore in 1945. Nevertheless, the Irish somehow managed to win 15 games in those two seasons while losing only four and tying one.

The 1946 Notre Dame team, however, would be a major rebuilding effort for Leahy. He did get Lujack back as his quarterback; he had a few linemen with experience but most of the line was new, as were most of the backs. Despite that, this group was loaded with talent: left end Jim Martin, left tackle George Connor, left guard Bill Fischer, running back Emil Sitko, and Jim Mello, a veteran fullback from the 1942–43 teams. These were mature men, not teenagers. Several had seen combat in the war; college football would be fun compared to that, even with the hard-driving Leahy at the helm. Lurking in the second unit was a right end, Leon Hart, listed at 6-foot-4 and 225 pounds as a freshman. Just as Leahy had coached two players who would win the Heisman in 1943, the 1946 team presented the same good fortune with Lujack and Hart as future winners of the most prestigious award in collegiate football. Lujack and Connor would be consensus All-Americans in 1946; two others also received All-American honors.

Leahy's "lads" opened with Illinois in Champaign, declared the No. 2 team by preseason prognosticators. The Illini were loaded with good players. Julie Rykovich was back with them, speedster Buddy Young (fifth in 1944 Heisman voting) had been driving defenses crazy, and Alex Agase (three-time All-American) led a tough lineman group. The Illini proved to be a tough outfit for most of the first quarter, but Sitko broke the stalemate with an 83-yard run past right end after taking a lateral from Lujack. Ironically, it was Rykovich who stopped him short of the end zone, on the 3-yard line. Bob Livingstone slammed in from there for the first score. The Irish added to their lead with a three-play drive late in the second quarter: Mello for 30 yards, Sitko for 11 more to the 14, then Mello running it in for the TD from there with a run around right end. The Illini kept up their stiff resistance for a scoreless third quarter, but they put the ball on the turf for reserve Irish tackle Gasper Urban to recover in the fourth quarter and Terry Brennan scored a few plays later from the 4-yard line. Mike Swistowicz had two interceptions in the game, his second giving fullback Cornie Clatt a chance to score for the 26–6 final tally. Rykovich earned his team's only score with a 63-yard TD pass to Bill Heiss. The game showed the makings of a great team defeating a good team; it also revealed the depth of talent that Leahy had, with not much difference in talent among the first three units. "Six Yard" Sitko more than doubled his nickname claim when he averaged 14.4 yards per carry for the day, taking advantage of a highly efficient set of linemen. In contrast, Leahy's defense held Buddy Young to 40 yards on 11 frustrating carries. The Irish also showcased three outstanding quarterbacks: Lujack, George Ratterman, and Frank Tripucka, all three of whom would eventually play pro football.

Notre Dame's 1946 home opener was against the Pitt Panthers. The early October weather was hot and humid, but the Pitt team held their own for most of the first quarter. The Irish were moving, but not scoring until Lujack saw some openings early in the second quarter, hitting right end Jack Zilly with a 12-yard strike before completing a 24-yard scoring pass to Bob Livingstone. Center George Strohmeyer intercepted a Pitt pass, Lujack connected on two passes, and Terry Brennan charged into the end zone from the Pitt 7. Both PAT tries were missed, so Pitt was still within calling distance at the half. The play-by-play attrition of meeting a great Irish team resulted in a Pitt fumble in the third quarter, Jim Martin recovering. Lujack quickly converted the turnover into a TD pass to Mello. Leahy, unforgiving with mistakes in execution, inserted veteran Fred Earley for the PAT, and he made it 19–0. Mello added a TD to that score, hauling the mail, untouched, from the Pitt 8. Earley made the PAT kick. In the fourth quarter, an eight-play drive ended with a Terry Brennan TD and an Earley PAT for the 33–0 final score. For the day, Leahy's offense racked up 19 first downs and 468 all-purpose yards. The Notre Dame defense virtually choked Pitt's offense into submission—they allowed only four first downs and 42 yards of total Pitt offense.

The Purdue Boilermakers traveled north to visit the Domers but went home with a stinging 49–6 defeat. As is often the case, the visitors came out of the tunnel with a lot of fight in them, and they were able to sustain that for much of the first quarter. It wasn't a cheap shot by Purdue, but starting running back Bob Livingstone was injured and helped off the field in the first frame, a vision that seemed to arouse the somnolent Irish. Mello promptly slammed from his 34-yard line for 33 yards. John Panelli struck for 18, then 10 more. Mello powered in from the 1 for the first Irish score and Earley, not wearing any shoulder pads, came in to make the first of seven PATs for the day. The teams traded fumbles in the second quarter, then it was Brennan's turn to spark a drive with excellent running—27 yards, then 9, then 6. Clatt exploded in from the 1-yard line for the second Irish score. Before the half ended, a Purdue punt resulted in a 47-yard punt return by Jerry Cowhig down to their 33. After a 5-yard gain, Lujack snapped a 25-yard TD pass to Brennan for the 21–0 halftime score. The Irish were just getting started. Purdue lost a fumble to Jim Martin on their own 18 early in the third quarter. From that spot on the field, sophomore John Panelli, the third team fullback, took a reverse from Lujack around left end, dropped some would-be Boilermaker tacklers with a good move, and blasted past the safety for a TD. Later in the quarter, Panelli kept up the pressure with a nifty 42-yard run, followed by Lujack's TD pass to Jack Zilly, who made a great fingertip catch in the end zone. The Irish were probably mentally adding up their accumulated points when the Purdue quarterback, John Galvin, escaped their defensive notice and zoomed 52 yards for the only Boilermaker TD of the day. The Irish knew that a lapse like that would not be tolerated by Leahy, so Bob Skoglund speared a Purdue pass and took it in for the score. By this time, Leahy was using all ambulatory fourth-string players; Billy Gompers scored the final Irish TD with a 20-yard run in the game's final minutes, reaching the 49–6 final score.

Ranked second nationally, the Irish met Iowa (ranked No. 17) on their turf. Notre Dame had not enjoyed the luck of the Irish in Iowa City, having lost games there in 1921 and 1939. Leahy, ever the student of football history, wanted to build on his team's 1945 home demolition of the Hawkeyes (56–0) by breaking their string of bad luck at Iowa Field. It didn't take long for Leahy's lads to assert their dominance. In the third minute of the game, Lujack heaved a 65-yard TD strike to a wide-open Terry Brennan, and the rout was on. The next Irish scoring drive featured a one-handed catch of a Lujack pass by massive freshman end Leon Hart, good for 43 yards to the Iowa 11-yard line. Three plays later, Panelli bolted in from the 1 for Notre Dame's second TD. Earley's PAT attempt was blocked, but the Irish led, 13–0. On the next Irish drive, Lujack completed passes to Hart and Swistowicz to move the ball from his 20 to the Iowa 47 but then fumbled the ball. The luck of the Irish took over at that point when he quickly recovered his own fumble and took off for the Hawkeye end zone, earning Notre Dame's third TD of the day. Iowa used a bad pass interference call to reach Notre Dame's 10-yard line, scoring from there four plays later to make the halftime score 20–6. In the third quarter, a trio of Irish running backs—Coy McGee, Sitko, and Mello—moved the ball downfield to the Iowa 3-yard line, with Sitko getting the scoring honors from that point. In the opening minutes of the fourth quarter, Pete Ashbaugh speared Emlen Tunnell's pass on the Irish 15 and ran it back 38 yards. Lujack hit Hart twice with passes, reaching the Iowa 13. From that point, Lujack handed off to Sitko three straight times and Red crashed through for the TD on the third try. Leahy ended up using his reserves and tried to keep it simple, but Gompers managed to get loose around left end for a 25-yard TD run, making the final score 41–6. The Irish piled up 392 yards of total offense to Iowa's 170, good enough for the win they wanted in Iowa City.

Enough for fancy football stuff for Notre Dame. Leahy was looking at Navy next, in Baltimore, and then Army, at Yankee Stadium. He wanted to keep his cards close to his chest playing the Middies. Not surprisingly, Army had been a supremely powerful team under Red Blaik in 1944 and 1945, demolishing the Irish, for instance, 59–0 and 49–0. Like Leahy's teams of the era, they had two players who would be Heisman winners—the immortal running backs Glenn Davis (halfback, Mr. Outside, Heisman in 1946) and Doc Blanchard (fullback, Mr. Inside, Heisman in 1945). In their careers, they would score a total of 97 TDs for the Cadets.

Just contemplating this upcoming Army game, its talented personnel, and the high stakes involved would be enough to distract anyone from giving their full consideration to the actual next foe, Navy. Somehow, Leahy managed to keep it all in perspective and had his team ready for the Middies. They were so ready for Navy, in fact, that observers at the game thought that the second and third units looked better than the starters.

The Midshipmen played Notre Dame tough enough for the first eleven minutes, but a patient drive moved the ball to the Navy 31 and Jerry Cowhig rumbled past his left end to pay dirt and a 7–0 Irish lead. Leahy took his foot off the pedal but fourth-string right halfback Floyd Simmons saw his opportunity and slammed in two TDs as Notre Dame took a 21–0 halftime lead. Leahy's team played vanilla football until near the end of the fourth quarter when two more subs sparked a 6-play drive with Tripucka at quarterback, Gompers blasting in from the Navy 2 for the 28–0 final score. Even with third and fourth-string players and a basic plan of attack, Notre Dame racked up 444 yards of total offense to Navy's 139, while piling up 27 first downs to Navy's eight. It was total domination, but could they crank it up this well against Army?

The immovable object meets the irresistible force. Which one gives? In the case of the 1946 Notre Dame-Army game, neither side capitulated and the teams played one of the all-time great football games to a 0–0 tie. This was not a "game of the decade." It was a game for the ages. The team that won the 1943 national championship would be clashing with the 1944–45 national champs, owners of a 25-game winning streak. Both teams had two players who would be able to claim the Heisman (Blanchard and Davis, Lujack and Hart). Both were loaded with talent and stars. Army would field three consensus All-Americans: Blanchard and Davis, of course, but also end Hank Foldberg. The Irish had two—Lujack and tackle George Connor. Both teams included other players recognized by various All-American voters: Army's other end, George Poole, quarterback Arnold Tucker, and guards Arthur Gerometta and Joe Steffy and tackle John Mastrangelo and center George Strohmeyer for the Irish. This does not even count several players on Leahy's team who would earn such honors later in their careers under the Dome.

No Army team had ever scored against a Leahy-led Notre Dame team. This game would not change that pattern. Nor would Army keep up its torrid scoring pace from '44 and '45 against the Irish when Leahy was serving in the Navy. As with most football fans in the country, the 74,000 spectators in Yankee Stadium fully expected a great game. They were not disappointed, if you don't mind defenses overwhelming offenses. That was the story of the game. The statistics were about equal. The Irish had the only sustained drive, an 85-yard effort that fizzled at the Army 3. Both teams had the same distance for the longest run—21 yards. Then

Two Heisman winners, with Lujack saving the day for the 1946 Irish as he targets Army's Doc Blanchard.

Doc Blanchard threatened a breakaway TD on a counter play to the left, but as he lumbered past the left edge of the Irish defense he was downed with a picture-perfect tackle by Lujack from his safety position on the Irish 36-yard line. Legend has it that Lujack's tackle was the only time in Mr. Inside's career that he was brought down in the open field. Army completed only four passes, the Irish only five. Leahy had taken enough players for three full units to play but he never used up much of that depth. His top-line players had to gut it out against Cadets who were doing just that as well.

With the battle of the titans behind them, the Irish could look forward to competition with mere mortals such as the Northwestern Wildcats. The Irish unleashed a powerful running game on its first possession, featuring a 34-yard sprint by Sitko and good running by Livingstone and Mello, before Sitko crashed into the end zone from a yard away. Earley made the PAT. In terrible, wet weather conditions Notre Dame's backs pretty much had their way throughout the game, but they were not able to add to Sitko's score for nearly 44 minutes, until well into the fourth quarter. Both teams had negligible passing attacks. The Wildcats did reach Irish territory four times in the first half, but two interceptions detonated their scoring hopes. Northwestern really toughened up, however, as the Irish closed in on the Wildcat end zone, neutralizing several good drives after Sitko's score. The Domers reached the Northwestern 10 in the third quarter but lost 13 yards, and Leahy called on Earley for a rare field goal try, which he missed. Leahy then started using his reserves at that point, with Ratterman at quarterback, and he promptly led two scoring drives of 43 and 59 yards, with Panelli registering the TDs to cap both drives. With Tripucka in the driver's seat late in the game, Emil Slovak burst around his left end for an 18-yard scoring run to finish the Irish scoring in their 27–0 win. Irish dominance was very clear: 423 yards gained rushing to 52 for the Wildcats; 27 first downs to four. And half of the game found the Irish starters standing in their rain gear on the sidelines.

The Irish dropped a 41–0 whipping on Tulane in New Orleans, surfing through the Green Wave for 552 yards of offense, with 428 yards picked up in a brutal running attack (a costly one though, as both Sitko and Ernie Zalejski were lost for the season with injuries). Lujack brought his "A" game by hitting his first six passes, leading to four pounding runs from the 20 before Mello's TD blast. Tulane wilted on their possession, and Lujack went right back to work, hitting Terry Brennan with a TD pass for a 13–0 lead at the end of the first quarter. Leahy put in the second string and after some self-inflicted adversity, freshman Ernie Zalejski zipped 24 yards for his first Irish TD. A four-play Irish drive quickly covered 49 yards, with Zalejski again running it in. In the third quarter, Lujack was back in the game, and he led an 81-yard march which included a perfectly executed Statue of Liberty play, with Gompers gaining 23 yards off that play. The Irish soon thereafter used a hook-and-ladder play with Zalejski gaining 11 more. Mello capped the drive with one of his patented TD bursts and a 34–0 lead after three quarters. In the fourth quarter, Mike Swistowicz pulled off some good runs, setting up Coy McGee for a 5-yard TD run off right tackle and the 41–0 final score.

The USC Trojans made a late-season trip to Notre Dame (a pattern that changed after the 1960 season) for the finale. Leahy missed the game due to an illness, but Moose Krause filled in for him. Leahy was known for his intensity and ability to focus totally on the task at hand. He even kept a cot in his office for the many nights when he would not be going home. Moose, who would become the Notre Dame athletic director in 1949, came to the USC game wound up rather tightly. Someone asked him who would be starting for the Irish. Moose thought it over for a second or two and proclaimed with his deep voice, "Who are we gonna start? Why, we'll start everybody!!"

Despite Moose's reply, the eleven men Notre Dame had on the field at any one time during the game were able to whack the Trojans, 26–6, and complete an undefeated season. USC held their own for the first quarter, but they couldn't sustain that level of proficiency against the talented Irish. Part of their problem was an Irish player they could not have prepped for (he was not even in the game program)—Coy McGee. He was all over the place and the Trojans had a hard time containing him. They didn't actually contain him; he gained 146 yards on six carries. McGee (after losing an 80-yard TD kickoff return to a penalty) led the first decent Irish drive with various runs that befuddled USC, but on the 17-yard line, a fumble stopped the Irish advance. The USC punter blasted an amazing 83-yard effort shortly thereafter. McGee went to work again; taking a lateral from Ratterman, he skipped past his right end and then jetted 77 yards for the first Irish TD. With the Trojans having their hands full trying to stop a bevy of Irish runners, Ratterman fired a 22-yard TD to Leon Hart. Earley made up for his first PAT miss with a good one this time for the 13–0 halftime score. USC looked good to start the second half and, with the help of a referee's call, found the ball on the Irish 1-yard line. Johnny Naumu, from Hawaii, scored the TD from there. A missed PAT left it at 13–6. The Irish starters handled the rest of the quarter and may have pulverized the Trojans enough for Moose to put in the reserves again. Ratterman led a march sparked by Floyd Simmons's 49-yard foray around left end, then capped by McGee's second TD on a hidden ball play. For the last scoring drive,

Pete Ashbaugh delivered a 35-yard punt return, reaching the Trojan 25. Simmons repeated his run past left end for 10 yards, then Gerry Cowhig pulled of a "lulu" according to observers, scoring through a cavernous hole on his first run of the game, a 15-yard TD for the final 26–6 score.

Leahy, the Irish, and the countless fans had their undefeated season!

In Philadelphia, on that same November Saturday, Navy beat Army, 21–18. Perhaps the stupendous 0–0 contest three weeks earlier with Notre Dame had taken some of the starch out of the Cadets. In any case, Notre Dame was subsequently declared the national champions for 1946. Accolades showered down on four All-Americans: the peerless quarterback, Johnny Lujack, an all-time great at tackle, George Connor, guard John Mastrangelo, and center George Strohmeyer.

1947

If the 1946 edition of the Fighting Irish was loaded with talent, what can be said about the 1947 outfit? Only three starters had graduated; Leahy had to fill the right guard, right end (he had sophomore Leon Hart, who would be declared an All-American for his remaining years of eligibility for this), and fullback positions. His 1946 reserves had played so many minutes that any man moving up would quickly become part of the smoothly efficient machine. Marty Wendell won the right guard spot, and Panelli moved up as starting fullback, part of an impressive, powerful stable of running backs.

With sky-high expectations, the Irish started their 1947 campaign on the road against the Pitt Panthers. The Irish did not impress anyone on a steamy, hot day, least of all Frank Leahy. He had to be almost apoplectic watching his stalwarts fumbling six times as the bevy of outstanding running backs only managed a little over 200 yards on the ground. So how did Pitt get creamed 40–6? Two words: Johnny Lujack. He sparked the first drive with a spot-on 34-yard pass to Jim Martin reaching the Pitt 14. A few plays later, Brennan lugged it in for the score from the Pitt 3. The first Irish fumble happened when Tripucka was hit on his 21-yard line and Pitt recovered. A few plays later, their quarterback, Carl DePasqua, rammed in for a short-yardage TD, but ND held the lead at 7–6. Lujack led the next drive, with a 21-yard scramble at the Pitt 30 putting the team in the red zone. He missed Brennan with a pass but hit end Doug Waybright on the next play for the score and a halftime lead of 13–6. It would be all Notre Dame in the second half: in the third quarter, Lujack found left end Jim Martin wide open on a fourth down play for a 65-yard TD pass. His next TD pass went to Hart in the fourth quarter. Coy

McGee and Lancaster Smith tacked on the final two TDs, the latter from 17 yards out. Earley had added five good PAT kicks for the 40–6 final tally.

If the Irish thought they were going to rest on their laurels for Purdue, they were mistaken. A feisty Boilermakers squad cut the Irish down to size a bit but lost, 22–7. Their eventual defeat seemed foredoomed on their first play from scrimmage when an observant Panelli saw an errant Purdue lateral and jumped on it at their 21-yard line. The Irish didn't make it easy on themselves but used seven plays—and were back at the 21 again—when Lujack fired a pass to Brennan for the score. Steve Oracko tacked on the PAT. Purdue came right back, using a friendly pass interference call, to move down to the Irish 9-yard line. The Irish held them right there for three plays but on fourth down, quarterback Bob DeMoss found Harry Szulborski open for the TD. The PAT tied it at 7–7 (it was the first PAT made by an opponent since the end of the 1945 season). Still in the first quarter, a Purdue fumble on the Notre Dame 29 put the ball back in Lujack's talented hands, and he led the Irish on a scoring march, with a long pass to Larry Coutre to the Purdue 21 (again). Lujack dropped to pass but thought better of it and scrambled the 21 yards for a TD. The PAT went awry, but Notre Dame led, 13–6. In the second quarter, Purdue's defense held the Irish for much of the frame, until they reached the 11. On fourth down from there, seeing the stiff Purdue defense, Leahy called for a field goal and Oracko boomed it through for the 16–7 halftime lead. It was the first successful field goal for the Irish since 1942. In the third quarter, Coy McGee returned a punt 40 yards to the Purdue 17. After several runs, Floyd Simmons barged in for the TD from the 3-yard line, ending the scoring for the day. The Purdue defensive scheme basically took away wide runs past the ends, but this left them vulnerable to the passing game, which Lujack and Tripucka were able to exploit sufficiently for the 22–7 end result.

The relatively unimpressive showing against Purdue dropped the Irish to the No. 2 position in the polls as they prepared for their first home game of 1947 against ancient foe Nebraska. The teams were dead even in the series—five wins each to go with a tie. They had not played since 1925, an Irish loss. Nebraska boasted of having a bunch of huge linemen, but the Irish were no slouches in that department either. Cornhusker hopes had to be high, given what appeared to be a lull in Notre Dame's season momentum.

The battle of the highly-touted lines turned out to be a rout for Notre Dame, as the Irish dominated all phases of the game in plastering the Cornhuskers, 31–0. McGee, Sitko, and Brennan, among other running backs, had the Huskers pretty much befuddled all day with a very effective ground game to go with passes by

Lujack and Tripucka. The first Irish score was due to a slashing running game by a backfield committee, a 74-yard drive punctuated by Panelli's 8-yard TD burst. In the second quarter, Swistowicz started a 55-yard drive with three straight runs off right tackle once the Irish saw how their tackle on that side, Ziggy Czarobski, was manhandling his man. From the 33-yard line, Tripucka zipped a pass to Brennan for 22 yards. Swistowicz, the man who started the drive with three runs, used three more runs to cover the 11 yards needed for Notre Dame's second score. Oracko had missed the first PAT and he missed this one as well. Leahy took notice. Later in the second quarter, the Irish struck with three lightning-like plays—a McGee punt return of 35 yards to midfield, a Lujack to Swistowicz pass for 36 yards to the Nebraska 14-yard line, and McGee again, this time on a quick opener that propelled him into the end zone untouched. Leahy called on Earley for the PAT, and he made it. Nebraska then kept the Irish out of their end zone until the fourth quarter when Tripucka led a 91-yard march. Sitko dashed for 33 yards before shorter runs kept the march going. Tripucka spotted freshman Bill Gay for a 20-yard strike and two passes later Waybright scored on a 14-yard pass from Tripucka. Moments later, the Huskers fumbled the Irish kickoff and Strohmeyer recovered near the red zone. Sitko, Gay, and Simmons hammered at the line on three plays, then Sitko wrapped it up with a 10-yard TD sprint around left end. Earley's PAT was blocked and the Irish wrapped up their 31–0 drilling of Nebraska.

The pundits still had the Irish as the No. 2 team in the country (behind 4–0 Michigan); the next hopefuls came from Iowa, the Hawkeyes. They must have had stage fright because they fumbled on the third play and Billy Walsh recovered on the Iowa 29. Brennan zipped off tackle twice for 16 yards, Lujack hit Martin with a short pass, and Brennan wrapped up the short drive with a TD run. On the next Irish possession, a great punt return by McGee reached midfield, Sitko bulled his way to the 18, and Brennan swatted away four Iowans on his TD run from there. Earley made both PATs. The Hawkeyes experienced their one thrill of the game early in the third quarter when Emlen Tunnell slanted between Notre Dame's Connor and Martin and broke loose for a 65-yard gain before Lujack and Brennan corralled him near the Irish 10. Embarrassed by the lapse, the Irish defense stopped Iowa's further advance. The final Irish score came at the end of a meticulous 98-yard drive with Larry Coutre taking the scoring honors from the Iowa 1-yard line, finalizing the 21–0 score.

Two consecutive shutouts over quality opposition launched the Irish back to the top spot in the polls as they met Navy in Cleveland. Even though it was November 1, the weather cooperated beautifully to give Lujack and Tripucka great opportunities to display Notre Dame's passing attack, and that's exactly what they did. Following Hart's fumble recovery, Lujack fired a 29-yard dart to Brennan for the first TD, and Tripucka then found Hart for a 31-yard TD strike. In the third quarter, Terry Brennan scored from the 1 for the third Irish TD and Livingstone rambled 42 yards with an interception to wrap up the scoring in Notre Dame's 27–0 victory. Lujack had the best run of the day, a 72-yard excursion, but he ended the play with a fumble. Overall, Army's scouts knew that they would have their hands full.

Those scouts reported that the Irish passing attack, second-most proficient in college football after five games, was a devastating weapon. Army also knew that postwar conditions would not give them the advantage they had enjoyed in the war years, and after this game there would be a temporary break in the series. So when the teams met at Notre Dame a week after the Navy game, the Irish used their ground game to smash Army's defense for 361 yards rushing and a 27–7 win. Terry Brennan set the tone with the opening kickoff. Snagging the ball with an over-the-shoulder catch, he used the stadium's west sideline and a series of obliterating blocks to reach the Army 25 and then turned on the jets to finish the run and establish the early lead. Army could not move the ball on its next possession, so they punted and Lujack started a drive from the Notre Dame 20. Thirteen plays later, with Brennan hauling the pigskin one-third of the time, including a run for his second TD of the quarter, Notre Dame took a 13–0 lead. Army fumbled the second-half kickoff and never was able to establish decent field position. The Irish kept up a steady pressure, and Livingstone burst in for a TD from the 6-yard line to conclude a 47-yard drive, giving Notre Dame an insurmountable 20–0 lead. As the third quarter faded into the fourth quarter, Army patched together a drive that resulted in a short TD run, ending Notre Dame's scoreless streak at 18 consecutive quarters. The Irish took umbrage and spliced together an 80-yard march that featured the running skills of Swistowicz and Coutre, the latter scoring from the Army 11-yard line to finish the day's scoring at 27–7.

No team, no matter how talented, can sustain the level of intensity to dominate opponents as the Irish had in their first six games of the 1947 season. No one should have been surprised that there was a dialing down of that intensity at some point. The Irish made the short trip to Chicago to meet Northwestern and encountered the miserable kind of weather that afflicts the Windy City as winter conditions set in. Nevertheless, the Irish scored within the first seven minutes and then scored again mere seconds later. It was 13–0 in the blink of an eye. Perhaps it was too easy because Northwestern put up a heck of a fight from there.

The first score came near the seven-minute mark of the first quarter, a 60-yard drive with Panelli doing most of the work, earning a 9 yard TD run for his efforts. Earley missed the PAT. The Wildcats fumbled Notre Dame's kickoff, and the Irish recovered on the 8-yard line. With his third pass, Lujack zipped an 8-yard TD to Brennan. The PAT was good, and it looked as though a scoring avalanche would ensue. Northwestern made its move late in the first quarter with an interception. With the ball on the Irish 15-yard line, they passed for 10 yards. From the Irish 5, it took four tries, but they scored, missing the PAT, on the first play of the second quarter. The Irish responded late in the first half as Tripucka found Lancaster Smith in the end zone, but he had stepped out of bounds. OK, try again. Tripucka then went back to Smith, who made a great catch for a 37-yard score. Earley's PAT was good, and the Irish had a 20–6 halftime lead. The teams traded long drives in the third quarter but it was the Wildcats that scored on theirs, with a 9-yard pass for a TD, Brennan having slipped on the end zone mud, leaving the receiver wide open. The Irish defenders blocked the PAT, but Northwestern had pulled to within 20–12. In the fourth quarter, Lujack engineered a long drive, ending it with a 6-yard TD pass to Hart. Northwestern took its turn blocking the PAT. The game's scoring ended with a Wildcat interception of a Tripucka pass (the receiver slipped again) and return for a TD. Leahy had seen enough and quickly inserted his starters in the final minutes to choke off any further scoring threats. The Irish drove to the Northwestern 1-yard line but fumbled, Northwestern recovering. Obligingly, they fumbled on the next play, and the game ended seconds later. With that fumble recovery, Notre Dame had shut down the Wildcats to win a close one, 26–19.

Maybe it had been the wet weather in Chicago, or perhaps it was Leahy's unbelievably intense drive for perfection that ravaged his physical constitution, but in any case he was knocked out of the next game, with Tulane visiting the Dome, and Moose Krause handled the coaching for a 59–6 obliteration of the Green Wave. Brennan got it going with an interception and return to the Tulane 5; Sitko pounded it in from there on his second try. The PAT was missed. The Irish kicked off but the Tulane deep men let the ball roll around, and Jim Martin took possession on the 20. Lujack promptly fired a pass to Sitko, who caught it in midstride for another TD. Tulane soon had to punt; Sitko stormed for 30 yards to the Tulane 18 and Brennan refused to be tackled from that point as he ran into the end zone, although four Tulane men hit him. On Tulane's next possession, Oracko tipped a pass that Hart gathered in on their 37. Gompers took the handoff, sprinted past left end, cut back, and scored from there, untouched, for a 26–0 first quarter lead. Tulane managed to reach the Irish 40 in the second quarter but conveniently dropped the ball for Czarobski to recover. Using mostly runs, the Irish moved to the Tulane 5 at which point Lujack passed to Brennan for a 32–0 lead. Earley was having his worst day attempting and missing PATs, not that it mattered in this game. Tulane tightened up their chin straps, seeing that the game was virtually out of reach and pieced together an 83-yard march from their 17, running in a TD from the Irish 4 making the halftime score 32–6. In a way, however, they had not seen the half of it. They dodged a bullet early in the third quarter when Gompers romped 76 yards for an apparent TD, but a clipping call brought it back. So rather than do it all in one play, the Irish went on an incremental drive with Panelli scoring from the 1-yard line … 39–6. Tulane was finding out that the Irish defense had no intentions of letting them roam around the stadium, holding them to 19 yards of total offense in the second half. After they punted, Notre Dame tacked on another score after another "one play at a time" drive, with Livingstone tallying a TD from the 4-yard line … 46–6. To complete the scoring, Moose was using up the entire bench in the fourth quarter, with Cornie Clatt zipping in from the 4-yard line; later, fifth-string running back Jim Brennan, Terry's brother, trotted 11 yards for the last TD and the 59–6 lambasting was mercifully over. The Irish had romped for 24 first downs and 559 all-purpose yards of offense, but there was a price for this victory as the Irish saw Sitko go down with an ankle injury and Terry Brennan lost to a torn knee ligament. It should be noted that the final three home games for Notre Dame in 1947 (Iowa, Army, Tulane) were televised by Channel WBKB of Chicago—a possibility originally envisioned, allegedly, by Rockne in his planning for the stadium that opened with the 1930 season.

Two weeks after the Tulane game, the Irish visited sunny southern California and played USC in the LA Coliseum before nearly 105,000 fans. The war years had seen very few cross-country games to the West Coast, so the Irish players were new to the venture. The extra week also gave Sitko an opportunity to recover from his ankle injury. Things started out well for Notre Dame when Trojan quarterback George Murphy dropped the ball at his own 9-yard line right after the kickoff, with massive George Connor recovering the spheroid. The Trojans fought back like madmen and held the Irish to an 18-yard field goal by Earley. A punting duel ensued until early in the second quarter when Lujack got the Irish motor to function on all cylinders during an 87-yard march featuring pounding runs by Livingstone and Panelli until Sitko exploded for the TD from the 1-yard line. Early made the PAT for a 10–0 lead. Murphy made up for his earlier fumble when he intercepted a pass that soon led to a TD to close the gap, but that was it for USC scoring that day. The rest belonged to the Irish. Early in the third quarter, Sitko showed off his healed ankle with a 76-yard TD romp, courtesy of a pulverizing George Connor block at a key point in the run. Lujack grabbed a Trojan pass to start the next scoring drive, with Sitko and Panelli sharing the ground duties with Panelli crossing the goal line for the score, making it 24–7. USC put together a good drive that reached the Irish 8 but Bill Walsh broke up their fourth-down pass. Livingstone broke the Trojans' back from that spot with a scintillating 92-yard TD run. In the fourth quarter, as USC was relying on a desperate passing attack, fourth-string Irish tackle Al Zmijewski intercepted a lateral and rumbled 30 yards for the final Irish score in their 38–7 triumph, locking in the kind of undefeated season not seen since Rockne's last teams. Lujack won the Heisman Trophy and was joined by two other consensus All-Americans—tackles George Connor (who had already been recognized with the 1946 Outland Trophy) and Bill Fischer, to go with those who also received votes, tackle Ziggy Czarobski and end Leon Hart.

1949

Notre Dame's postwar successes and depth in 1946, 1947, and 1948 (26–0–2, a .964 winning percentage) meant that the program could withstand the graduation loss of a Heisman Trophy winner, an Outland Trophy winner, or assorted All-Americans yet still be able to fill the spot and not lose a beat. Backups were provided ample opportunities in those years to see significant playing time and often exceeded the results of the starters. Basically, the team was almost overstocked with talent (but would any coach be willing to admit that?). Leahy, in his typical fashion, would tell the press things like making a first down would be a serious challenge for this year's edition of Notre Dame football.

The Irish had three returning linemen from the '48 edition: Jim Martin moved from left end to left tackle, Ralph McGehee switched from left tackle to right tackle, and Leon Hart held down the right end position. Otherwise, reserves moved up into starting positions. In the backfield, Leahy's good fortune in having talented quarterbacks such as Johnny Lujack and Frank Tripucka in previous seasons seemed to hold up with Bob Williams and John Mazur. Frank Spaniel and Larry Coutre moved up from the running back reserves, and Sitko switched to fullback. Starting with this season, and lasting until 1952, collegiate football allowed for a two-platoon configuration. For Notre Dame, several of the players on offense (all linemen) continued to play two ways while the running backs did not start in the defensive secondary. Overall, this team had good speed at the key spots, excellent size (Leon Hart was a force unto himself, especially when unleashed on end around plays), and enough veteran experience to keep the ship steady when it encountered a storm.

The Indiana Hoosiers provided the season-opening competition in a game played under the Dome. The usual first-game nerves manifested for both teams with nearly back-to-back fumble exchanges early in the first quarter, but the Irish were the first to put together a scoring drive, with Bob Williams finding Coutre open for a pass that reached the Hoosiers' 17-yard line. Sitko slammed it in on the third play from there for the season's initial score. A stiff Irish defense forced a punt from the Indiana end zone, but it was blocked by Bob Toneff for a safety. The Hoosiers seemed to recover from that misfortune to cobble together a scoring drive, but it was neutralized just before the halftime by a Williams pass to reserve back Bill Gay, who made a stunning catch and kept his balance for a 28-yard TD. Oracko made the PAT and the halftime score stood at 16–6. Early in the third quarter, Sitko started the scoring landslide for Notre Dame with a 6-yard TD blast past left tackle. Gay returned a punt 50 yards, and Coutre scored from the Hoosier 13. Sitko repeated his 6-yard TD run late in the third quarter for the 36–6 count. In the fourth quarter, Swistowicz piled in from the 1-yard line, and sub quarterback John Mazur closed out the scoring with a 71-yard pass to Bill Wightkin, making the final score 49–6.

The team made the long trip to Seattle to meet the Washington Huskies, who they had demolished, 46–0, in 1948. With that outcome still stinging the Huskies, they played a great first half of football to achieve a 7–7 halftime score. They scored first, following a Notre Dame fumble, with a 55-yard TD pass from Don Heinrich to Roland Kirkby. The Irish had some difficulty trying to match that as the West Coast officials were calling a much tighter game with regard to holding than the brand of football practiced in the Midwest. Several long penalties killed Irish possessions until late in the first half. Irish backs scraped together 40 yards on the ground, reaching the Huskies' 21. From there, Williams dropped back to pass and hit Hart for the TD and a halftime tie, 7–7. The teams traded punts in the opening moments of the third quarter, but Bob Toneff came up with a block of the Huskies' second punt, with Bill Flynn capturing the ball on the Washington 14. From that spot, first, the usual: Sitko slamming inside for 6 yards. Then the Husky nightmare: huge Leon Hart on an end around, running parallel to the line of scrimmage, then turning his route towards the end zone, clobbering various reluctant Husky defenders on the right side, before scoring the go-ahead TD. After a non-scoring Husky drive, the Irish jumped on another Washington fumble at their 36. On the second play from there, Coutre and a convoy of blockers sped 30 yards to pay dirt and a 20–7 lead. Leon Hart made his presence known again, this time on defense, when he slammed into Husky quarterback Don O'Leary, causing a fumble on the Washington 18. The Husky nightmare promptly returned as Hart rumbled on another end around for 12 yards to start the drive. On the first play of the fourth quarter, sophomore fullback Jack Landry scored the game's final TD from the 3 to make the score 27–7. It was the 30th straight win for the Irish.

The Purdue Boilermakers usually put up a pretty good fight against their in-state rivals, especially when playing at home. They thought they had done their homework, but Emil Sitko proved otherwise in short order. Immediately following Frank Spaniel's 55-yard burst on the first Irish possession, Sitko blasted off for a 41-yard TD run. Later in the first quarter, Coutre and Sitko used their legs to get the team deep into Purdue territory. From the 9-yard line in the opening seconds of the second quarter, Coutre powered into the line for 5 yards, then Sitko sealed the deal with his second TD of the game and a 14–0 lead. Purdue fought back, reaching the Irish 33 but they fumbled there, and John Petitbon took possession. The usual assortment of running backs plus Leon Hart moved the ball to the Purdue 9-yard line, at which point Sitko blasted in for his third TD of the day and a 21–0 lead for Notre Dame. Later in the second frame, Bill Gay found himself hugging a Purdue pass and knew exactly what to do—61 yards later, his interception return gave the Irish a 28–0 lead. In the third quarter, yet another interception led to the final TD, this time the theft conducted by linebacker John Helwig, who hauled it back to the Purdue 46. The short drive from there ended with Billy Barrett's TD run and a 35–0 lead. Purdue scored two consolation TDs for the 35–12 final score.

Newly ranked No. 1 in the country, the Irish next met Tulane (for some reason, ranked No. 4). Such rankings make for good dramatic effect and help build fan interest, but the Irish lambasted their opponents from New Orleans anyway, 46–7. Head coach Frank Leahy, a professional pessimist, went so far as to say that this would be the toughest game in his Notre Dame tenure to date. With all that fanfare, however, Larry Coutre took all the drama out of the contest with three TDs in the first quarter: a 14-yard dash right up the middle, then 81 blistering yards with a pitchout for his second TD, and a 2-yard TD plunge following a great pass from Williams to Wightkin. Spaniel added the exclamation point to the first quarter rout with a 38-yard TD pass from Williams. In the second quarter Leon Hart made the halftime score 33–0 by catching a 20-yard pass from Williams. Tulane earned their only score on a 76-yard pass play in the third quarter. Spaniel responded to that on the next possession to cap a good drive with an 11-yard TD run over right tackle. Barrett finalized the 46–7 score with a 59-yard TD run off left tackle and a cutback move that dropped a couple of would-be Green Wave tacklers. Coutre ended the day with 101 yards gained on four runs; meanwhile, the Irish defense stuffed the Green Wave running game for minus-23 yards. So much for being ranked fourth.

The Irish next went to Baltimore to play Navy. Irish quarterback Bob Williams was able to play before his hometown fans in Babe Ruth Stadium (Ruth, also from Baltimore, had died the year before, and Memorial Stadium was renamed in his honor). Leahy was ill again and did not travel with the team but managed to get to the game in time thanks to a friend's offer to use a private plane for the trip. It was a good thing that Leahy made it in time because Williams struck for a score within the game's first four minutes—a 48-yard TD catch and run with Ernie Zalejski on the receiving end. Oracko made the PAT. The teams traded long, non-scoring drives until the second quarter when Coutre outraced the Middies on a 91-yard TD jaunt. Shortly after that stunning play, Sitko broke loose on a 44-yard trip to the Navy 25; a few plays later he made one of his signature bursts for 16 tough yards and a TD, giving Notre Dame a 21–0 lead. A Williams to Zalejski TD pass made the halftime score 27–0. Leahy took out the starters for most of the second half and had the team use running plays only. Jack Landry sprinted for a 14-yard TD, and Zalejski ended the scoring with an explosive 76-yard run to the end zone for the 40–0 final tally. With this convincing victory the Irish set a collegiate record for the day with its 33rd consecutive game without a loss.

In East Lansing, Notre Dame met a gritty Michigan State team that took the opening kickoff and carefully maneuvered on a drive that reached the Irish 5-yard line. Two plunges by Spartans fullback Jim Blenkhorn ended up with a fumble with Hart recovering the ball for the Irish on their 2. The Irish then wiggled out of that predicament, trading interceptions with the Spartans, before Williams took charge and tightened up the sloppy work. Punting from his own 46, he got the ball to stop dead at the MSU 4-yard line. The Spartans eventually punted, and Gay returned it to the Spartans 24. Coutre banged into the line for 5 yards, then Williams spotted a wide open Zalejski who took enough undisturbed steps to score ND's first TD of the day early in the second quarter. It was not all heroic stuff for the Irish quarterback; a bit later he fumbled at his own 5-yard line, the Spartans recovered, and a few plays later had their own TD for a 7–7 standoff. Williams took charge after that score to lead a scoring drive. He completed a pass from his own end zone and then found Wightkin with a jump pass on a fourth-down play. Wightkin broke a tackle and took the ball to the MSU 22. Williams then turned it over to his backs, with Coutre banging in for the TD and a 14–7 halftime lead.

Williams continued his leadership on Notre Dame's possession of the third quarter, a 79-yard drive that he finished when he faked a lateral to Sitko and dashed 40 yards for his own TD and a 20–7 lead. On the first play of the fourth quarter, Sitko did get the ball, faked out a Spartan defender, and scored from the MSU 12. The desperate Spartans failed on a fourth down play on their 36, and Williams struck instantly—a pass to Wightkin and a TD pass to Hart. MSU scored two late TDs to make the score a more respectable 34–21.

With Army no longer a regular on their schedule, the Irish had gone in search of a suitable replacement for a game to be played in Yankee Stadium. It turned out to be North Carolina, and they also turned out, for a half at least, to be a very worthy foe, as they worked mightily to earn a 6–6 halftime deadlock with Notre Dame in their first scheduled contest and did this despite missing their star player, Charlie Justice. Unranked, they put the Irish in trouble early in the game by blocking a punt attempt from the end zone, taking possession at the 10. Running back Dick Bunting carried twice and scored the TD. Near the end of the first quarter, Spaniel broke loose for a 78-yard TD run but the Carolinians blocked the PAT try for the 6–6 halftime score. To be honest, it would prove to be almost impossible for *any* collegiate team to continue to keep the Irish scoring machine penned up like this, and, sure enough, the second half turned out to be a scoring festival for Notre Dame. Williams completed a pass to Hart, who had attracted half of the Wolfpack defense, so he lateralled the ball to Barrett who in turn blasted off for the second Irish TD. Hart soon thereafter caused a safety when he stripped the ball from Bunting. The fourth quarter was all Irish: an 11-yard Williams TD pass to Spaniel … a 29-yard Williams pass to Barrett for a TD … Swistowicz zoomed 85 yards with an interception for another TD … and, finally, Barrett again with a TD pass from sub quarterback Johnny Mazur following Oracko's fumble recovery at the North Carolina 23-yard line. Final tally: 42–6. The Irish defense once again completely choked off an opponent's running game, holding the Wolfpack runners to minus-5 yards on the ground.

Iowa was next up. The Irish recorded an early TD following Gay's fumble recovery at the Hawkeye 32 as Williams lofted a 20-yard TD pass to Spaniel. The teams played to a stalemate until the early moments of the second quarter when Iowa benefited from an Irish fumble to generate their only TD drive of the game. With most of the second quarter gone, the ever-present Leon Hart blocked a punt out of bounds at Iowa's 22-yard line. Williams threw a pass to Hart for 14 yards, and Barrett took it the rest of the way for a TD and a 14–7 lead for the Irish at halftime. In the third quarter, the game returned to the stalemate mode it had been in until a penalty had Notre Dame backed up on its 5-yard line. Rather than pout, the Irish went to work to assemble a 14-play, 95-yard drive that pretty much took the wind out of the Iowa team. Williams sparked the drive with a 36-yard pass to Spaniel, who later scored on a 6-yard jaunt. Then it was back to the stalemate until the final 45 seconds of the game when Williams targeted Hart with a TD pass and the 28–7 final score. Irish fans had grown accustomed to seeing Leon Hart manhandle his opponents and now the scribes were also beginning to notice how many times Hart had a major impact. Also, in this game, Williams, the nineteen-year-old Irish quarterback, broke Angelo Bertelli's single season passing yardage total.

Notre Dame then matched up with the Southern Cal Trojans for the 21st time, and this one turned out to be the largest blowout to date in the series started by Rockne, 32–0. Irish runners churned out 316 yards on the ground while the defense was stifling the Trojans' run game, holding them to 17 yards rushing. Mortal teams just did not have much of a chance against the Irish in 1949. The game was into its twelfth minute before Notre Dame broke the ice of the frigid November weather as Williams found Hart with a perfect pass good for a 40-yard TD. Less than two minutes later, Petitbon leaped for a Trojan pass, hauled it in, and dashed 43 yards down the sideline to the end zone and a 13–0 lead. The second quarter revealed a new weapon for Notre Dame: Leon Hart as the fullback. One

Leon Hart (82) leading the way to an undefeated 1949 season.

wonders what went through the minds of the Trojan linebackers and defensive backs when they saw this frightful innovation. Something like: *Someone's gonna have to tackle this guy. Will it be me?* They found out soon enough following a fumbled punt on the USC 30-yard line. Barrett rammed through for 19 yards, and then Hart lined up in the backfield with the ball on the USC 11. Hart carried the ball, along with several startled Trojans, for a 7-yard gain. Then, with the Trojan defense looking at Hart looming in the backfield, Williams handed off to Sitko, who sprinted around left end for the TD. The PAT failed and the score stood at 19–0 at the half. Notre Dame cranked it up in the third quarter with a 60-yard march in 12 plays; Spaniel barged in from the 2 for the TD. In the fourth quarter, Williams snapped a pass to Barrett for a 32-yard gain, Hart thundered from the fullback position once again moving the sticks to the 15, Zalejski reached the 6, and Williams handed off to Barrett twice from there for the final TD and score of 32–0.

They saved the best game for the last one in 1949—Notre Dame versus Southern Methodist University in Dallas. Kyle Rote was the Mustangs' well-known star, but they would be missing their other All-American, Doak Walker. Despite his absence, they put up a terrific battle, tying the game, 20–20, in the fourth quarter before Notre Dame was able to score the winning points and turn back a determined SMU response in the game's waning moments. The Irish came out of the gates fast with Williams throwing TD passes of 42 yards and 35 yards to Wightkin and Zalejski respectively, the latter coming off a deflection by a defender. Both drives followed Irish interceptions. It had all the appearances of another blowout. In the second half, however, Zalejski fumbled twice to put an end to promising drives. Rote started to run effectively after the second drop—18 yards, then 23 yards, capped by a 2-yard TD plunge. Sophomore Jim Mutscheller picked off a Rote pass on their 22, then Barrett smashed over right tackle for a TD. Within a minute, however, Johnny Champion hauled in a Rote pass and ran it inside the Irish 2-yard line before Rote scored from there. The Irish offense was stymied, and a good punt return left SMU a short field. From the 14, Rote ran three times and scored the tying TD. Jerry Groom blocked the PAT. After Spaniel returned the kickoff to the Irish 46, Sitko and Barrett hammered the line for five runs to the SMU 26. Hart, from the fullback spot, smashed for 6 more yards, gaining the attention of every Mustang. Then it was Barrett and Gay for 6 yards each, and Barrett for 2. The last 6 yards were covered by the speedy Barrett, swinging outside the containment for the winning TD. Oracko made the PAT. But it wasn't over yet. With Rote leading the way, SMU reached the ND 5-yard line. He tried a desperation jump pass from there but it was intercepted by Irish linebackers Jerry Groom and Bob Lally, who grabbed the ball at the same time to end the threat.

With this thrilling win, Leahy's four championship teams had compiled a stunning record of 36–1–1. Leon Hart deservedly won the Heisman Trophy, only the second lineman to do so. All-American recognition went to Sitko, Martin, Hart, and Williams. From the 1949 Notre Dame roster, NFL teams would draft 29 players.

1966

The 1965 season, Ara Parseghian's second with the team, had not been as exciting or fulfilling as the 1964 campaign, when the Irish went 9–1. Some of the key players from '64 were still on hand—Alan Page, Jim Lynch, Nick Eddy, Pete Duranko, and Tom Regner, to name a few—but Heisman winner John Huarte was gone as was his favorite receiver, Jack Snow. In fact, in 1965, Ara found himself between seasons of having the kind of quarterback he liked: the graduated Heisman winner or the two freshmen he saw every day in practice, Terry Hanratty and Coley O'Brien, who would not be eligible until the 1966 season. So Ara had to make do with the players on hand. In doing so, he was able to will the team to a 7–2–1 record.

Another 1965 freshman was Jim Seymour, a rangy, speedy wide receiver. Parseghian could see that Irish defenders in practice were having trouble covering the passes thrown to Seymour. The freshmen quarterbacks had superior arms, quick releases, and were able to read defenses as well as a senior could. Two other freshmen also stood out—George Kunz at tackle and Bob Kuechenberg, who could play both sides of the ball as a lineman. It had to be frustrating for Parseghian to see the talent on hand that he could not use for a year.

The coaching staff had to have a strong sense that the 1966 unit was talented across the board. As it turned out, nine of the starting eleven on offense and seven of the defensive starters would play pro ball, several would be NFL All-Pro selections, and defensive end Alan Page would be a Pro Football Hall of Fame inductee in 1988. Overall, the team had excellent size, good speed and quickness, and several players who were simply dominant at their positions, such as Page at defensive end.

The 1966 Notre Dame team was unveiled in a home game against a talented Purdue team, led by quarterback Bob Griese and all-purpose star Leroy Keyes. The game got off to a strange start. Purdue had the first possession, and on the first play Griese came up under center, took a look at the Irish defense, and checked off. Irish middle linebacker Jim Lynch shifted the D. Griese checked off again.

Lynch adjusted. Frustrated, Griese stood up and called for a time-out. This sequence revealed just how well-prepared this team would be. In fact, as the season developed the Irish defense would register six shutouts and give up only 38 points. Purdue would score 14 points that day, more than one-third of the total that Ara's defense would give up in the remaining nine games. Purdue struck first when Keyes fielded an Irish fumble in midair and sprinted 95 yards for a 7–0 lead. It didn't last long. Nick Eddy took the ensuing kickoff and after a couple of cat-like moves that left various Boilermakers lunging at air, reached pay dirt 97 yards later, tying the game. Shortly after that explosive play, Hanratty found Seymour wide open for a 42-yard gain, but the drive fizzled. The long gain showed, however, that Seymour could lose defenders with ease. Ara and Hanratty had not forgotten that play. On the next possession, looking at a 3rd-and-14 situation from his own 16-yard line, Hanratty zipped a pass to Seymour, who took it to the end zone for an 84-yard score and the lead. In the third quarter, the young duo connected again for a 39-yard score. The teams traded TDs after that for the final score of 26–14. With this opening win the Irish had served notice to the collegiate football world that this sixth-ranked team had loads of well-coached talent and would be a force to reckon with.

Northwestern thought it had a plan from scouting reports—hard blitzes on Hanratty from their ends and double-team Seymour. This worked well enough to keep Seymour out of the end zone but he still snagged nine passes for 141 yards. The Irish runners (fullback Larry Conjar, Nick Eddy, and Rocky Bleier) and cornerback Tom Schoen did the scoring in their 35–7 win. Eddy and Bleier weren't touched by the Wildcats on their scoring bursts. So much for scouting.

Two teams had scored 21 points on the Irish already. The next three would suffer shutouts. Army was first up, and Ara turned loose the offense for a 35–0 rout by halftime; he used subs after that and the score stayed the same. The running game did it again—Bleier scored first, then Hanratty reminded people that Seymour could score, too, hitting him with a perfect throw for a TD. Hanratty took one in for himself and Eddy blasted in twice. Army was basically helpless—a mere shadow of the glory days under Heisman winners Blanchard and Davis.

North Carolina totally ran out of luck in the span of four plays the following week when all three of their quarterbacks went down with injuries; they had to use a fullback at quarterback. This did not bode well for Tar Heel success. Indeed, Notre Dame kept the shutout streak going with a 32–0 pasting. Conjar blasted in twice, Seymour hauled in a 56-yard TD pass from Hanratty, Eddy breezed 52 yards for another, and running back Bob Gladieux took a pitch from fellow reserve Coley O'Brien 5 yards for a score to wrap it up.

The Irish by this time had convinced the scribes and other coaches that they were worthy of the No. 1 ranking. They had not had a serious test yet. Tenth-ranked and undefeated Oklahoma was next. With two shutouts of their own so far, they would test Notre Dame's mettle for sure. Instead, the powerful Sooners laid another egg, losing 38–0 at home. The game itself was a contrast of two foot-ball philosophies—the Sooners (much like Bear Bryant's Alabama teams of those days) featured light, quick players who were utterly dogged at pursuit. A good example was their noseguard, Granville Liggins, one of the fastest players of the day at 6-foot, 225 pounds. Facing him were George Goeddeke, 6-foot-3 and 253 pounds, and guards Tom Regner at 6-foot-1, 255, and Dick Swatland at 6-foot-2, 225. Clearly, the Irish emphasized much bigger but nevertheless fast players who were often fifty pounds, or more, heavier than the man they were facing. All of the scoring took place in the second and third quarters: Eddy and Hanratty scored on short runs after patient drives, then the Irish added a field goal. In the third quarter, the total dominance persisted with TDs by Eddy, Bleier, and O'Brien. The Irish did not escape Norman unscathed, however, as several of their reliable receivers were injured in the game.

They wouldn't need them against Navy. As freshmen, the seniors on the team had seen Navy's Heisman winner Roger Staubach demolish the Irish in South Bend during the disastrous season before Parseghian was hired. Well, the tables were turned as Notre Dame had its way with the Midshipmen, 31–7, but their three-game shutout streak was broken. One Notre Dame player did catch three balls—linebacker John Pergine, with interceptions of Navy passes (one tipped to him by fellow linebacker Jim Lynch). Navy's lone score came off a blocked punt. Navy totaled 36 yards rushing and, with Pergine's theatrics, only 28 yards passing. Hanratty scored two TDs, Conjar and Gladieux one each, and kicker Joe Azzaro added a field goal to complete the scoring.

The Irish returned to their habitual shutout mode (although the defense did shut out Navy) with a 40–0 shellacking of Pitt. The Panthers kept the game score-less until the very end of the second quarter before they fell apart. Hanratty scored on a short run and Eddy got the second half started with an 85-yard kickoff return for a TD. Defensive back Tom Schoen took back a punt 63 yards for a score. Eddy broke loose for a 51-yard ramble, but he hurt his shoulder. Parseghian started using odd combinations of players—two quarterbacks and two fullbacks, just to give the scouts something to worry about. Fullbacks Larry Conjar and Paul May combined for three TDs with May scoring twice.

The final home game of the '66 season gave Ara an opportunity to put on a full display of the team's talent and depth, with the Duke players serving more or less as innocent bystanders: he played 64 players, 29 of them seniors. The halftime score was 43–0. At one point, Ara's sense of the dramatic urged him to honor the front four from the '64 team by putting them in the game to a standing ovation: Page, Kevin Hardy, Tom Regner, and Pete Duranko, all seniors. The unit had not played together in more than two years, but they stuffed Duke's play anyway. Nick Eddy got the scoring started on the game's second play—a 77-yard run to the end zone untouched. Linebacker John Horney intercepted a Duke pass and had the presence of mind to lateral the ball to defensive back Tom O'Leary, who then took it to the house from the 25. Rocky Bleier slammed in for two TDs, then Conjar added one. Hanratty started a drive with a 50-yard run, then he hit Seymour for a 43-yard score to wrap it up. Three reserves added the last TDs for the final tally of 64–0.

Next up were the Michigan State Spartans. They had defeated Notre Dame in South Bend in 1965, 12–3. They were one of the most dominant teams of the decade, if not all time. Every Spartan opponent that year did not win their following game. After the 1965 drubbing, Notre Dame did the best it could by pulling out a 0–0 tie with Miami. The '66 Spartans were still loaded with talent on both sides of the ball: Bubba Smith, Clinton Jones, Gene Washington, George Webster, and Charley Thornhill to name a few, and they were all veterans of tough, high-stakes campaigns.

The game was played on a bitterly cold day. The Irish lost All-American halfback Nick Eddy before the game ever started when he slipped on ice as he departed the team's train in East Lansing, reinjuring his shoulder. Hanratty went down early in the game after Bubba Smith sacked him. The Irish center, George Goeddeke, rolled an ankle on a punt play and did not return. The first quarter was scoreless, although Parseghian unveiled a new weapon: defensive tackle Kevin Hardy, at 6-foot-5 and 275 pounds, was given the punting duties. Hardy, a three-sport collegiate athlete (basketball and baseball were his other sports) boomed towering punts that nullified the Spartan return game. In spite of that impressive punting show, Michigan State took the lead in the second quarter with a 5-yard run by Regis Cavender and a field goal by barefoot kicker Dick Kenney, one of Duffy Daugherty's prize recruits from Hawaii. With the starting center, quarterback, and halfback not in the game, the replacements had some time to acclimate themselves both to the brutal cold and the Spartans. The Irish got on the scoreboard later in the second quarter when Coley O'Brien tossed a perfect pass over the MSU defense for a 34-yard TD to Bob Gladieux, making the halftime score 10–7. Those ten points in the second quarter would be the grand total for the Spartans as the Irish defense kept them scoreless the rest of the game, never allowing MSU's offense to move beyond ND's 45-yard line, a stunning performance led by Tom Schoen's two interceptions. Jim Lynch had another one, but he fumbled after a devastating tackle. Somehow, Notre Dame managed to put together a scoring drive in the fourth quarter, earning a Joe Azzaro field goal after a Schoen interception that tied the game at 10–10.

College football fans will forever debate the ending of the game. Parseghian chose to give MSU no chance for some fluke turnover as the time waned. More to the point is the fact that Coley O'Brien had only recently been diagnosed as diabetic. He played well for the better part of three quarters, but in the fourth quarter his passes were falling incomplete. His insulin intake had not been regulated yet; he was being given candy bars on the sideline to keep his blood sugar up. It is likely that his depth perception was diminishing the longer he played in the demanding conditions. So Parseghian, looking at MSU in a prevent defense, with the ball on the ND 30, relied on the ground game to maintain ball control and, perhaps, bust one open to give Azzaro another chance (he had just missed by scant inches what would be the game-winning field goal following Schoen's second interception). Three runs resulted in a 4th-and-1 play; O'Brien ran it for two yards. After a Spartans time-out, the Irish ran an option play but Bubba Smith smothered it. On the last play, O'Brien ran it again.

Parseghian never apologized—and did not have to. He kept O'Brien's medical condition private, protecting the young man's dignity, and taking the heat that followed. He showed that he was a much bigger man than the critical armchair quarterbacks.

Notre Dame had one more game—the season-ending every-other-year funfest with USC. The Irish were a few years away from the school's change in bowl game policy, so this was it for the season. It is not to be minimized that the seniors on this team, as sophomores, had suffered through a gut-wrenching loss to USC in 1964 when they were only 93 seconds away from a perfect season. They weren't going to let it happen again. Given that sharp focus, the team came together to support the subs who had to replace the starters lost in the MSU game, and together they demolished the helpless Trojans, 51–0, a stunning score that cemented the Irish in the No. 1 spot they richly deserved.

Notre Dame used about all the ways possible to score against the Trojans. O'Brien had a great day—completing 21 of 31 passes for 255 yards. He found Seymour 11 times for 150 yards and two TDs. The USC defense was stubborn on a scoring drive, making the Irish earn a Conjar TD after 17 grueling plays. Schoen was back in form with an interception that he took back 44 yards for a TD. Eddy's sub, Dan Harshman, scored, as did Eddy. Linebacker Dave Martin snagged a Trojan pass and returned it 33 yards for the last TD of the game and the season.

Notre Dame won the national championship with an unbelievable defense, a strike-from-anywhere offense with runs or passes, opportunistic special teams play, and some of the best coaching in collegiate football history. Eight players received All-American honors: running back Nick Eddy, linebacker Jim Lynch, guard Tom Regner, defensive end Alan Page, along with fellow defensive linemen Kevin Hardy and Pete Duranko, wide receiver Jim Seymour, and tackle Paul Seiler. These eight illustrious players (one of whom, Page, would be declared the NFL MVP in 1971 and inducted into the Pro Football Hall of Fame in 1988) represented the single largest collection of such honors in Notre Dame's honored history.

1973

Can a miracle emerge out of a total disaster? Can it happen twice?

We have already seen the glorious 1966 team emerge from the frustrations of the 7–2–1 1965 campaign. The great, undefeated team of 1973, similarly, emerged from the ashes of the last two games in 1972, disasters in which USC and Nebraska trampled the Irish by the respective scores of 45–23 and 40–6, numbers that indicate a major breakdown in the team's defense. Parseghian always seems to have been able to use crushing adversity to the team's eventual advantage.

The 1973 Fighting Irish brought Ara to the top of the collegiate football world for the third time in his ten seasons as Notre Dame's head coach, if you count the 1964 and 1966 seasons in which the Irish were a combined 18–1–1 (a .925 winning percentage). In those seasons, the Irish totally dominated virtually every team they met and were seven points away (or less) from running the table. A few seasons later, Ara did it again, winning 21 games and losing only two in 1973 and 1974 (a .913 winning percentage). In both seasons, there were enough veteran players from the 1972 disasters to keep the competitive fires burning for all the players.

Several key players from 1972 were major contributors to the 1973 unit—quarterback Tom Clements, a tackle who shifted to tight end, Dave Casper—a move that eventually led to his induction into the Pro Football Hall of Fame—guard Gerry DiNardo; on defense, linebacker Drew Mahalic and left tackle Steve Niehaus. New starters added extra punch to a team seeking to redeem itself: split end Pete Demmerle, Art Best and Eric Penick, both with outstanding speed, at running back, Wayne Bullock at fullback; on defense Ross Browner, an all-time Irish great started at left end with Mike Fanning, Jim Stock, and Willie Fry also in the trenches, Drew Mahalic starting again as outside linebacker, and a very talented Luther Bradley at strong safety. Many of these players went on to NFL careers; such was the depth of talent for this team. Ara had to be pleased to see the combination of veteran starters and highly talented newcomers, all capable of making a major impact on either side of the ball.

The Irish started the 1973 campaign with a 44–0 demolition of Northwestern; the halftime score was 37–0. The Wildcats had minus-8 yards rushing at that point. Browner blocked a punt for a safety, and Clements led a balanced running/passing attack. A tough Purdue team held the Irish to 20 points but could only generate one TD of their own. Best jetted for a 64-yard run and, later, a 9-yard TD burst. Wayne "The Train" Bullock slammed in for the final Irish TD, with a field goal to follow. Purdue's runners managed a total of 33 yards for the game, a good sign that the Irish front four were going to be a difficult problem for future opponents. Michigan State, always up for Notre Dame, came to the Dome and fought a great battle before eventually bowing, 14–10. Northwestern had already defeated the Spartans, so perhaps the Irish were a bit complacent. After scoring opportunities fizzled in the first quarter, the Irish marched 80 yards, all on the ground, with Bullock pushing in from the 1-yard line for the first TD. Clements helped the Irish finish their scoring with a 30-yard screen pass to Casper and a 10-yard TD pass to Demmerle. The Irish defense held on for dear life in the second half, allowing only a field goal. An interception return gave the Spartans their only TD. With the outcome in doubt, cornerback Tim Rudnick killed MSU's hopes with an interception as time ran out.

Next up, Rice was unable to score, going down 28–0; the Irish running game was on full display, with Bullock scoring twice, Casper once with a Clements pass, and backup quarterback Cliff Brown scampering 38 yards for the final TD. The Irish defense was so suffocating that Rice was held to minus-14 yards in the second half. Army, whose glory days were a distant memory, imploded by a 62–3 tally, easily the most points the Irish ever scored against the Black Knights. Army held Notre Dame scoreless in the first quarter before an avalanche of TDs overwhelmed them, including a 73-yard punt return for a score by freshman Tim Simon. USC made its biennial trip to Notre Dame and kept it close until Eric Penick used his blazing speed for an 85-yard TD to start the second half. Anthony Davis had run wild in the 1972 game; this time, it was Penick's turn as the Irish defense held Davis to 55 yards on 19 carries. Penick, meanwhile, gained more yards on one run than the Trojans earned for the entire day. In the third quarter, with the ball on the Irish's 15-yard line, and anticipating a Trojans blitz, Clements pitched out to Penick in motion to the left from the slot and he turned the corner untouched, blazing 85 yards for one of the most important runs in Irish football history. The Trojans were held to a total of 66 yards on the ground, compared to Notre Dame's 316 yards that led the way to the 23–14 win. Stopping the vaunted Trojan running game in its tracks was one more measure of how stout Parseghian's defense could be. The Irish then sank the Midshipmen of Navy, 44–7. Parseghian played the whole bench, using twelve runners to rack up 447 yards on the ground and sharing the scoring opportunities. Pittsburgh fell on its home field, 31–10, but their star, Tony Dorsett, cruised for 209 yards on 29 hard-earned carries (his career total against Notre Dame came to an amazing 1,139 yards). Defensive takeaways and the usual Notre Dame running game offset Dorsett's theatrics. Fullback Wayne Bullock powered in for three Irish TDs to cap the victory. Next, Air Force surrendered three fumbles in the first quarter, and Notre Dame scored on three short drives. A poor Falcons punt led to a fourth Irish TD and a 28–0 lead before the first quarter was over. Parseghian managed to get sixty of his players into the game. Notre Dame ran wild for 414 yards, led by Best's 125 yards to round out a 48–15 win. At one point Air Force felt so stymied that they even tried a 62-yard field goal. To finish the regular season, Miami—obviously not the kind of team it would soon become—provided a perfect bookend to the season as they lost 44–0, the same score that opened the campaign back in September. Ten Irish runners stomped through the Miami defense for 477 yards. Demmerle led the TD parade with three, and the team locked up the first perfect regular season since the Leahy era.

But the season wasn't over yet. Three years earlier, Notre Dame's administration had decided that its self-imposed bowl ban following the 1925 Rose Bowl win over Stanford could be rescinded and the team had played in several bowls starting with the 1970 Cotton Bowl. The third-ranked Irish had to meet Bear Bryant's top-ranked undefeated Alabama team in the Sugar Bowl on New Year's Eve. Surely, the team had its haunting memories of the horrible Orange Bowl loss to Nebraska a year earlier.

The first quarter saw Alabama's wishbone offense completely stuffed by the Irish defense … zero yards in 12 plays. The Irish had plenty of experience defending the wishbone due to previous games against Texas. Parseghian had come up with a defense that forced the bone runners to make the decision, rather than the defenders, nullifying the main advantage of this type of offense. On the other hand, the first scoring drive for the Irish revealed that Clements could pick apart the Alabama pass defense as he hit Demmerle with three completions of 19, 26, and 14 yards to set up Bullock's 6-yard TD blast, ending a 64-yard drive. The PAT was missed, but Notre Dame had the lead at 6–0. The teams traded scores in the second quarter as Alabama's wishbone started to operate more efficiently. The Tide's Randy Billingsley slammed in from the 6 for a TD, and the PAT gave them the lead. It didn't last long, however, as Notre Dame's Al Hunter took the Tide's kickoff and dazzled the 85,000 spectators with a 93-yard return for a TD. Clements then threw a pass to Demmerle for a two-point conversion and a 14–7 lead. Alabama cut that to 14–10 with a 39-yard field goal. Early in the third quarter Bear Bryant's team put together an impressive 93-yard drive in 11 plays, capped by Wilbur Jackson's 5-yard TD scamper. The PAT was good and 'Bama had a 17–14 lead. The teams then settled into a bit of a stalemate for almost all of the third quarter until Irish linebacker Drew Mahalic snagged a Tide fumble in midair and took it to the 12-yard line. Eric Penick jetted in from there on a counter play behind Casper's block for a 21–17 lead. In the fourth quarter, the teams traded fumbles until Alabama scored on a snazzy play, with halfback Mike Stock throwing back across the field to a wide-open quarterback Richard Todd for a 25-yard score. The PAT was missed, which would turn out be crucial, and Alabama nursed a 23–21 lead. The Irish had to answer, and they did. With a 3rd-and-8 situation deep in their own territory, Ara called for a pass to Casper, but he was covered and it went instead to little-used tight end Robin Weber. It was a gutsy call, and Alabama was not prepared for it as Clements hit Weber with a 35-yard pass from his end zone. Weber snagged it and was hit out of bounds on the unhappy Alabama sideline. It was Weber's only catch of the championship 1973 season, although Clements had earlier in the game missed seeing him wide open in the end zone on a busted play. This memorable (miraculous?) play sparked a 79-yard drive that ended with a 19-yard field goal by Bob Thomas to seal the 24–23 win and the national championship for Notre Dame.

Two Irish players earned All-American status in this championship season: Dave Casper, the tackle who had converted to tight end, and defensive back Mike Townsend.

1977

Notre Dame head coach Dan Devine never had a problem following famous acts and personalities. Three cases in particular during his Hall of Fame career revealed his willingness to tackle a good opportunity under difficult circumstances: (1) he became head coach of the University of Missouri team in December of 1957 following the legendary Don Faurot's retirement; (2) he tackled the position of head coach for the NFL Green Bay Packers only three years after Vince Lombardi left the team; (3) he took on Notre Dame's head coach position immediately after Ara Parseghian's departure.

Many Irish fans were shocked and disappointed when Ara announced his retirement at the end of the 1974 season. He was only a year away from leading Notre Dame to a unanimous national championship season and his team had defeated Bear Bryant and Alabama in consecutive bowl games. He was leaving a team well-stocked with talent and enjoyed the adulation of Notre Dame's countless fans and admirers. His eleven Irish squads had made claims on three national titles: 1964, 1966, and 1973. He was only fifty-one years old, not much older than Frank Leahy was when he left the job in 1953. Ara's .836 winning percentage at Notre Dame put him in an august Irish circle: Rockne's .881 and Leahy's .855.

The 1977 team was Devine's third under the Dome. Previous coaches had set precedents in their third seasons, notably Leahy and Parseghian, both of whom had won national titles—Leahy in 1943 and Parseghian in 1966. The ingredients for a title were definitely there: the offense showed great potential with a big, mobile line, superior running backs, excellent wide receivers, and a gaggle of quarterbacks, including Joe Montana. The defense had Ross Browner (the '76 Outland Trophy recipient), back from an earlier suspension and a veteran of the '73 national champs, along with defensive end Willie Fry, middle linebacker Bob Golic, and Luther Bradley (shifted to corner), amid other talents.

Notre Dame's first game was against the 1976 national champs, Pittsburgh, sans Heisman winner Tony Dorsett. It was not an auspicious first half, as both teams showed first-game jitters, with Pitt taking a 9–6 halftime lead. Irish starting quarterback Rusty Lisch passed for the lone Irish score to tight end Ken McAfee, but the PAT was botched. The turning point may have already happened when Fry put a hit on Pitt quarterback Matt Cavanaugh that broke his left wrist and knocked him out of the game. Cavanaugh's throw was good for a TD but that was the only one Pitt would score that day. Indeed, the Irish defense held the Panthers to a total of 21 yards after that play, but the Notre Dame offense had to come out of hiding before the Irish could claim a win. More help came from the defense in the third quarter when Bob Golic recovered a fumble at the Pitt 16, resulting in the tying field goal. The defense kept at it with Ross Browner coming up with a fumble recovery leading to another field goal and the lead. The last Irish score came after

Ross's brother, Jim, picked up yet another Pitt fumble, with halfback Terry Eurick slamming in from the 4-yard line.

Ole Miss was not so charitable, and the Irish had to play in a rare 100-degree game, losing, 20–13. Jerome Heavens tallied the lone Irish TD after a Jim Browner interception. Dave Reeve kicked two field goals, but the offense was not hitting on all cylinders by any means.

Still looking for the right combination, the Irish used three quarterbacks to beat Purdue—the season starter Lisch, then the unfortunate Gary Forystek (broken collarbone), finally Joe Montana. Highly-touted Purdue freshman quarterback Mark Herrmann directed the game's first scoring drive, throwing for 60 yards, the final 10 for a TD. The Irish offense still seemed stuck in first gear, so the defense came to the rescue, harrying Herrmann enough to make him retreat deep in his end of the field where he should have thrown the ball away but didn't. Doug Becker snagged the errant throw to set up a Lisch to Eurick TD pass. Herrmann had no quit in him and led Purdue to a 24–14 third quarter lead, firing two more TD passes. Lisch had located Eurick again for the other Irish TD in the second quarter. Devine had to try to spark the offense, so he had inserted Forystek to start the second half. The new quarterback did get the Irish offense to move more efficiently but took off on a run from the Purdue 30, gaining 13 yards before the Boilermakers tracked him down. The gang tackle there broke his collarbone. Insert Joe Montana who, in 1976, had engineered a couple of comeback wins but also showed some physical fragility. Devine could not be sure what was going to happen; he didn't need another injured quarterback.

Montana couldn't fully capitalize on the drive Forystek started, but the Irish managed a field goal to make it 24–17. Devine had ten minutes to get the job done. The defense stepped up yet again; Luther Bradley grabbed a Purdue pass, and Montana started to pick the defense apart with passes to McAfee and Kris Haines, then McAfee again for the tying score. The Irish defense stayed stout, and Montana got the ball again with a bit more than three minutes left. Four passes to McAfee and Haines put the ball on the Purdue 10. Two runs from there completed the comeback, with halfback Dave Mitchell registering the winning TD in Notre Dame's 31–24 victory.

Against a feisty Michigan State team, Montana opened up with a 45-yard completion to McAfee, sparking a drive deep into Spartan territory. There the team showed that it couldn't stand too much prosperity and a fumble gave the Spartans the ball near their own goal line. The Irish defense held and a good punt return put them back in business deep in enemy territory—but Montana threw one of his

All-American Luther Bradley taking one of his 17 career interceptions to the house in 1977 action.

three interceptions on the day, which eventually led to a field goal and an early 3–0 lead for the Spartans. So far, the Irish had been equal opportunists for turnovers; next up was Jerome Heavens who found himself unattended 40 yards from the line of scrimmage. Montana saw him and fired a perfect pass to his big fullback, who promptly dropped it. A Dave Reeve field goal tied it in the second quarter, but the next turnover fell to running back Dave Waymer on a nifty double reverse when he simply dropped the ball. Finally, another short drive clicked when Heavens made up for his drop with a 24-yard romp, capped by Mitchell's 9-yard TD run, giving the Irish their first lead, 10–3. Golic intercepted on the first play in the second half but the clumsy Irish nullified any chance for a TD with a penalty so Reeve booted another field goal. The teams traded field goals after that for the 16–6 Notre Dame win. It wasn't pretty (the teams shared seven interceptions and three fumbles, so the defenses were paying attention), but it was a win against one of the major historic opponents on the schedule.

After a bye week, the Irish slammed Army with a much better performance, winning 24–0. This was Jerome Heavens's day, as he became the first Irish back in the modern era to rush for 200 yards. Gaining 43 of the 47 yards needed on a short drive in the second quarter, Heavens scored from the three. Luther Bradley intercepted an Army pass to deny them a TD. Dave Reeve tacked on a field goal.

Mike Whittington's interception allowed Montana and Heavens to pound away, the drive ending with a Terry Eurick TD run. Eurick added another TD run in the fourth quarter.

Dan Devine had an idea before their highly anticipated matchup with USC. The Trojans had been having their way too often with the Irish. Notre Dame had been sluggish and mistake-prone for most of the season so far. He arranged for the team to do its pregame warm-ups only to return to the locker room to find new green-and-gold uniforms. The team went nuts right there and the fans soon went berserk when the green-clad Irish emerged from the stadium's tunnel. The Trojans had to know right then and there that this was not going to be easy. Indeed, it wasn't, as the Irish pasted the Trojans, 49–19. USC had the first scoring opportunity but missed a field goal. Montana then led a composed and confident offense right downfield, with no mistakes, good running by Heavens, and sharp passes by Joe, capped by a short TD run by Mitchell. Eurick fumbled deep in ND's territory to give USC a cheap TD, but the Irish later jumped on a Charles White fumble to give Montana a 1-yard TD sneak six plays later. As luck would have it, the PAT snap went awry, but the Irish converted a two-point play instead when holder Ted Burgmeier more or less heaved a "pass" to an open Tom Domin in the end zone.

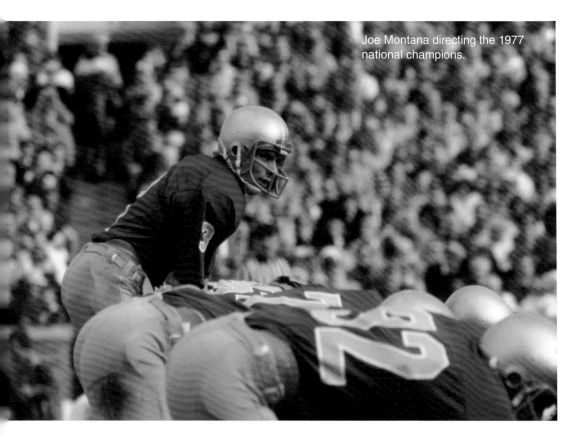

Joe Montana directing the 1977 national champions.

The Trojans had to be wondering about all this. They had more to wonder about when Bradley snagged his 16th career interception, tying an Irish record that he would eventually break. The drive stalled, but a fake field goal let Burgmeier get loose for a 21-yard gain. Montana flipped a 12-yard TD pass to McAfee, who literally towered head and shoulders above the small USC defensive backs. In the second half, Golic blocked a punt and tackle Jay Case rumbled 30 yards for the score, a lineman's dream come true. Montana tossed a 1-yard TD to McAfee, then added a 1-yard TD sneak before backup Lisch hooked up with Kevin Hart for the final TD. USC's scores were less than half of what they needed. The game showcased a powerful Irish offense and a defense that just wouldn't quit against a quality opponent, allowing the 11th-ranked Irish to defeat the fifth-ranked Trojans.

The Irish took over USC's No. 5 spot in the polls and had five games left to make a national statement. They blasted Navy, 43–10, dismantled Georgia Tech, 69–14, blanked Air Force, 49–0, and muzzled Miami, 48–10, showing an almost unstoppable offensive force and a defense that simply throttled their opponents. One game turned out to be a squeaker—in between Georgia Tech and Air Force the Irish had to go back to the South, the region where they had lost the second game of the season, in this case Clemson's Death Valley.

Notre Dame came out of the gates quickly, with a Jerome Heavens 5-yard TD romp in the first quarter. The second quarter belonged to Clemson, however, as they tallied a field goal and a 10-yard TD run by quarterback Steve Fuller while ND missed a field goal. Clemson held off the Irish's first possession in the third quarter and used a short field to march to the Irish 2-yard line. On 4th-and-1 from that spot, Fuller pitched to tailback Lester Brown veering left and the head linesman executed a perfect brush block on Burgmeier, the only Irish defender able to stop the play, allowing Brown to score. It was the kind of officiating error Devine feared going into Death Valley; he was later handed a 15-yard penalty for unsportsman-like conduct after he verbally blistered yet another *faux pas* by the officials that threatened to kill a good Irish drive. That drive had started with a fumble recovery by defensive tackle Mike Calhoun but the Irish running backs had to do double duty for yardage—make a nice gain, penalty, do it again, penalty. Montana managed to overcome a 2nd-and-31 situation with a long pass to McAfee, then earned another set of downs by going back to the tight end for a 16-yard gain. Montana finished the drive with a 2-yard run. Déjà vu all over again with nine minutes to go in the fourth quarter—Calhoun snagged another fumble, and the Irish marched in for the game's winning score on Montana's 1-yard TD plunge to clinch a 21–17 thriller.

Part Two

Ranked fifth in the nation, Notre Dame accepted a Cotton Bowl bid to play the top-ranked Texas Longhorns and their star running back, Heisman winner Earl Campbell. Texas was undefeated going into the game and acted like it in the various pre-bowl activities. At one banquet, the Texas team was given the seats of honor, and the Irish were stuck in the back of the room. Devine later said he knew right then and there that the Irish were not taking it lightly. He kept monitoring the team's attitude closely and knew that they were in a perfect mental state coming down the tunnel for the kickoff. He was confident they would do well.

And well they did—causing six turnovers and keeping Campbell penned up. He did gain 116 yards, but the Irish backs, Jerome Heavens and Vagas Ferguson, both had 100 yards or more each to counter that. Middle linebacker Bob Golic later said that he "wore Campbell in my pads," he hit him so often as part of his 17 tackles in the game.

The teams probed and prodded for much of the first quarter, resulting in a 3–3 standoff. The Irish field goal came off an errant pitchout to Campbell on the game's fifth play, Ross Browner recovering. This was an early indication of how it was going to go for the Longhorns. A patient Irish drive that started late in the first quarter led to a Eurick TD run of 6 yards to start the second quarter. It proved to be a disastrous frame for Texas, as Notre Dame would score two more TDs—another Eurick TD from 10 yards out and later a Montana to Ferguson 17-yard throw and catch. Texas managed a TD pass on the last play of the half, then the Irish defense shut them out the rest of the way. In the third quarter, linebacker Steve Heimkreiter speared a Texas pass on their 26-yard line, leading to a short Ferguson run after Montana found some wide-open receivers. In the fourth quarter, with the Longhorn offense badly outclassed, the Irish finished the scoring with a two-minute drive, capped by Ferguson's dandy 26-yard run. The Irish offense had stampeded the Longhorns for 26 first downs, 247 yards rushing, and 156 yards passing. Maybe next time Texas wouldn't seat the Notre Dame team at the back of the banquet hall.

Seven Notre Dame players from this great championship team were honored as All-Americans: defensive end Ross Browner, tight end Ken MacAfee, defensive back Luther Bradley, guard Ernie Hughes, nose guard Bob Golic, defensive end Willie Fry, and defensive back Ted Burgmeier. How Joe Montana was not recognized is one of college football's great mysteries. In spite of that slight, he did make it into the Pro Football Hall of Fame in 2000.

1988

The ebbs and flows of collegiate football certainly have afflicted the history of Notre Dame football as much as any other team with a prominent history. Knute Rockne set the standard for excellence, but his tragic death at age forty-three in 1931 left the football program to drift somewhat while trying to find the kind of leader as a head coach who could rekindle the spirit and success that Rockne's years enjoyed. Frank Leahy turned out to be that man when he left Boston College to serve as Notre Dame's head coach in 1941. He had an unbelievable string of success, winning four national titles and producing four Heisman winners. His departure left yet another vacuum and mediocrity set in for a decade. Ara Parseghian revitalized the program with his very first season, almost going undefeated that year, 1964, and winning it all in 1966 and 1973. The cupboard was not bare when he left after 1974; Dan Devine won the title in 1977 with Joe Montana and a bevy of other stars and threatened to do it again in 1980. The Gerry Faust era at first found Irish fans beside themselves, salivating, knowing of his amazing success at Moeller High School in Cincinnati. While creating and sustaining Moeller's football program, Faust's won-loss record was a stunning 178–23–2 (.882 winning percentage). That exalted level of success, however, simply never materialized for Faust under the Dome. He had great players and unbounded enthusiasm and is still a beloved figure at the school, but the complexities and intricacies of game management and tactics never reached the level of sophistication that is needed in major college football. (A case can be made that Notre Dame twice hired great high school coaches who had only mediocre careers under the Dome—Terry Brennan, at Chicago's Mt. Carmel before coaching freshmen at Notre Dame, followed Leahy and Faust, of Moeller High School in Cincinnati, followed Devine.) So these lulls happen but then another "savior" appears for the Irish. After Faust, that savior turned out to be Lou Holtz.

As history would have it, the 1988 version of the Fighting Irish was Holtz's third team under the Dome. He was hired just as the Irish were in the process of losing the 1985 season-ending game with Miami by the horrific score of 58–7. He had to be wondering what he had just gotten himself into. Indeed, his 1986 first edition of the Holtz era ended up with the same record as Faust's 1985 team—five wins, six losses. His 1987 team showed considerable improvement, registering an 8–3 regular season and a Cotton Bowl loss to Texas A&M. They also lost to Miami, but the score was 24–0—a modest improvement over the 1985 debacle.

Third seasons at Notre Dame have had a bit of allure to them because of certain precedents. Jesse Harper's third team in 1915 lost only to Nebraska by one point, 21–20. Rockne's third year was undefeated and produced a national title (but his second year's team had done the same). Leahy's third team won his first national championship and garnered the school's first Heisman winner in Angelo Bertelli. Parseghian's third team went undefeated and won a national title (although his first team, the '64 squad, made a serious bid for the title and was recognized as such by several pundits). Other coaches were not so lucky, but the optimists don't dwell on their outcomes. There is just enough of a trend for the fans to pay close attention—and the head coach hears about it, to be sure. It also means that by the time that the third campaign comes around, the players and the coaching staff have had enough time together to mesh as a productive unit, not to mention implementing successful recruiting appeals and the like. It might not be fair, but the third season for a coach at Notre Dame has become a barometer of success or, possibly, mediocrity or even failure. It is perhaps not a coincidence that the 2012 Irish team, Brian Kelly's third season there, went undefeated in the regular season, lost to Alabama in the BCS Championship Game, and still took third or fourth place in the postseason rankings.

Holtz faced two major problems as he looked to the 1988 season: he would have to replace the entire offensive line as well as a Heisman Trophy winner (flanker Tim Brown). His backfield was intact and had some excellent new players in the pipeline. Tony Rice as an option quarterback would grow into the role more completely as the season progressed, although he did not enter the season as a serious passing threat. He was, however, a master of the option read, and if he kept the ball, he was a slick runner with breakaway speed. His backfield mates included fullback Anthony Johnson, running back Mark Green, and flanker Ricky Watters. His tight end was 6-foot-7 Derek Brown and the split end was Rocket Ismail. As a unit, there was plenty of speed in this group. Holtz once said that Ismail was so fast, he was the only guy he knew who could play tennis with himself. This was not the kind of offense that used the run to set up the pass; it ran the ball and took the occasional pass opportunity when it was there, or absolutely needed. The team's rushing yardage ratio to passing yardage was virtually 2:1 at the end of the season.

The defense was loaded with big, fast players and had excellent depth. In fact, the defense was truly the heart of this team. The linemen and linebackers could shut down a running game while the defensive backs could nullify most passing attacks. Pick your poison. Overall, the team would produce three consensus All-Americans: Andy Heck at tackle, after having moved from tight end; Frank

Stams at defensive end; and linebacker Michael Stonebreaker. Two more defenders would see honors—nose tackle Chris Zorich and linebacker Wes Pritchett, along with flanker Ricky Watters. The NFL would draft twenty-four players from this team in the 1989–91 drafts.

The first game of the 1988 season, a home game at night, for 13th-ranked Notre Dame was against long-time rival Bo Schembechler's Michigan Wolverines, ranked No. 9. Both teams had players of huge dimensions, but the man who won the game was less than half the size of many of the starters and was even smaller than some of Rockne's pet projects, such as 149-pound starting guard Bert Metzger on the 1930 team. The hero turned out to be Reggie Ho of Kaneohe, Hawaii, a walk-on kicker for Notre Dame, who stood 5-foot-5 and registered 135 pounds— in truth, not much smaller than his coach, a former college linebacker. Ho would kick four field goals in the game, tying the Irish record, the last one with 73 seconds left in the game, defeating the Wolverines, 19–17.

Ricky Watters got it going with a rousing 81-yard punt return for the first Irish TD in the opening frame, a sort of tradition for the Irish against Michigan (Ismail would do the trick twice in 1989 against the Wolverines). Just before the first quarter expired, the undersized Ho followed a 16-yard Watters punt return with a 31-yard field goal for a 10–0 Irish lead. Mere seconds into the second quarter, defensive end Arnold Ale landed on a Michigan fumble near the red zone; Michigan stopped any further advancement, and Ho blasted another field goal, 38 yards, for a 13–0 lead. The answering Michigan drives were sparked by a 59-yard kickoff return, capped by fullback Leroy Hoard's 1-yard TD plunge, making the halftime score 13–7. Michigan scored in the third quarter thanks to a fluky break when their punt grazed Watters and they recovered on the Irish 14-yard line. Quarterback Michael Taylor gained the last yard for a TD and a one-point lead for Michigan. In the fourth quarter, a 12-play 68-yard Irish drive ended with another Ho field goal of 26 yards and the Irish had the lead again, 16–14. Michigan's Mike Gillette answered that kick with his own ten minutes later, a booming 49-yard effort, as the lead returned to Michigan, 17–16. The Irish had plenty of clock left and worked a careful 71-yard drive, Rice escaping for a 21-yard gain, to set up Ho's winning kick, a 26-yard effort with 1:13 left. Michigan had enough time to give Gillette another opportunity, but his kick went wide right as the clock expired.

Having escaped a loss to Michigan at home, the No. 8 Irish next went to East Lansing to do battle with the country's leading defense against the run in 1987, Michigan State. The Irish passing game was nonexistent, so if they were going to have a chance, they would have to do it on the ground. They did, gaining 245 bruising yards on 54 rushes, even after losing two fullbacks to injuries and switching tailback Tony Brooks to fullback, who then played the second half with a broken bone in his foot. The Irish held a 6–3 lead at halftime as Reggie Ho banged two field goals in the second quarter to counter MSU's one field goal made in the first quarter. Rice hit one of his two completions in the game when he spotted tailback Mark Green for a 38-yard gain, setting up Ho's first field goal. With less than five minutes left in the second quarter, Ho hit another field goal, thanks to Ismail's block of a Spartan punt. Up to that point, the Irish offense seemed to be operating in first gear. Holtz decided at halftime to run more option plays and that's exactly what they did. In the third quarter, Brooks powered for a 37-yard gain to set up Rice's 8-yard option TD run. Linebacker Michael Stonebreaker sealed the deal with an interception and 39-yard return for a TD and the 20–3 final score. The Irish running game piled up 195 yards on the ground in the second half; the defense held the Spartans to 89 yards on the ground. Green accounted for 125 yards on 21 carries to lead the parade.

Still ranked eighth, the Irish continued their mastery over Big Ten rivals, this time Purdue. Holtz knew he had to get more production out of the passing game. (Rice had only two completions for 50 yards in nine attempts versus MSU, and a matching number of interceptions. The Irish were ranked last in Division I passing.) Everything worked, however, in a 52–7 rout of the Boilermakers, one of Notre Dame's oldest rivals. It was their seventh straight win over a Big Ten opponent. Purdue was never in the game; the halftime score was 42–0, and Holtz emptied the bench after that. The scoring parade included Rice's 38-yard TD on an option play; two TD passes, the first to Derek Brown for 8 yards and then to Ismail for 54 yards; Green had a 7-yard TD burst; Watters slashed 66 yards with a punt return; Brooks' 34-yard reception from sub quarterback Steve Belles; Rodney Culver scoring on a 34-yard sprint … all to go with seven PATs and a field goal. Notre Dame gained 321 yards on the ground and 147 yards via passes. The opportunistic Irish defense picked off five Purdue passes.

Moving up in the national rankings to No. 5, the Irish met Stanford at home and continued the scoring onslaught, winning 42–14. Rice showed that he could pass with accuracy by hitting ten throws in a row (the last four versus Purdue, the first six in this game). He attributed his success to throwing darts, as recommended by Holtz. He also led the eleven runners the Irish used with 107 yards, scoring the first TD of the game early in the first quarter with a 30-yard run. The PAT failed. In the second quarter, linebacker Ned Bolcar jumped on a Stanford fumble conveniently dropped at their 1-yard line. Mark Green hurdled into the end zone and

Rice then ran for two points to make it 14–0. Tony Brooks scored from the 5 not long after that. Stanford shows signs of life with a 68-yard scoring drive, but that was nullified by an 80-yard march that concluded with Anthony Johnson scoring from the 1-yard line. The second half showed that the Irish defense could completely choke off an opponent's running game, as they allowed Stanford only a net of five yards. Rice darted a 3-yard TD to his tight end, Derek Brown, in the third quarter and then showed his own running skills with a 21-yard breakout that led to his own 6-yard TD scamper in the fourth. Stanford scored once with a consolation TD to make it 42–14.

Still ranked No. 5, they wanted to play No. 1 Miami. But first, the Irish had to play at Pitt. The Irish had to be careful about looking past a team that had beaten them in their last three meetings. And that's exactly what happened as the Panthers fought doggedly in a game that Notre Dame won 30–20. Pitt scored first with a 42-yard pass from Darnell Dickerson to Reggie Williams, but the Irish countered with two TDs on short bursts by Rice and Anthony Johnson. Rice's score followed a 52-yard rumble by Brooks. Pitt scored again in the second quarter with another Dickerson aerial for 33 yards, and they held the Irish to a 37-yard Ho field goal even though Ismail made a great 40-yard kickoff return to start the drive. In the second half, the Irish turned to their superior running game (310 net yards for the day) to play keep-away with the ball as they mounted a 2:1 time of possession advantage. But Pitt kicked a field goal after a Watters fumble before Braxston Banks snagged a 30-yard pass to lead to Rice's 1-yard TD plunge at the end of the third quarter. Arnold Ale's timely interception had ended a Pitt scoring threat, and Mark Green punctuated the last Irish scoring drive with an 8-yard TD gallop good for the 30–20 final score.

Miami had dominated the Irish in recent years and was riding a 36-game regular season winning streak when they flew into South Bend. The Irish were ranked fourth as they faced the top-ranked team in the country. It would be crucial for the defense to harass the Miami quarterback, Steve Walsh, as much as possible. They did just that yet Walsh still managed to pass for more than 400 yards. Miami would win most of the statistics, gaining 481 total yards to Notre Dame's 331, but they coughed up four fumbles and lost three interceptions, wrecking those Hurricane possessions and indicating the hard-hitting deployed by the Irish.

Rice got the festivities started near the end of the first quarter, spotting Ismail with a 22-yard pass and eventually running for a 7-yard TD. Walsh matched that score in the second quarter with an 8-yard TD pass to Andre Brown. Rice and Ismail hooked up again, this time for a 57-yard bomb that set up a 9-yard TD pass

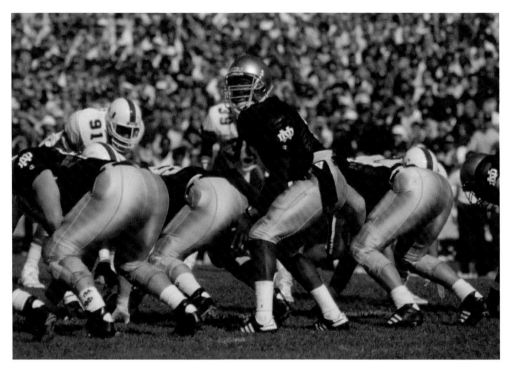

Tony Rice, the last Notre Dame quarterback to win a national championship, in 1988 action.

from Rice to Banks. Two minutes later, one of those miraculous plays happened when Irish free safety Pat Terrell intercepted a Walsh pass and zoomed 60 yards to pay dirt and a 21–7 Irish lead. The lead didn't last long as Walsh fired two TD passes in the final minutes of the half for a 21–21 tie at halftime. In the third quarter, Miami tried a fake punt near midfield, but the Irish snooped it out, recovered possession, and Rice zipped a 44-yard pass to Watters, followed by a 2-yard TD run by Pat Eilers. Defensive end Jeff Alm intercepted a Walsh pass near the end of the third quarter, and Ho booted a 27-yard field goal when the drive ended. Miami scored twice in the fourth quarter, a field goal and a Walsh TD pass. With the score 31–30, Miami went for a two-point conversion, but Terrell tipped the pass attempt to deny the conversion. Miami tried an onside kick, but Anthony Johnson covered it. Frank Stams, Irish defensive end, was a key figure in the game as he tipped the pass that Terrell took to the house, caused two fumbles, recovered a fumble, and helped lead the Irish run defense that allowed only 57 net yards rushing and two first downs earned on the ground. Millions watched the game on a national broadcast, a thrilling contest that deserves to be right up there as a "game of the century."

For four dismal encounters in the mid-'80s before Holtz arrived, Air Force had prevailed against the hapless Irish (in 1986, Holtz's first Irish team snapped the streak, beating the Falcons decisively, 31–3). These Falcon teams did not field a single player that the Irish had tried to recruit, but they took the measure of the bigger, faster players and beat them at their own game. In some ways, this is a measure of the state of affairs within Notre Dame football, or any major college program for that matter. Do the better athletes actually improve their skill set over time, or not? Are they provided the tactical wherewithal to win games consistently over time when they have the dominant players against lesser athletes? These matters were in doubt before Holtz arrived, just as they had been in doubt in all the other "lulls" in Irish success on the gridiron.

Air Force, with the talented Dee Dowis at QB and the highly respected Fisher DeBerry as head coach, was leading the nation in rushing, using a triple option offense that racked up 432 yards per game on the ground. The Irish were coming off the exhaustion and excitement of the big win over Miami and were now ranked No. 2 in the country behind UCLA. Air Force got the scoring started with a field goal, following a typical Dowis escape act for a 22-yard gain. The Irish used the last six minutes of that quarter to construct an 11-play drive covering 71 yards, with Mark Green blasting in from the 7-yard line for a 7–3 lead. Air Force patched together a 41-yard drive for another field goal in the second quarter, using a reverse to keep the Irish defense honest. Watters made a good kickoff return, then snagged a 22-yard pass from Rice, with the Irish quarterback then taking it in from the 4 for a 14–6 lead. The Irish used two big plays to add their third TD: Watters broke loose for a 36-yard punt return and Johnson busted one for 27 yards before wrapping it up with a 12-yard TD run. The kick failed, and Notre Dame led, 20–6. The Falcons kept chipping away, however, using a 60-yard kickoff return to give them a short field near the end of the half. Five plays later, and with less than one minute remaining, Andy Smith stormed in from the Irish 3 to pull the Falcons within a TD at halftime. During the half, middle linebacker Wes Pritchett took the team to task for letting the Falcons stay in the game. His appeal worked in spectacular fashion—the Irish defense allowed only 39 yards rushing by Air Force in the second half, totally choking off their primary means of moving the ball and controlling the clock. The Irish took the second half kickoff and drove 81 yards in nine plays, with Anthony Johnson busting loose for a 42-yard TD romp. He gained more yards on that one play than Air Force would generate during the entire second half. Late in the third quarter, Air Force knew it was in a desperate situation and tried a fourth down run, needing two yards but they got only one. Four plays later, Watters took in a great pass from Steve Belles after an option fake and sped past the clutching Falcons 50 yards for a TD. In the fourth quarter, it was Notre Dame's turn to go for it on a fourth down. They needed one yard but Rodney Culver picked up four. Not long after that, Rice passed to Watters for a 28-yard TD and the final 41–13 score.

Still sitting at No. 2, the Irish came a cropper against Navy. They managed to win the game played in Baltimore, but the receivers dropped five passes, ballhandlers lost two fumbles, Ho missed a PAT, one punt went only 10 yards, and the team was hit with 90 yards of penalties. Every team will have a bummer like this, but it's not a good idea to do it against a team like Navy, an outfit that never quits, always plays above their skill level, and is opportunistic. To be frank, the Irish dodged a bullet with this 22–7 win. If there was a bright spot, it was Notre Dame's defensive effort, allowing Navy only 192 yards of total offense and giving up precisely one pass completion. In spite of their problems, the Irish piled up a 22–0 lead before Navy scored in the third quarter. Most of the first quarter was gone before Navy fumbled on their 27-yard line; on the sixth play after the fumble Derek Brown caught a 10-yard pass from Rice for a TD and a 7–0 lead. Rodney Culver rambled 22 yards for a second-quarter score, but Ho's PAT was missed. As the half ended, Ho split the uprights to register a 29-yard field goal to make it 16–0. Reserve fullback Ryan Mihalko finished Notre Dame's scoring on a 1-yard plunge for the 22 Irish points. Punter Jimmy Sexton's 10-yard shank led to Navy's only score near the end of the third quarter.

No. 1 UCLA lost to Washington State, 34–30, the same day, so the Irish ascended to the top spot. The win over Navy showed what a powerful team could still do even though not hitting on all cylinders. Against Rice, however, the entire engine was operating at peak power, so Notre Dame shelled the Owls to the tune of 54–11. Rice kicked a field goal to end its first possession; their lead lasted for 13 seconds. Ismail threaded his way through a good running lane while the Irish blockers did the rest during his 87-yard TD kickoff return. On the next possession, the Owls lost sight of Mark Green while he was running for a 40-yard gain; Anthony Johnson wrapped up the drive with a 2-yard TD burst. In the second quarter, Johnson went in again from the Rice 3 after a 41-yard pass from Rice to Brown. Jeff Alm intercepted a Rice pass and returned it to the 18 to set up Brooks's 1-yard TD plunge. The teams traded field goals in the final moments of the half as the score reached 31–6. Following Wes Pritchett's fumble recovery, Rodney Culver scored the only TD in the third quarter on a 19-yard cruise. The Owls added a field goal but then Ismail did it again—83 yards with the kickoff return for a TD. The Irish added a field goal and a 6-yard TD run by reserve running back Joe Jarosz. The Owls blocked the PAT and ran it back for two more points and the 54–11 final score. The Irish defense completely paralyzed Rice's running game, allowing 32 yards in 34 rushing attempts.

Next was a revenge game against Penn State. The Nittany Lions had defeated the Irish three consecutive times, but they were in a bit of a downturn in 1988, coming to Notre Dame with a 5–5 record. A loss would lock in their first losing season in fifty years. The Irish would ring up some big numbers on them but the score stayed at a modest level, 21–3. The only Penn State score came at the end of the first half, aided by a Notre Dame penalty. The Irish scored one TD in each of the first three quarters, on their way to 502 yards of total offense. Tony Rice sparked his own 2-yard TD scamper with a 31-yard ramble as part of an 87-yard drive. In the second quarter, Rice caught Watters open in the secondary and led him perfectly with a pass good for 27 yards. Mark Green got the scoring honors with a 2-yard run. Ismail scored the third of Notre Dame's TD with a 67-yard catch and run on a nice throw from Rice. The Irish defense broke up 10 Penn State passes and intercepted two more. Defensive end Jeff Alm earned his third interception of the season. Penn State managed only 105 yards rushing on 31 carries and completed only five passes in 24 attempts.

The undefeated No. 1 Irish met the undefeated No. 2 USC Trojans at the Coliseum in LA in the last game of the regular season. The Trojans had gaudy press clippings lauding their achievements: a Heisman candidate in quarterback Rodney Peete, a stifling No. 1-ranked run defense that allowed only 68.1 yards per game, and an offense that cranked out 472 yards per game. Before the game, Holtz suspended two of his workhorses—Tony Brooks and Ricky Watters—for disciplinary reasons. Ismail served notice on Notre Dame's first possession when he hauled in a pass from Rice for 55 yards but stumbled at the end of the long gainer. The Irish waited for the first ten minutes of the first quarter to expire before they struck again—and it was Tony Rice on a 65-yard TD gallop. Before the quarter ran out, Stams recovered a Trojan fumble, and Mark Green took advantage with a 2-yard TD run with less than two minutes remaining. In the second quarter, Peete swung into action with a 26-yard pass completion to set up a 1-yard TD run by Scott Lockwood. They looked to be back in the game, but Irish defensive back Stan Smagala saw his big opportunity with a Peete pass floating unattended when the target receiver fell down. He picked it and sped 64 yards for an Irish TD and a 20–7 halftime lead. Peete was injured by Stams's blindside block on the play. USC wrapped up its scoring for the game with a field goal in the third quarter, but the Irish countered that early in the fourth quarter with a 70-yard march capped by Mark Green's 1-yard TD plunge and the 27–10 final score. The Trojans more or less won the battle of the statistics, except for the scoreboard. They lost two fumbles, gave up two interceptions, and had 50 yards in penalties. Half of their turnovers led directly to Notre Dame scores. Notre Dame's 11–0 regular season record marked the first time the Irish had won that many games in one season.

Irish defender Todd Lyght breaking up a Trojan pass in 1988. *AP Photo/Reed Saxon*

Undefeated Notre Dame went on to meet undefeated No. 3 West Virginia in the 1989 Fiesta Bowl in Tempe, Arizona. The Mountaineers were a high-scoring bunch led by the talented Major Harris at quarterback. They had run up bigger scores than the Irish had against two shared opponents—Pitt and Penn State, winning 31–10 and 51–30, respectively. West Virginia's hopes suffered a setback when Jeff Alm and Stonebreaker tackled Harris on the game's third play, injuring his left shoulder. He stayed in for much of the rest of the game but his effectiveness was reduced. Notre Dame earned the first three scores of the game: a 45-yard Billy Hackett field goal shortly after Rice roamed for 31 yards; an Anthony Johnson short plunge for a TD after Rice struck with a 23-yard pass to Brown; and in the second quarter, after yet another Rice to Brown hookup of 47 yards, Culver slashed in from the 5-yard line to give the Irish an imposing 17–0 lead. West Virginia managed two field goals in that quarter, but they sandwiched and were nullified by Rocket Ismail's 29-yard TD pass from Rice for the 23–6 halftime score. Ho booted a 32-yard field goal in the third quarter before Harris led a 74-yard drive for a Mountaineer TD that cut the lead to 26–13. In the fourth quarter, Rice's passing produced the last Irish score, as he lofted a pass to Watters good for a 57-yard advance, then found Frank Jacobs with a 3-yard scoring pass. Rice added the two-point conversion with his run. Late in the game, Harris was out of the game, but the Mountaineers didn't quit, using 11 plays on a 59-yard drive for a 3-yard TD run and a two-point conversion to make it 34–21 at the final gun. The Irish racked up 455 yards of total offense to 282 for West Virginia. Don Nehlen, the Mountaineers' head coach, later said that watching film did not help him and his staff properly assess Notre Dame's overall team speed. They were not prepared for that.

With the win, Notre Dame won its 11th undisputed national championship. Stams, Heck, and Stonebreaker were consensus All-Americans; Zorich, Pritchett, and Watters were also recognized. Surely, this team can legitimately be considered as one of the top five in Irish football history.

Part Two

PART III

MIRACLE COACHES

Knute Rockne

Knute Rockne would have made an outstanding postal worker. He had a superior work ethic, a keen mind, excellent rapport with folks, and enough energy for three people. He loved sports and was gifted enough in track and field. He was a late-comer to football, a sport frowned upon by his Norwegian parents, but he did give it a try in high school. Perhaps a formative influence on him was the fact that he lived in the tough Logan Square neighborhood of Chicago, where kids from widely different backgrounds more or less made a habit of picking on each other. Rockne quickly learned to defend himself. After high school, the dutiful, diligent Rockne applied himself for four years as a mail dispatcher in the Chicago Post Office, saving enough money to help afford the expenses of a college education. He had heard of this place called Notre Dame. Football's imminent gain was the postal service's eventual loss. He gave the school a try, entering as a twenty-two-year-old freshman in 1910.

He never left the place.

If there was ever a polymath, Rockne broke the mold. At Notre Dame, he pole-vaulted, played the flute, acted in campus theatrical productions, played football, boxed, dabbled in school journalism, majored in chemistry, and earned graduation honors. That is merely a partial list—and he continued multitasking for the rest of his life. He also captained the football team in 1913 and came to the attention of the reigning authority on all things football, Walter Camp, enough so that Camp bestowed third-team All-America honors on him as an end that year. Beating Army, 35–13, on the plains of West Point made an impression on Camp, who favored East Coast teams and players in his various selections. But intercollegiate football was changing in many ways, and the spirited Rockne was a major part of that. He would eventually come to personify the game itself as it evolved in the years ahead.

No prediction is ever fully guaranteed to work out, but it's fairly safe to say that Rockne's unparalleled record after thirteen seasons at Notre Dame (105–12–5, a winning percentage of .881) is not going to go down easily. This is the highest winning rate for any coach in both major college football and the NFL. In the simplest terms, his competitors could not catch up with him—and no one has surpassed him in the intervening years and decades. They did use the rulebook against him (seen every time a penalty is called for an "illegal shift"—more on this later). But Rockne's feet were not stuck in concrete; he was as nimble as a coach as he had been as a player. He was fully capable of changing his tactics to meet changing times. A case in point is to compare his running backs from 1924 and 1930. The Four Horsemen, dripping wet, did not break an average of 160 pounds per man as a group. The 1930 backfield starters, on the other hand, averaged 182.5 pounds, nearly 25 pounds heavier in a few short years. Rockne knew that he had lost the advantage the Notre Dame shift gave his smallish backfields at the point of attack, so he changed his recruiting to attract bigger running backs who still had plenty of speed.

Rockne stayed on after commencement in 1914 to work as a chemistry graduate assistant under Father Julius Nieuwland, the inventor of synthetic rubber. But there was a proviso: he could also work as an assistant to football head coach Jesse Harper. This arrangement held true until Harper retired after the 1917 season, during which Harper unveiled a tremendous asset—George Gipp. Thus began Rockne's tenure as Notre Dame's head coach.

He inherited a team that had produced six shutouts in its eight games in 1917, allowing the opponents only nine points *total* for the whole campaign. Gipp had shown flashes of brilliance, but a broken leg ended his season midway through. Even with this very solid and talented legacy for Rockne from the Harper years, the 1918 football season was beset by a worldwide crisis—the tragic flu epidemic that killed millions. The US government instituted strict travel limitations to avoid spreading the contagion. Teams curtailed their travel, canceled games, and generally operated on a very tentative basis from week to week. Rockne's Irish played only six games that season, ending up with a 3–1–2 record. There was only one home game—a fact that indicates the stringent travel restrictions other teams faced.

In typical Rockne fashion, he didn't let the crisis create a setback for his program. With Gipp playing better than any other human on the planet, the Irish ran off back-to-back undefeated seasons in 1919–20, winning twice each against the likes of Nebraska, Army, and Michigan State. In those two undefeated seasons Rockne's teams pounded the opposition for 479 points—better than 26 points a game, but allowed only 91, barely over 5 points per game. Other teams were simply stifled: seven shutouts, reaching double figures only three times, with 13 points being the most scored against Notre Dame in that stretch of wins. There was the Rockne formula: an overwhelming defense and an offense that was designed to score from anywhere on the field. Rockne tinkered with "shock troops"—starting a game with the second-string unit, allowing the starters to take in the action and see what they were up against. His other initiative, a refinement of a Harper tactic, was the "Notre Dame shift"—explained to me personally in 1980 by Paul Castner, his fullback from 1920 to 1922. The four backfield men would be arranged in a "box" formation. The center could snap the ball to any of them just at the split second that all four might start in motion, giving the Irish a tremendous advantage as the runner followed his backfield mates into gaps in the line, or out wide beyond the ends. Of course, the shift also allowed for a deadly passing game. Defenses were in a world of hurt against this scheme; if they overloaded to attempt to stop the run and negate the Irish blocking scheme, the passing game would kill them. If they spread out to defend the pass, the running game would gouge them for huge gains.

Rockne had thus refined the game and made obsolete what he considered to be "bovine football"—the old mass play tactics from the nineteenth century. With his innovations and refinements, modern football was born. He could even have fun with it, as he did in a 1924 game by employing an anachronistic nineteenth century "flying wedge" to start the second half returning the Princeton kickoff—more or less thumbing the collective Midwestern Irish nose at the eastern cradle of football in the Irish's 12–0 victory. Did I forget to mention that Knute Rockne had a very good sense of humor?

Coach Knute Rockne in his element—surrounded by Irish players and coaches.

To achieve his stunning winning percentage, Rockne coached undefeated teams in five of his 13 seasons: 1919, 1920, 1924, 1929, and 1930. (The 1929 season was particularly noteworthy because the Irish never played a home game; all games were on the road while the new stadium was being built for the Irish.) The Irish lost only one game each in the seasons of 1921, 1922, 1923, 1926, and 1927. Notre Dame thus had only three losses in the six seasons from 1919 to 1924. Rockne was either undefeated or had only one loss in ten seasons—an unbelievable, unmatched record of achievement. One season, however, really stands out as an exception: 1928. In that difficult season, Rockne's charges won only five games while losing four. One-third of Rockne's career losses were suffered in that single season. This is also the season, the Army game specifically, when Rockne called upon the ghost of George Gipp to motivate his players to play beyond themselves, which they did. Irish halfback Jack Chevigny, upon scoring Notre Dame's first TD in the third quarter, reportedly cried out, "That's one for the Gipper!" When John O'Brien hauled in the TD pass that won the game, the injured Chevigny is said to have cheered from the sideline, "That's another one for the Gipper!"

Rockne's 1929 and 1930 teams were mere perfection. He was making his adjustment to the rules encroachments that were designed to hobble his shift, but Rockne stayed ahead of his peers and demonstrated that he was perfectly capable of coaching any system or variation. And he was doing this even as he seemed overcommitted in his non-football life. He had been serving as Notre Dame's athletic director, conducted football clinics around the country, served as a spokesman for South Bend's Studebaker Corporation, sat on various collegiate football committees, and became involved in the film industry.

With the 1930 regular season completed and the Irish recognized as the consensus national champs, there was one more game for The Rock—a charity game to benefit the unemployed in New York City. Mayor Jimmy Walker put the deal together, knowing full well that Rockne's brilliant reputation, the glamor of the Fighting Irish all-stars, and the attraction of the Giants, the second-place team in the NFL, would be a great combination. Some 55,000 fans saw the game on December 14 in the Polo Grounds, helping to raise well more than $100,000. The 13–4 Giants proved to be too much for the Irish all-stars as they triumphed, 22–0. Rockne basked, however, in the afterglow of having so many of his Irish stalwarts making a statement on behalf of a just cause as the Depression raged.

Ever busy, Rockne had to go to the Mayo Clinic for further treatment for the phlebitis he suffered in his legs, due to a collision on the sideline of the Indiana game a year earlier. After that, he managed to take the family to Florida for a January vacation. From there, he returned to the campus to help set up the spring practice schedule, dropped in the Studebaker offices to visit friends, Paul Castner among them, then went to Chicago to visit with his mother. From Chicago, he took the train to Kansas City to see his sons who attended a private school there, but the meeting never took place as planned. Disappointed, Rockne went to the airport to take Transcontinental Western Airline flight 599 to LA. He was planning on being involved with a movie being produced called *The Spirit of Notre Dame*.

The plane was a Fokker tri-motor, made in the Netherlands, and was state of the art for passenger planes in 1930. It seated ten passengers to go with two pilots. For this flight, however, there were only five passengers. The weather in the vicinity was ominous. The plane took off in spite of the conditions and headed for Wichita to pick up mail. The plane never made that scheduled stop, however, as the weather proved too vicious for a poorly designed wing structure and materials. The plane crashed near Bazaar, Kansas, with no survivors. March 31, 1931, became the date on which the most famous airline passenger at that point in history was killed in a crash.

The Basilica of the Sacred Heart at Notre Dame arranged for the national mourning over the tragic 1931 death of Knute Rockne.

The shock and grief were immediate, both in the US and overseas. CBS created the first nationwide radio network to broadcast the funeral from the basilica on the Notre Dame campus. President Hoover issued a statement lamenting the national loss. The King of Norway knighted Rockne posthumously. Memorial tributes flooded the campus and plans for a building in honor of Rockne materialized almost overnight. Virtually every newspaper in the country editorialized over the tragedy.

Had Lars Rockne not left Norway with his young family in 1893, had son Knute decided to play it safe and make a career of the post office job … these and many other crucial nexus points could have kept Rockne from enrolling at the University of Notre Dame in 1910. And even with his enrollment things could have turned out differently. It is possible that Notre Dame would have become the household name we know of today. The track record prior to Rockne's presence there was a pretty good one, but it is clear that the Irish took a quantum leap in its success on the gridiron and in its public recognition for excellence both there and in the classroom, recognition largely motivated by Knute Kenneth Rockne.

Frank Leahy

One of the most famous coaches in American football history had an inglorious start to his Hall of Fame career—in a hospital bed after two frustrating years as a substitute lineman on Rockne's last two teams in 1929–1930 (both undefeated). Of course, there's more to the story. Frank Leahy was laid up in a bed at the Mayo Clinic for treatment of an injury that had curtailed his involvement in Notre Dame's 1930 national championship season. He had a roommate at the clinic—head coach Knute Rockne—who was also at the clinic for further medical care regarding the phlebitis that had set in following a sideline crush of players slamming into him during the 1929 Notre Dame-Indiana game. This injury kept him from full involvement as the head coach for the balance of that season. Yet this confluence of injuries turned out to produce the most fortuitous and illustrious pair of Notre Dame coaches. Perhaps wallowing in some self-pity, the sometimes Irish lineman from Winner, South Dakota, was likely brooding and complaining about his rotten luck. Rockne, ever the optimist, seems to have spent valuable time encouraging his protégé to stay in the game and give coaching a try. That kind of encouragement is all that Leahy needed.

After graduating from Notre Dame in 1931, Leahy followed Rockne's advice and served a year at Georgetown as that school's line coach; for the 1932 season, he held a similar position at Michigan State. Then he moved on to Fordham where he served under former Four Horseman Jim Crowley. During his tenure at Fordham, Leahy tutored the Seven Blocks of Granite in their amazing 1935 to 1937 seasons, a period in which Fordham posted an impressive record, losing only two games in those three seasons. More to the point is that one of those blocks of granite was an undersized guard named Vince Lombardi, who would later be the head coach for the Green Bay Packers, a team founded by yet another Notre Dame football player, Curly Lambeau, who had played under Rockne in 1918. See a pattern there? Rockne and Lambeau, Rockne and Leahy, Rockne and Crowley, Crowley and Leahy, Leahy and Lombardi. It might also be noted that one of Leahy's parting gifts to Notre Dame was a running back he recruited late in his years as leader of the Irish—Paul Hornung, who, of course, went on to a great career under the Dome, earning the 1956 Heisman, and eventually also played at Green Bay—under Lombardi. (Notre Dame can boast of seven Heisman winners. Leahy coached four of them in their trophy-winning seasons—Angelo Bertelli, Johnny Lujack, Leon Hart, John Lattner—and recruited the fifth, Hornung, whose freshman year was Leahy's last year as head coach at Notre Dame.) Leahy also had the good fortune to coach Fordham's Alex Wojciechowicz, yet another Pro Football Hall of Fame member.

After Fordham, Leahy took the head coaching position at Boston College, where he instituted the T-formation and led BC to a 20–2 record in the 1939–1940 seasons, capped by a 19–13 victory over General Robert Neyland's Tennessee Volunteers in the 1941 Sugar Bowl to conclude an undefeated campaign.

Rockne's tragic death just months before Leahy graduated from Notre Dame had left a void at the school that was almost impossible to fill, not that the stalwarts who tried to sustain the school's prominence didn't try. First, one of Rockne's all-time greats, Heartley "Hunk" Anderson, took over the coaching reins. He had been an integral member of the coaching brain trust under Rockne but was apparently not cut out for head coaching duties, compiling a 16–9–2 record in three seasons. Another former Horseman, Elmer Layden, took over for seven seasons starting in 1934. Both men remained true to Rockne's tactical methods, but the evolution of the game was beginning to move away from the traditional Notre Dame box formation. Layden was not the firebrand that Rockne had been, nor was he as intense as Leahy who would follow him. He did manage to produce an 8–1 record in 1938, but his teams were not particularly flashy or overwhelming as he led the Irish to a 47–13–3 record (a .769 winning percentage).

Leahy's success at Boston College brought him to the attention of his alma mater, and he desperately wanted to return, but BC's officials held him to his contract. Leahy pulled every lever he could find, ultimately convening a press conference at which he announced that he would be going to Notre Dame as the new head coach. An exasperated BC senior administrator quickly called him on the phone and gave him his release.

Leahy would coach the team in two groupings of seasons: 1941 to 1943 and 1946 to 1953, with the 1944–1945 campaigns being handled by two interim coaches while Leahy was serving in the U. S. Navy. He stayed true to Rockne's box formation for the 1941 season, but then made the bold decision to scrap that relic and move to the modern T-formation, a decision that was not unanimously supported under the Dome. Whatever doubts may have lurked were dispelled in short order as the Irish lambasted opponents, winning a national title in 1943 and capturing the school's first Heisman trophy award in the person of Angelo Bertelli, the Springfield Rifle.

A smiling Frank Leahy as he takes over the Irish reins in 1941. *AP Photo*

Five of Leahy's seasons, separated by the war years, are perhaps the highwater mark of Notre Dame football—1943, 1946, 1947, 1948, and 1949. Under Leahy's demanding leadership, the Irish compiled an unbelievable record of 36 wins, one loss, and two ties (a .949 winning percentage). This was done more than two decades before the Irish would ever grace another bowl game; otherwise Leahy could have tacked on even more victories. In four of those seasons, Notre Dame went undefeated. They won undisputed national championships in four of those years, missing a title only in 1948, thanks to a season-ending tie with

USC. In three of those campaigns, the Irish ended up with a Heisman winner, with Leahy on three occasions coaching two Heisman winners or winners-to-be on the same team (Bertelli/Lujack, and Lujack/Hart twice).

Aside from the immortal Rockne (who had five undefeated seasons of his own), it is very likely that no other Irish coach—much less coaches elsewhere—will ever again string together such miracle seasons with so many luminaries.

Ara Parseghian

The Notre Dame football team faced some frustrating seasons in the immediate aftermath of Frank Leahy's retirement from coaching. Although a young Terry Brennan was able to put together four winning seasons in his five years as head coach following Leahy's departure from coaching following the 1953 season, even having a Heisman winner in 1956, Paul Hornung, could not take the edge off that 2–8 season. Brennan was gone after the 1958 season, replaced by Joe Kuharich. As the former head coach of the NFL's Washington Redskins, and as a Notre Dame alum who had played for Elmer Layden from 1935 to 1937, Kuharich had the kind of experience and Irish connections that seemed to promise a return to the glory years of Rockne and Leahy. After all, he was honored as the Coach of the Year in the NFL in 1955. Irish fans are hard to please in any case, with the exalted expectations they had developed over the years. But Kuharich was unable to string together the kind of wins and seasons that would satisfy the alums and the student body. In four seasons, he had three 5–5 records (1959, 1961, 1962) and a repetition of the disastrous 1956 season with a hapless 2–8 record in 1960. Kuharich became the only Irish coach in the school's football history to finish with a losing record (17–23) and his consecutive shutouts of Southern California in 1960–61 were not enough for him to keep the head coach position. He resigned in the spring of 1963; Hugh Devore became the interim head coach, a position he had filled once before, in 1945, while Leahy was still in the service. Devore inherited a stable of some very large players and an incoming freshman class that would eventually rank with one of the best in Irish annals. Alas, they were not eligible to play varsity football under the NCAA rules of the day.

Kuharich ultimately had proved unable to make the transition from the NFL to college football. NCAA football was still, in those years, a one-platoon game, with stringent substitution rules. Kuharich was given to recruiting and playing NFL-sized players rather than the smaller, quicker players typically found in college football in those days (see Bear Bryant's Alabama teams from those years, for instance). For example, he had recruited a behemoth backfield, with running backs Paul Costa and Jim Snowden both in the 240-pound range and Pete Duranko as a 235-pound fullback.

While Notre Dame was in the doldrums, Ara Parseghian was at Northwestern from 1956 to 1963. He followed Lou Saban, who coached the Northwestern team to a 0–8–1 record in 1955. The Irish were 2–7 in 1963 and might have lost one more but the game was canceled due to the assassination of President Kennedy. So Ara was no stranger to rebuilding college football programs. Furthermore, Ara had led Northwestern to four consecutive victories over the Irish: 30–24 in 1959, 7–6 in 1960, 12–10 in 1961, and a blowout 35–6 win in 1962. Athletic director Moose Krause had to have noticed that an undermanned team with few marquee players was making life difficult for the Notre Dame football program. Notre Dame was a lackluster 17–23 in those years while Parseghian was 22–14 with a school that had similar academic expectations for its athletes but was much less of an attraction in comparison to the history and former luster of the Irish.

Ara made the initial contact with Notre Dame, calling Father Edmund Joyce, the university's vice-president and chair of the athletic board. The loyal Hugh Devore had served his alma mater as the interim coach (as he had in 1945) in the '63 season, but his second stint was very different compared to his successful results in '45. Parseghian broke the mold as Notre Dame coach in that he was not a Catholic; Father Joyce had other priorities.

Parseghian immediately infused a spirit of hard work, commitment to the task at hand, unmatched physical conditioning, and optimism. He took one look at the huge runners he had inherited and swiftly turned them into first-rate linemen—Snowden operating as an offensive tackle with Costa and Duranko switching to the other side of the ball as defensive lineman. All three played as linemen in the NFL after graduation from the Dome. With an unranked and largely unknown Irish squad, the team met a lauded Wisconsin team at Camp Randall Stadium in the 1964 season opener and demolished the Badgers, 31–7, unveiling a stifling defense and a highly efficient quarterback-receiver combo in John Huarte and Jack Snow. Huarte racked up more passing yardage in this single game than did the starting quarterback for the '63 team for that entire dismal season. The Irish were back!

The 1964 Irish defense never gave up more than 15 points until they met USC in the finale. They recorded three shutouts—UCLA, Navy, and Iowa—while the offense racked up 92 points in those three games. During the lean years, Notre Dame had lost eleven of the last twelve contests with Michigan State, but the '64 squad took care of that with a 34–7 rout of the Spartans. Head coach Duffy

Part Three

Daugherty said that if there was a better team in the country, he wouldn't want to play them.

In the season finale, Ara took the team west to meet long-time nemesis USC. In a thrilling game, the Irish came within 93 seconds of achieving an undefeated record, but they ran out of time with a wrenching 20–17 loss to the Trojans. Nevertheless, Notre Dame won the Macarthur Bowl trophy by the National Football Foundation as national champs. Ara knew it was an asterisk situation. The sophomores on the team vowed that it would not happen again on their watch, a list led by Alan Page, Kevin Hardy, Tom Regner, and Jim Lynch.

That near miss in 1964 was a superb harbinger of greater success to follow—the impressive 1966 national champs and the 1973 national champs. With these teams, Parseghian displayed his recruiting prowess, his amazing attention to detail, his very keen eye for talent and where to place that talent on the field, and his unwavering demand that his teams will always generate an absolutely stifling defense. The '66 unit, for example, pummeled opponents into six shutouts,

Two all-time greats—Bear Bryant and Ara Parseghian (right), meeting before Ara's team would take down the Tide in the 1973 Sugar Bowl. *AP Photo/Joe Raymond*

including a demolition derby rout of USC, 51–0, while surrendering only 38 points all season. Ara also had the good fortune of Notre Dame's decision to return to bowl games, after a forty-five-year hiatus following the 1925 Rose Bowl win over Stanford. His teams played in five bowls, winning three—including consecutive bowl wins over Bear Bryant's Crimson Tide. His other bowl win was over No. 1 Texas in 1970, a game that showed America how to stuff the wishbone offense so popular at the time. Ara's Irish teams never lost consecutive regularly scheduled games in the eleven seasons he led the team, a testament to his ability to keep his players ready for the long haul and proof that he was not kidding when he told the student body in January 1964 that Notre Dame's players would always be in outstanding physical condition. In the annals of Irish football, Parseghian stands out for his amazing ability to field outstanding quarterbacks: John Huarte, Terry Hanratty, Coley O'Brien, Joe Theismann, and Tom Clements. And when Ara made the decision to retire from coaching, he had Joe Montana on the shelf for future reference.

After eleven grueling seasons under the Dome, Ara's teams had compiled a 95–17–4 record, a .836 winning percentage. He was honored for his accomplishments by induction into the College Football Hall of Fame in 1980.

Lou Holtz

Exercising the "Notre Dame clause" in his University of Minnesota contract, Lou Holtz became the 25th Irish head coach in late November 1985, following Gerry Faust as the leader of the university's football fates. He had to be wondering what he was getting into as he watched the last game of the 1985 Irish campaign as the University of Miami dismantled an Irish squad that was apparently incapable of stopping the Hurricanes, much less ramping up an offense of their own. The 'Canes flat-out whipped the Irish, 58–7, on national TV with Holtz offering some bemused halftime comments on a phone call with the game's broadcasters.

One of Holtz's maxims (there are many) is that "Pressure is not being prepared." After seeing the train wreck of the Miami game, he knew he was going to be facing lots of pressure to make the Irish return to respectability.

With a background that included being an assistant coach under Woody Hayes at Ohio State in their 1968 national championship season, and then as a head coach at Arkansas with yet another Hall of Fame coach, Frank Broyles, as his athletic director, and including a season as the head coach of the hapless New York Jets, Holtz had seen some of the game's best and worst. Known as both a disciplinarian and a powerful motivator, the self-deprecating Holtz knew he would need to use every trick in the book to get the Irish players to start believing in themselves and playing to their full potential.

The university had hired Gerry Faust to follow Dan Devine starting with the 1981 season. They hoped that Faust would duplicate for the Irish his amazing success at Cincinnati's Archbishop Moeller High School, a national powerhouse in high school football under his leadership.

Alas, it was not to be. The university should have learned its lesson when the Terry Brennan experiment in the 1950s did not work as planned. Brennan had been schooled by Frank Leahy and had taken his talents after graduation to Chicago's Mt. Carmel High School, where he promptly led his team to three straight city championships. He was only twenty-five years old when the Irish elevated him from his position in 1954 as Notre Dame's freshman coach following Leahy's retirement. As it turned out, Brennan had lots to learn as a new, first-time college head coach. Faust, at least, was in his mid-forties when he was hired, with two decades of coaching behind him. Holtz, however, had several successful years under his belt as a college head coach at William and Mary, North Carolina State, Arkansas, and Minnesota. He knew the ropes and got started right away to turn this team around.

It was no accident that Holtz, a devout Catholic, would have had Notre Dame in the forefront of his thoughts as he moved up the coaching ladder. He was eleven years old, living in East Liverpool, Ohio, when he was listening to a radio broadcast of the famous Notre Dame-Army 0–0 game in 1946. He was thrilled when he heard the excited announcers rhapsodize over Lujack's amazing tackle of Army's Doc Blanchard in the open field. That single moment stuck with the wiry little kid through the years, until he was a wiry little linebacker for Kent State. Add his 1968 experience in the shadow of Woody Hayes, perhaps the ultimate disciplinarian, and the making of head coach Lou Holtz was well underway.

He inherited a team that had gone 5–6 in 1985. There were some bright spots—the quarterback, Steve Beuerlein, and a big, speedy wide receiver named Tim Brown. It remained to be seen if the available talent would be enough to make up for the graduation of Allen Pinkett, Notre Dame's all-time rushing leader, who had put together three 1,000-yard seasons as the tailback on his way to a career total of over 4,100 yards, a mark that wasn't broken until Autry Denson did it twelve years later.

The 1986 season for Holtz and his Irish ended up with the same won-loss as Faust's last season—5–6. Notre Dame played five teams ranked in the Top 20, losing four of those games, including a character lesson from No. 2 Alabama, coached by Ray Perkins, a Bear Bryant protégé. The saving grace was a rousing 38–37 defeat of USC to end the season. A last-minute loss to Pitt in the middle of the season was the game that kept the campaign in the losing column. Overall, though, the Irish played tougher and were in most of the games.

Holtz knew a good player when he saw one, and he turned Tim Brown loose in 1987. With a first-time starter option quarterback at the helm, Tony Rice, it was clear that Brown was not going to be catching a ton of passes. Still, he was good for 39 receptions and 846 yards through the air. But it was his kick returns that showed his multiple skill set: 23 kickoff returns for 456 yards and 34 punt returns for another 401 yards. Holtz also used his wide receiver 34 times to carry the ball, tacking on another 144 yards. In total, Brown zipped through opponents 130 times for 1,847 yards and 7 TDs, helping the Irish to an 8–3 regular season record and capturing the Heisman Trophy before Texas A&M took the blush off the rose in a Cotton Bowl loss.

Irish coaches have to live with high expectations and a new Irish coach typically encounters the mounting hopes of the students, alumni, subway alumni, and administration in their third season. Rockne saw it; Leahy saw it; Parseghian saw it—all of them winning a national title in their third Notre Dame campaign (Rockne, not surprisingly, duplicated the success of his second team). Lou Holtz did not disappoint, forever winning the hearts of the Irish faithful with a perfect 12–0 season in 1988 as Notre Dame excelled in all phases of the game, taking down teams that had run roughshod over them in prior campaigns, including the thrilling 31–30 victory over No. 1 Miami. The wins included Holtz's third straight defeat of Air Force, a pesky service team that had defeated the Irish in four consecutive games before Holtz took charge, and a decisive 27–10 pasting of No. 2 USC in LA to cap the regular season. The Irish wrapped up the national title in the 1989 Fiesta Bowl by taking down West Virginia 34–21 to earn Notre Dame's first-ever 12-win season.

Holtz showed that the Irish had returned to the pinnacle of college football in the five seasons that followed, going 12–1, 9–3, 10–3, 10–1–1, and 11–1—one of the best stretches in Notre Dame history, one that has not reappeared since then under four different head coaches. In those six seasons from 1988 until 1993, Holtz led the Irish to 64 wins, nine losses, and two ties for a winning percentage of .867, within shouting distance of Leahy's dominant run that started in 1943. These Holtz teams were loaded with offensive explosiveness headlined by Rocket Ismail, Ricky Watters, and Jerome Bettis, with Rick Mirer handling the quarterback spot after Rice graduated. Watters and Bettis went on to rush for 10,643 and 13,662 yards in the NFL respectively. Once again, as with Tim Brown, Holtz's keen eye, not only for talent but how best to turn that talent loose, shows in all of these cases. Holtz's defenses also lived up to their billing, often completely strangling opponents' hopes of mounting anything resembling a coherent offensive scheme.

When the Holtz era was all said and done, he accumulated 100 wins for Notre Dame, against 30 losses and two ties, a winning percentage of .765. Having an ebullient personality, a bundle of energy, and loving the thrill of the big challenge was not quite enough fuel for Holtz to go beyond the 1996 season under the Golden Dome. Had he done so, the seven games won in 1997 under his successor, Bob Davie, would have put his total wins at two more than Rockne's 105, a looming historical burden in itself. Holtz played his cards close to his vest regarding his reasons for leaving Notre Dame. At a midweek press conference held in late November 1996, with two games left on the schedule, Holtz told the assembled reporters, "I feel worse than I've felt in a long time .... I do not feel good about this at all. But I do feel it's the right thing to do."

Without a doubt, it is the toughest college football job on earth and it had to have worn him down. It was just time to go. Both Frank Leahy and Ara Parseghian, who had faced those same intense pressures, would have agreed.

An exuberant Lou Holtz on the shoulders of his triumphant Irish players after beating West Virginia in the Fiesta Bowl to claim the 1988 national championship. *AP Photo/Rob Schumacher*

PART IV

NOTRE DAME'S HEISMAN WINNERS

Angelo Bertelli, 1943

World War II was raging in all theatres of the conflict in 1943 as college football played its last recognizable season until the hostilities ended. Frank Leahy was in his third season under the Dome as head coach, and his team was loaded with talent, so much so that he would be fielding the 1943 Heisman winner, Angelo Bertelli, and when he was not decimating opposing defenses, there was a star sophomore named Johnny Lujack, who would return to ND after the war and take home his own Heisman in 1947. A further measure of the depth of this team was that running back Creighton Miller (of the famous Miller clan) was voted fourth in the Heisman balloting and lineman Jim White snagged ninth, no small accomplishment considering that Otto Graham was also on the ballot.

Bertelli was born in West Springfield, Massachusetts, in 1921 to Italian immigrants. He was recognized as an all-state player in football, baseball, and hockey. His classmates also elected him as their class president. Leahy had a good chance to assess his skills before starting him as a sophomore in 1941, although he had some reservations about his potential as a runner. Bertelli spent his first year on the varsity as a single-wing tailback, but his forte was passing the football. He led the nation in passing, hitting 56.9 percent of his passes for 1,027 yards and eight TDs, and was thus a major factor in an undefeated season, the only blemish being a scoreless tie with Army. His performance that season was impressive enough that he garnered Heisman attention, placing second in the balloting. In 1942, Bertelli again racked up more than 1,000 yards passing and added 10 more TDs, but the Irish slipped to 7–2–2 and he finished sixth in Heisman voting. Bertelli's accomplishments were so well-known as a senior that he was able to take home the trophy in 1943 despite playing in only six of Notre Dame's games due to his being called up by the US Marines from the reserves. But those six games proved to be enough, as he led the Irish to these convincing victories:

41–0, Pittsburgh
55–13, Georgia Tech
35–12, No. 2 Michigan
50–0, Wisconsin
47–0, Illinois
33–6, No. 3 Navy

Notre Dame's first Heisman Trophy recipient, Angelo Bertelli.

Oddly, Lujack's stats as Bertelli's sub during the '43 campaign made him Notre Dame's passing leader for the year. Bertelli completed only 25 passes in the six games he started, but 10 of those were for TDs; with 40 percent of his completed passes for scores, this was surely one of the best percentages on record in any era.

Having starred as a single-wing tailback for Leahy in his sophomore year, Bertelli had to make the considerable adjustment to a new set of duties following Leahy's successful lobbying effort with the Notre Dame administration to modernize the Irish team's approach to the offensive game. In short, Leahy sought to abandon the single-wing offense (a vestige of Pop Warner's years at Carlisle and Rockne's famous box version) in favor of the new-fangled T formation. For Bertelli, this meant taking the snap directly from the center, and it reduced the need to use him as a blocker on running plays. In the single-wing offense, the center's snap could be to any of the backfield men. With this major change, the modern football quarterback may be recognized as the team's primary passer, the one player assigned the task of distributing the ball to runners or receivers. For instance, missing from the single-wing's set of duties for players like Bertelli was blocking at the point of attack, leading the way for the left halfback. This smart change to the T formation helped make Bertelli Notre Dame's first Heisman winner.

Johnny Lujack, 1947

Notre Dame's campus mail delivery system was encountering overload work in the fall of 1947 due to the sheer quantity of mail being sent from around the country to a student in a certain dorm, often reaching fifty letters a day. Johnny Lujack, of Connellsville, Pennsylvania, was that student and his countless admirers were bombarding him with letters, congratulations, and offers of various kinds as he led a great Irish football team through an undefeated season. Lujack somehow found the time to respond to each missive. He was already permanently etched in the minds of Irish fans for his role filling in for a wartime absentee Heisman winner, Angelo Bertelli, in 1943, capturing a national title that year as the team's leading passer. Then, after two years of anti-submarine warfare hunting for German U-boats in the English Channel during World War II, he was an important spark for an undefeated 1946 Notre Dame team, saving the season with his famous tackle of Army's Doc Blanchard (another Heisman winner) just as the big fullback was building up a head of steam towards the Irish end zone around left end, preserving a 0–0 tie and the national title. He started 22 games at quarterback in 1943–46–47, in addition to halfback duties in 1943 before Bertelli left the team after six games, and his record in that span was 20–1–1. Highly respected football historians rank Lujack as the all-time best of Notre Dame's impressive stable of quarterbacks.

Lujack was a splendid combination of numerous qualities and talents needed for success as a football player and team leader: he had charisma, discipline,

Heisman winner Johnny Lujack, perhaps Notre Dame's greatest quarterback.

excellent speed, a strong arm, a killer instinct, a certain calmness under fire (why not, as a WWII veteran?), and a willingness to throw his body into the fray—as he did when his tackle in Yankee Stadium was the only time Blanchard went down in the open field after one man's hit. In addition to his football heroics, Lujack also played baseball and competed on the track team for Notre Dame. As a senior he completed 61 of 109 passes for 777 yards, nine for TDs. He rushed 12 times for 139 yards and pulled down three interceptions, returning them for 44 yards. It's important to keep in mind that this was one-platoon football; Lujack was seldom on the sidelines. In the Heisman voting that year, he garnered 742 voting points to Michigan running back Bob Chappuis's 555. It was a very strong class of players, including Doak Walker, Charlie Conerly, Bobby Layne, and Chuck Bednarik. Lujack played four NFL seasons for the Chicago Bears as a quarterback and defensive back, passing for six TDs and 468 yards in one game, setting a record at the time. He was inducted into the College Football Hall of Fame in 1960.

Leon Hart, 1949

Not many athletes can make the claim that the 1949 Heisman Trophy winner could make: In four years of major college varsity football, he never lost a game. His record from the 1946 to 1949 seasons came to 36–0–2. He is one of two linemen (on defense) to earn the Heisman (the other was Yale's Larry Kelley in 1936).

He is one of three in the history books to win the Heisman, a national championship, and become the first overall NFL draft pick within a calendar year along with Notre Dame's Angelo Bertelli and Auburn's Cam Newton.

Leon Hart was a starter almost as soon as he arrived on the Notre Dame campus. Standing 6-foot-4 and weighing 225 pounds at age seventeen, he was much larger than the typical end for his era. He would top out at 245 pounds for his senior year, and Leahy would occasionally put him in the fullback position, or (worse yet for the defense) turn him loose on an end-around running play. In some ways, he was the template for the modern tight end. He played with a Heisman winner, Johnny Lujack, his sophomore year in 1947, on an undefeated national championship team.

Hart was a one-platoon player his first three years and was just as dominant when playing defense as he was when Notre Dame had the ball. In his senior year, college football went briefly to a two-platoon system, but head coach Frank Leahy made sure that Hart still played on both sides of the ball, mangling blocking schemes and putting constant pressure on opposing quarterbacks.

1949 Heisman winner Leon Hart, one of the most dominant players of his era.

In 1949, he served as the captain of the undefeated national championship team and won the Maxwell Award in addition to the Heisman. For the second year in a row he was recognized as a consensus All-American, in addition to being on some All-American ballots as a sophomore. His 1949 statistics show that he carried the ball 18 times for 73 yards and one TD, caught 19 passes for 257 yards and five TDs, blocked a punt and recovered three fumbles. For his career, he averaged 12.2 yards every time he ran with or caught the ball and scored a TD on 20 percent of those plays. The AP recognized him as the Male Athlete of the Year in 1949. He graduated from Notre Dame in 1950 with a degree in mechanical engineering and became the top overall NFL draft pick, going to the Detroit Lions and winning three NFL titles there in his eight-year pro career. In 1973, Hart was inducted into the College Football Hall of Fame.

John Lattner, 1953

The Heisman Trophy is awarded annually to "the most outstanding player in college football in the United States whose performance best exhibits the pursuit of excellence with integrity. Winners epitomize great ability combined with diligence, perseverance, and hard work." Sometimes it goes to the player who has the best sports publicity department, or the player who is most telegenic. Unlike the latter cases, John Lattner, the 1953 Heisman recipient, would seem to qualify in all respects according to the language quoted above.

After a brief flirtation with two-platoon football, college football returned to the one-platoon version in Lattner's senior year. Like Leon Hart, however, Lattner was sure to be on the field as often as possible. Unlike Paul Hornung in 1956, Lattner did not lead the Irish in any of the usual statistics—rushing, passing, receiving—in 1953. Instead, Lattner's gift was his ability, literally, to do *everything* with a certain flair. In addition to running and receiving, he could pass but also return punts and kickoffs, while recovering fumbles and making interceptions when playing defense.

Ironically, he was part of a game played in 1952 against Purdue in which the teams combined for the staggering total of 21 fumbles (the Irish recovered 15 of those). Lattner's lamentable contribution to this disaster was to drop five fumbles all by himself. Leahy was indignant and threatened (not too seriously) to take away Lattner's scholarship if he saw him without a football during the week after that fiasco. The urban legend has it that Leahy taped a football to Lattner's hand for the week following the Purdue game. In fact, a fellow student created a "handle"

Johnny Lattner, the 1953 Heisman winner, on the loose.

on the ball with tape, the better for Lattner to handle his books, notebooks, and meals, etc. In any case, he took it seriously and never again came close to losing the football like he did in the infamous game with Purdue. Leahy had made his point with his star player.

In his senior campaign, Lattner started at right halfback for a second season, carried the ball 134 times for 651 yards and six TDs, caught 14 passes for 204 yards and one TD, completed a pass for 55 yards, handled eight kickoff returns for 321 yards and two TDs, returned 10 punts 104 yards, made four interceptions, recovered one fumble, and punted 29 times. In his career, he made 13 interceptions for 128 return yards and recovered eight fumbles to give some indication of his presence in any phase of the game. Overall, his total offense came to 3,250 yards and 22 TDs. He was a consensus All-American in 1952 and 1953, won the Maxwell Award in both years, and the Heisman in 1953. He was a first-round NFL draft pick by the Pittsburgh Steelers and made the Pro Bowl in his one professional season. A knee injury suffered during his military service caused his premature retirement from pro football. Lattner was inducted into the College Football Hall of Fame in 1979.

Paul Hornung, 1956

Hailing from Louisville, Kentucky, where he was a three-sport star at Bishop Flaget High School, Paul Hornung chose Notre Dame over the recruiting appeals of the head coach at the University of Kentucky—Bear Bryant. According to the rules of the day, he was not eligible to play as a freshman but filled all backfield positions as a sophomore sub and added a monogram as a varsity basketball player that year. As a junior in 1955, he was fourth in the nation with 1,215 yards of offense and six TDs, and also played safety as part of the one-platoon collegiate system, earning the fifth spot in the Heisman voting that year. As a senior in 1956, Hornung played on a losing team, but it is hard to imagine what that 2–8 season would have looked like for Notre Dame without his heroics. He led the team in numerous categories: passing, rushing, scoring, kickoff and punt returns, punting, and passes broken up as a defender (he was second in interceptions and tackles). His total offensive production came to 45 percent of the team's total yardage. With only two wins in 1956, the school's athletics public relations director, Charlie Callahan, did not have much to promote, but it was obvious to his keen eye that Hornung was doing remarkable things on the gridiron. Callahan had plenty of experience looking for the right story; he had successfully promoted the exploits of four other Notre Dame players—Angelo Bertelli, Johnny Lujack, Leon Hart, and John Lattner—all of whom had won the Heisman on Callahan's watch.

At 6-foot-2 and 205 pounds, Hornung was a physical specimen seemingly designed for the game of football … with excellent speed, superior moves, a good arm, a great leg for punting and kicking PATs and field goals, and a hard nose for playing defense. He was also tough as nails. For instance, in a 1956 loss to USC, he played with two dislocated thumbs yet managed to return punts and kickoffs while also playing left halfback. One of his kickoff returns went for a 95-yard TD. Of course, he also played defense with his injured hands. Hornung's 1956 statistics reveal the degree of his total commitment to helping the team. He rushed 94 times for 420 yards and seven TDs, completed 59 of 111 passes for 917 yards and three TDs, leading the team in both categories (the first player since Bob Saggau in 1938 to do so for the Irish), had 16 kickoff returns for 496 yards and 1 TD, had four punt returns for 63 yards, made 14 PATs, had 55 tackles, and two interceptions (10 for his career). In his career, he gained 3,622 all-purpose yards and scored 28 TDs.

Hornung did not garner the most first-place votes in the Heisman voting (Oklahoma's Tommy McDonald had that distinction), but he did well enough with second- and third-place votes for a total of 1,066 points to surpass Johnny Majors's

Paul Hornung—the Golden Boy for the golden dome—1956 Heisman winner.

994 and McDonald's 973. In addition to being a consensus All-American in 1956, Hornung is a member of an elite group of Notre Dame stars who are enshrined in both the College Football Hall of Fame and the Pro Football Hall of Fame: Wayne Millner, George Connor, Alan Page, Dave Casper, and Tim Brown (also a Heisman winner).

John Huarte, 1964

At the beginning of the 1964 collegiate football season, he was perhaps the least likely football player to be considered a candidate for the prestigious Heisman Trophy, even though he was the starting quarterback for a downtrodden Notre Dame team.

He had never earned a Notre Dame monogram in his prior seasons of competition for his participation on Irish football squads in 1962 and 1963. And this was for teams that had won a total of seven games in those two seasons. Depth chart? He wasn't even in the building.

Then a new coach was hired after the disastrous 1963 campaign—Ara Parseghian of the Northwestern football program. The Irish had not played Northwestern in 1963, but the two teams had played in Evanston in 1962, and the Irish were obliterated by Parseghian's team, 35–6. The Irish quarterback in that game, the worst Irish defeat by a Wildcats team, would become known in the NFL as "The Mad Bomber"—Daryle Lamonica. He passed for 190 yards that day and the Irish needed him at the helm, not some untried, unknown sophomore named Huarte.

All this means that Parseghian had not one second of experience looking at game film of this quarterback while he was the Northwestern head coach. He may have never heard of him, after all, no one else in the football world had. And once he was the Notre Dame football leader, he would have very little game film with which to see John Huarte in action.

In 1962, Huarte was not even listed in the Irish depth chart. He did see some action, brief though it was: he fired exactly eight passes for Notre Dame, completing four of them, for 38 yards during the entire season. He was also sacked three times for minus-14 yards. The Irish record book thus shows him being involved in 11 offensive plays involving yardage for the whole season. This is far short of the playing time needed for a monogram award. Huarte was, however, listed as the third team quarterback on the 1963 Irish roster. He threw 20 completions in 42 attempts for 243 yards and one TD. He also kicked one PAT. Again, he did not earn a Notre Dame monogram for a team that had won two games.

So a well-known and successful head coach would be surveying his new roster and looking at game films, studying statistics, interviewing players, etc., to have some semblance of an accurate depth chart for spring football. The former head coach who had recruited many of the players in this group, Joe Kuharich, favored big, NFL-type players. The roster was dotted with such specimens. Huarte was not one of them. Parseghian would make a career at Notre Dame of creating outstanding quarterback-wide receiver combinations. With very few exceptions, sheer size was not the key factor. Speed and quickness, however, were prime values for him. He saw this in a running back named Jack Snow and promptly penciled him in as a split end. His quarterback cadre for spring ball was thin, to say the least. But Huarte caught his eye. He noticed that the little-used quarterback had very good hands on his fakes and handoffs, quick feet, a quiet demeanor, and an unusual delivery for his passes ... almost sidearm. But this quirk did not seem to impact his accuracy. Ara decided that he would not make any major adjustments in Huarte's delivery. He needed to get this team ready for the 1964 season and such changes

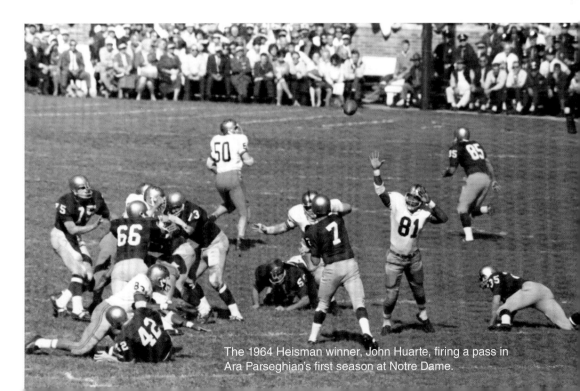

The 1964 Heisman winner, John Huarte, firing a pass in Ara Parseghian's first season at Notre Dame.

were not a high priority. He also told Huarte before spring ball was completed that he was going to be the starting quarterback in 1964.

The rest is history. Huarte came out of the gates quickly in the team's first game, a surprising 31–7 win on the road at Wisconsin, setting single-game Irish records with Jack Snow that day. Snow caught two long TD passes as he and Huarte combined for 217 yards through the air (amazingly, this was 33 percent of the total passing yardage for the entire 1963 season, a good indication of what Parseghian was up to with this Notre Dame team). In a home victory against Michigan State later in the season, Huarte completely bamboozled the Spartans with his ball faking on one signal play, dropping and looking to his left for a screen pass … so, the Spartans peeled off in that direction, then Huarte quickly rotated to his right and lofted a pass to a second screen for a short TD.

In his Heisman-winning season, Huarte led the Irish to a No. 1 ranking that no one in the country had predicted, and took the team to within seconds of being undefeated. The native of Santa Ana, California, completed 114 of 205 passes for 2,062 yards and 16 TDs, rushed 37 times for seven yards and three TDs, and caught one pass for 11 yards.

Tim Brown, 1987

Except for Paul Hornung, most of the great Heisman winners at Notre Dame were playing on utterly dominant teams in the year of their award and often before that. The teams prior to John Huarte's Heisman season had been mediocre at best, and their campaign in his junior year in 1963 was virtually as bad as Hornung's 1956 season—two wins. Parseghian turned that around immediately and Huarte was his man, a key figure in the rebirth of Irish football.

Tim Brown, on the other hand, played as a reserve split end on Gerry Faust's 1984 team that had won seven games, then was the starter at flanker for Faust's last team that went 5–6. Lou Holtz followed Faust in 1986, and Brown was the starter at flanker again, with future pro Steve Beuerlein the quarterback delivering the ball to Brown. That '86 team again went 5–6 again, with Beuerlein at the helm. But Holtz was getting it turned around; Brown's senior season in 1987 saw the Irish ranked No. 7 in the country until they hit a tailspin by losing the last three games, including a Cotton Bowl game in Brown's hometown of Dallas. So Brown did not experience disastrous seasons such as Hornung did in 1956, or the misery Huarte saw before his senior year campaign. Likewise, Brown did not play for the Irish at their peak of excellence, as Leahy's four Heisman winners did. Brown and the Irish were in a downturn period following the excellence of Parseghian and Devine, with Holtz not yet hitting his full, impressive stride. In fact, Tim Brown would be playing in his first season in the NFL, the year after his senior Heisman campaign, when Holtz's Irish would win it all in 1988. In some ways, coming to the attention of the Heisman voters in 1987 from the Dome would not be an easy task. Notre Dame did not have the undivided public attention of teams such as Miami, Florida State, and Oklahoma. And Brown was not in a position to dominate all of the team stats like Hornung did in 1956. He was in a grey zone as far as the Heisman was concerned.

One more item to consider is that in 1987 Brown did not enjoy the benefit of having a quarterback with a great arm such as Beuerlein's to direct a dedicated passing attack. In 1986, the Irish passed for nearly 2,500 yards and 14 TDs. After Beuerlein graduated, Holtz needed to find a new starter and, after a shoulder injury to starter Terry Andrysiak, he settled on Tony Rice, a great option quarterback but not a serious passing threat in 1987. The Irish running game would produce 33 TDs in 1987; the Irish reached the opponents' end zone only four times through the air and registered 1,400 yards, a drop of more than 1,000 yards in passing production from the year before. Brown would need to be productive in other areas and this he did—almost with Gipp-like proportions.

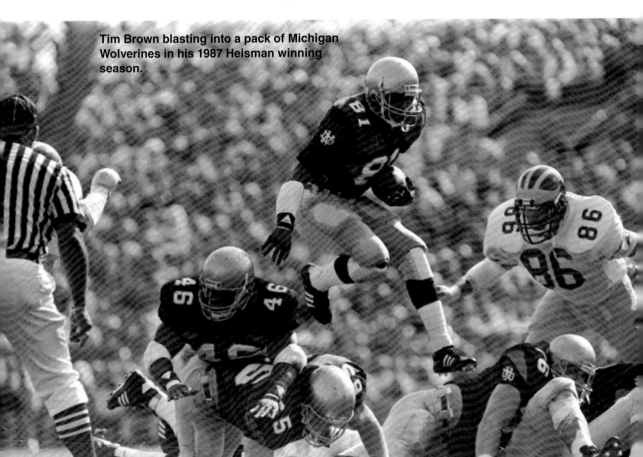

Tim Brown blasting into a pack of Michigan Wolverines in his 1987 Heisman winning season.

In his senior campaign, Brown's all-purpose yardage total came to 1,847 yards. He caught 39 passes for 846 yards and three TDs; he had 34 rushing attempts from his flanker position for 144 yards and a TD; he returned 23 kickoffs 456 yards and added 34 punt returns for 408 yards and three TDs. He averaged nearly 185 yards of all-purpose yardage every time he suited up for the Irish in 1987. In his entire Notre Dame career, Brown racked up 5,024 all-purpose yards. He was a breakaway threat every time he touched the ball. Defenses had to know exactly where he was on every play and often double-teamed him. His special teams duties put extraordinary pressure on the opponent just to try to control him, to minimize the potential damage he could inflict. With Brown's speed, size, and maneuverability, he did not need much of an execution breakdown to take it to the house.

The Heisman voters appreciated Tim Brown's manifold talents. He was not a one-dimensional player, and he thus stood out all the more in the modern era of highly specialized players. In addition to his Heisman honor, Brown also won the Walter Camp Award and the Timmie Award as the college back of the year.

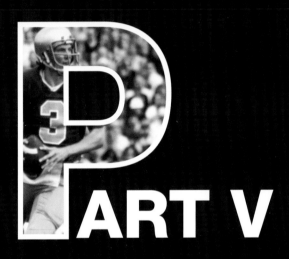

PART V

JOE MONTANA AND THE
MIRACLE COMEBACK

Joe Montana

Unless the rules change, Joe Montana will never be inducted into the College Football Hall of Fame, although he entered the NFL's Hall of Fame in 2000 immediately upon becoming eligible.

Why is he not in the College Football Hall of Fame? Well, it's a riddle wrapped in a mystery. The mystery is that Joe Montana was never honored as an All-American—at any level. Not first team. Not second team. Not third team. Not even honorable mention. Not in 1975, not in 1977 (as quarterback of a national championship team), and not in 1978 (even though he led the greatest bowl game comeback when the Irish defeated Houston, 35–34, in the Cotton Bowl). The Top-10 lists for the Heisman Trophy in 1977 and 1978 failed to include Montana, although his teammates Ken MacAfee and Ross Browner came in third and fifth respectively in 1977.

Montana played in 27 games for Notre Dame: seven in 1975, nine in 1977, 11 in 1978. The Irish media guide lists him as the number two quarterback in 1975 behind starter Rick Slager, Montana's sophomore year and the first year of Dan Devine's tenure as the Irish head coach. He missed 1976 with a shoulder injury. He is listed as the starting quarterback for the 1977 national champs (although he started the season third on the depth chart) and the 1978 team that produced a 9–3 record. In 1978, he was appointed a tri-captain, and his teammates elected him the MVP.

That's it for accolades during his college playing days for Joe Montana.

These apparent injustices would not bother Montana, be assured. He was not in it for external reasons such as national honors and awards. His motivation was *much* more attuned to intrinsic rewards—the outcome of brilliant execution on the field, the great teamwork, the competitive challenge facing the best teams in the country, piecing together a great comeback (he had several of these at Notre Dame). Beyond those accomplishments, Joe Montana never looked back with an ounce of regret.

Arriving at the Dome in the late summer of 1974, he found himself one of seven Irish freshman quarterbacks. It would turn out to be Ara Parseghian's final campaign as the Notre Dame head coach. The number one quarterback was senior Tom Clements, a starter ever since his sophomore year, the quarterback who beat Bear Bryant's Alabama teams in back-to-back bowl games to end the 1973 and

1974 seasons, winning a national title in 1973. Seventh among the freshmen—that's exactly where the new head coach, Dan Devine, found Montana when he came to the campus—buried deep in the freshman quarterback roster.

Montana was a bit of a free spirit, perhaps cut from the same athletic and competitive cloth as George Gipp five decades earlier, although he certainly was not a high-maintenance figure as was Gipp. In short, not a practice guy. He was a game guy. Any deviation in practice under Parseghian could be counterproductive for the player in question. In spite of Joe's position on the depth chart, Devine saw something in the young man that could be used advantageously for the team, although he stayed with the junior incumbent, Rick Slager, as the starting QB in 1975. Montana would see action in seven games that year.

Montana saw his first serious action in the third game of the '75 season, an Irish win over Northwestern. With starter Slager hurt, Montana threw one TD pass and added a 6-yard TD run in the 31–7 victory. Notre Dame lost the next game to MSU at home, 10–3; Montana had a pass intercepted in the end zone while the offense managed only the one field goal. The next game, at North Carolina, turned out to be the contest that started "The Comeback Kid" story for Montana. Slager started the game, but the Irish fell behind, 14–0, until speedster Al Hunter scored with two minutes left in the third quarter, but they missed a two-point try. Devine turned the game over to Montana with 6:04 left on the game clock. He immediately led a five-play drive with Hunter scoring from the 2-yard line. Montana hit the pass for two points and a 14–14 tie. The Tar Heels missed a 42-yard field goal attempt, and the Irish had the ball on their 20-yard line with 1:15 left in the game. The first play from scrimmage was supposed to be a draw play for the fullback, Jerome Heavens. At the line of scrimmage Montana saw that North Carolina did not have press coverage on his split end, so he audibled to a pass that Ted Burgmeier gathered in and bolted 80 yards for the winning score. Joe had completed three of four passes for 129 yards, the winning TD, and a two-point conversion in less than half of a quarter's work.

Montana missed the '76 season with a shoulder injury. His own personal comeback had ended with him as the third-string quarterback. Rusty Lisch started the 1977 season opener, a 19–9 victory at Pittsburgh, but the Irish lost to Ole Miss in triple-digit weather in Oxford the following week. Lisch was ineffective against Purdue, and Gary Forystek went in and managed to get the Irish to within 24–14 at halftime. Early in the fourth quarter, Forystek suffered a broken collarbone on a rollout play. Montana then worked the Purdue defense for a field goal and a 13-yard TD pass to tight end Ken MacAfee. The Irish defense contained Purdue and Montana went to work from his 30-yard line with three minutes left. Four passes later he had the Irish on the Purdue 10-yard line. Running back Dave Mitchell scored from the Purdue 5 for the 31–24 win. It was Joe's third comeback win. Devine kept him as the starter in the next game, a home brawl with MSU. It was a festival of fumbles and interceptions, but the Irish defense locked down the Spartan offense for a 16–6 win. Joe next led the Irish to a 24–0 win over a determined Army squad, then Devine pulled off his famous "green shirt" ploy to fire up the team against USC. Montana scored twice on short runs and threw two TD passes as Notre Dame blasted the Trojans, 49–19. Navy sank next, with Joe running for a TD and passing for another. Against Georgia Tech, Montana ran for another short TD and threw three TD passes, one to Dave Waymer for 68 yards, as the Irish mauled Tech, 69–14, and romped for 667 total yards. Against Clemson, the Irish had to overcome some home cookin' by the refs as well as their own miscues, but Joe sparked a 21–17 win with two short TD runs in the fourth quarter to erase a 10-point deficit. Irish runners did most of the work in a 49–0 dismantling of Air Force, but Montana chipped in with a 33-yard TD pass to wide receiver Kris Haines. Miami went down 48–10; the defense helped the offense with timely stops and recoveries,

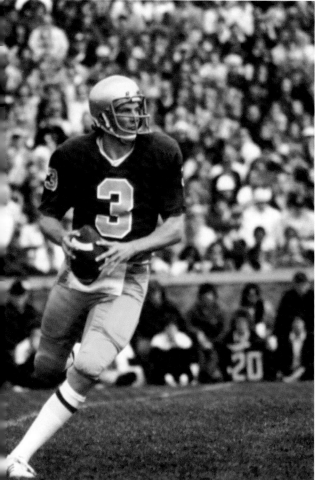

allowing Montana to throw 3 TD passes while Irish ball carriers ran wild for 404 yards. In the Cotton Bowl, Montana engineered a 38–10 win over Heisman winner Earl Campbell and the Texas Longhorns, passing for 111 yards and one TD, while handing off to two Irish backs who both chugged for more than 100 yards while the Irish defense gobbled up four Texas fumbles and made three interceptions. With this convincing win over the No. 1 team, Notre Dame was crowned the 1977 national champions.

The four All-American quarterbacks in 1977 were Guy Benjamin (Stanford), Doug Williams (Grambling),

Joe Montana in action against Southern Cal during the 1977 national championship season.

Matt Cavanaugh (Pittsburgh), and Derrick Ramsey (Kentucky). Williams, Benjamin, and Cavanaugh joined Rick Leach of Michigan as the four quarterbacks to be in the top ten of the 1977 Heisman Trophy voting.

Someone missed the miracle going on under the Dome in 1977.

In 1978, Montana led the Irish to a 9–3 record and a final national ranking of 10th. He started all the games, completing 141 passes for 2,010 yards and 10 TDs. He carried the ball 72 times for 104 yards and 6 TDs, making him the team's third leading scorer. His heroics in the 1979 Cotton Bowl were legendary. Suffering from the flu and hypothermia, he willed the Irish to a 35–34 win after trailing 34–12 with a mere six minutes left in the game. In his career, playing in 27 games, he completed 268 of 515 passes for 4,121 yards and 25 TDs, while running 129 times for 104 yards and 14 TDs. His career total for offensive production came to 4,225 yards and 39 TDs.

There may never again be another Irish player with Joe Montana's overall level of success and production who remains so far out of the normal picture for the various awards and honors that are typically handed out by the sportswriters and organizations.

The Greatest Comeback: The 1979 Cotton Bowl

Most Notre Dame football fans simply cannot stand to watch their favorite team lose any game and it hurts even worse when it's a really important game such as a bowl game or one of the team's major rivals in a potential championship season. It is not uncommon for these fans to watch a losing effort up to a certain point, and then switch the TV channel to something more comforting, less depressing.

Given that pattern (I plead guilty), millions of fans missed Notre Dame's greatest comeback win in the 1979 Cotton Bowl. They had watched a team that wasn't producing much offense and was only a minor irritation on defense to a talented Houston team that had piled up a 34–12 lead with 7:37 left in the fourth quarter.

Enter Joe Montana. He had missed most of the game's third quarter with hypothermia caused by the brutal blizzard-like conditions that had assaulted the Dallas area in the days immediately prior to the game and into the game itself. All serious Irish fans know that warm chicken soup administered at halftime had helped raise Montana's core temperature to the point where he could safely enter the game.

The quarterback had produced several impressive comeback wins in his up-and-down career under the Dome, and had also led the 1977 squad to a national championship. Originally recruited by Ara Parseghian, Dan Devine found Montana hidden deep in the roster—he was listed as sixth … among the freshmen! But Devine saw something in the Pennsylvania native, a competitive fire that blazed in competition and under pressure but less so in the daily practice routine. He was also as cool as the other side of the pillow in the heat of battle. Not an imposing physical specimen, Montana nevertheless had an arm that could make all the throws. He was not much of a running threat, but he was mobile enough to avoid most potential collisions. He was a quick reader of the defensive formations and, in general, operated surgically on most defenses. He also had a superior supporting cast in his linemen and running backs. The Irish receiving corps was efficient, with good hands, if it didn't have blazing downfield speed. Ultimately, the key element in his career was Montana's unbelievable ability to focus on winning. Surgical.

In the Cotton Bowl game, in spite of the horrible, frigid conditions, the Irish jumped out to a 12–0 lead before Houston scored to end the quarter at 12–7. Montana contributed timely pass completions to fullback Jerome Heavens and tight end Dean Masztak to set up his own 3-yard scamper for the first TD. Linebacker Bob Crable snagged a Houston fumble and Pete Buchanan rammed in from the 1-yard line six plays later. Joe missed on a two-point conversion pass. And that was it for Irish scoring until half of the fourth quarter was completed and Houston was having its merry way on both offense and defense.

The comeback started with a special team play, a blocked Houston punt that Steve Cichy returned for a TD, capped by Montana's two-point pass completion to running back Vagas Ferguson that made it 34–20. Montana took charge three minutes later on a drive of 61 yards, hitting Masztak for 17 yards and Jerome Heavens for 30 before the ND quarterback scooted into the end zone from 2 yards out. Then he found wide receiver Kris Haines with a two-point pass to make it 34–28. The clock showed 4:15 left in the game. The Irish defense held as Houston tried to

Joe Montana passing to Jerome Heavens in 1979 Cotton Bowl action.

kill the clock, stopping a fourth-down run on Houston's own 29-yard line. The clock showed 00:28.

Montana took off for an 11-yard gain, then fired a pass to Haines for 10 more yards. His next pass was to Haines in the right corner of the end zone was incomplete. There were two seconds left. Unbelievably, Notre Dame ran the same play again, with Haines snagging Montana's TD pass. 00:00. 34–34.

Kicker Joe Unis had to attempt the PAT twice, the second time after an illegal procedure penalty, but he made the kick, and the greatest comeback in Notre Dame's annals was in the history books.

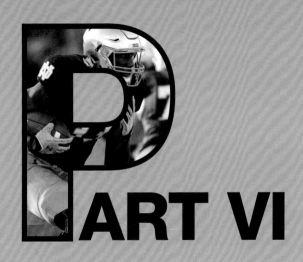

PART VI

NOTRE DAME'S
MIRACLE PLAYS

"The Perfect Play"

Knute Rockne was a firm believer in what he called "The Perfect Play." This can happen anywhere on the field at any time. It is actually the desired outcome for all plays. The Perfect Play means that the opponent's defenders have either been blocked out of making a play on the Irish runner or pass receiver or have been otherwise nullified—fooled by a great fake, badly out of position, late in reading what's happening and the like. Irish football annals are replete with examples of Rockne's Perfect Plays, both on offense and defense.

For example, Elmer Layden of the Four Horsemen scored twice in the 1925 Rose Bowl by intercepting passes thrown by Stanford's all-time great fullback and triple threat Ernie Nevers. Rockne had prepared Layden and the Irish defense to look for a pass when the big fullback swung a little wide towards the sideline from his normal route. Twice Layden spotted this "tell," and twice he snagged the ball and took it to the house, one for 78 yards, the second one for 70 yards, as the Irish prevailed over Pop Warner's team, 27–10.

A few years later, another defender, Jack Elder, won the 1929 contest with Army when he grabbed a Chris Cagle pass, intended for his left end, in the Irish end zone and jetted down the sideline 100 yards for the game's only score. His blazing speed did most of the work but his teammates knew exactly how to pave the way and make sure that yet another Perfect Play for Rockne would cinch this important game played before 80,000 fans in Yankee Stadium. It also concluded a perfect season for Notre Dame, a very tough test as there were no home games that year while old Cartier Field was being replaced by a new stadium.

That new stadium did not have to wait long for one of Rockne's Perfect Plays to happen. In the first game played there in 1930, with the Irish defending their 1929 national title, SMU scored on the game's first possession with a 48-yard pass. The ensuing kickoff went to the big Notre Dame fullback, Jumping Joe Savoldi, who bobbled the ball before slamming through the Mustangs' kickoff team, right up the middle of the field, for a 98-yard romp and the game's tying score. It was the first Irish play with the ball in their possession in the new stadium. The bobble may have marred the perfection of the play, but it also took the Mustangs slightly out of their coverage lanes and Savoldi and his blockers knew what to do next. The Perfect Play.

In a 1956 game with USC, Paul Hornung put on a display that did not win the game but might have clinched the Heisman Trophy for Notre Dame's Golden Boy. Late in the season, Hornung had dislocated both thumbs; he then moved from the quarterback position to the left halfback spot (the old spot for George Gipp back in the day, the premier backfield position under Rockne). In a losing but valiant effort, Hornung somehow fielded a Trojan kickoff with his injured hands at the 5-yard line and turned upfield, blasting through a wave of would-be Trojan tacklers at the 25-yard line, then using a great stiff-arm and elusive moves to ward off other Trojans as he rumbled 95 yards for an Irish TD.

Some players just have the knack. Nick Rassas, whose best Irish years were with Ara Parseghian, could execute his part of the Perfect Play either as a kick returner or defensive back. In a 1965 victory over Northwestern, Rassas showed his stuff within a seven-minute period by hauling an interception 92 yards for a TD and then rocketing 72 yards with a punt return for another Irish TD. Rassas did it again that season against Navy in an Irish victory when he turned on the speed for a 66-yard TD punt return in which the Middies were completely stymied by the perfect execution of Parseghian's players. The spirit of Knute Rockne must have been pleased.

Occasionally, the Perfect Play struck against the Irish, as happened in the opening game of the 1966 season. The Irish were marching on Bob Griese's talented Purdue team when a ball carrier fumbled on the Boilermaker 5-yard line, only to see all-everything Leroy Keyes snag the ball in midair and take off for the promised land. He reached it 95 yards later. Purdue's euphoria did not last long. They kicked off, and Nick Eddy fielded the ball at his 3-yard line. He hesitated for a split second to see what was headed his way, took a slight turn to his right, zipped through the first wave of Purdue's players, then juked to the right again before going straight for a 97-yard TD that helped lead the Irish to the opening 26–14 win of the undefeated 1966 campaign. Two back-to-back Perfect Plays.

Parseghian's teams, like Rockne's, seem to have had the knack for pulling off the Perfect Play. There is no better example than the one that struck against USC in their 1973 encounter under the Dome against the team that would win the national title that year. This was one of the best "rebound" years for the Irish. Their 1972 season had produced a record of 8–3, but two of those losses were extremely painful, blowouts by USC (45–23) and Nebraska (40–6 in the Orange Bowl versus Heisman winner Johnny Rodgers). So yet again the Irish were in a mood to revenge a loss to the Trojans. In this home game, the Irish were ranked No. 8 and USC No. 6. Southern Cal featured Lynn Swann and Anthony Davis, with quarterback

Pat Haden distributing the ball to the assembled talent. It was a close game into the third quarter. Notre Dame had a couple of field goals after bad Trojan punts to go with a TD; USC had two TDs, one each for Swann and Davis. Frank Alloco, ND's backup quarterback, had not been wasting his time on the sidelines; he had been watching the Trojan coaches signal in their plays and thought he might just have figured out the blitz sign. He mentioned this to the coaches who then started watching for the cue. Sure enough, they saw the blitz sign with the Irish lined up on their own 15-yard line; quarterback Tom Clements had running back Eric Penick lined up to his right in a wingback position. Penick started in motion to his left and Clements handed the ball to his 210-pound speedster on the 10-yard line as the Trojan blitz unfolded. Both Irish guards pulled to the left and sealed that portion of the formation; tackle Steve Neece took out the middle linebacker, and tight end Dave Casper, a former tackle, slammed into his man. The remaining Trojans were flailing and missing as Penick turned the corner, just past his guards, Gerry DiNardo and Frank Pomarico. A Trojan defensive back missed an arm tackle up

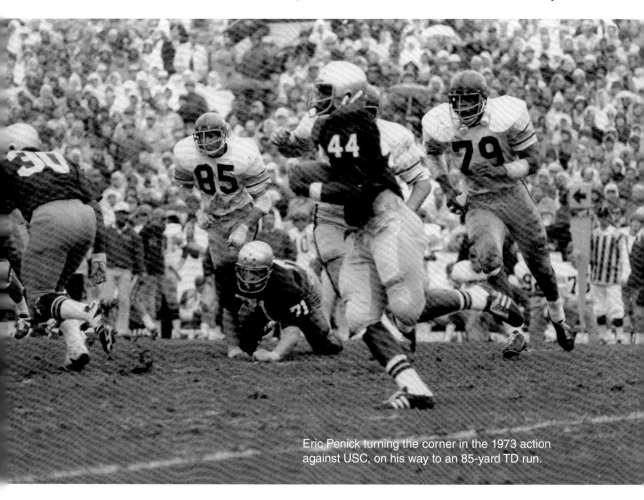

Eric Penick turning the corner in the 1973 action against USC, on his way to an 85-yard TD run.

high, the only tackle that might have at least slowed Penick down, but the DB kept his balance and chased the sprinting Penick for 60 yards or more before he missed him again. Penick crossed the goal line and disappeared into a mob of ecstatic Irish fans and students. This Perfect Play broke the back of the Trojan team as the Irish held them scoreless until the final gun and the 23–14 victory. Led by Penick's 85-yard score, Irish runners mangled the Trojans defense for 316 yards, while the stout Irish defense held the California superstar runners to 66 yards.

Lightning, in the form of the Perfect Play, *does* strike twice. In the same quarter, in fact. That's what Tim Brown did to Michigan State in his senior year (you think they might have noticed his skills before then) in 1987. His first TD went for 71 yards and was no accident. There was no Irish pressure on Spartans punter Greg Montgomery. His kick drifted to his right where Brown fielded it on his own 29-yard line. Instead of pressuring the punter, the Irish set up a wall for a return down the right sideline. Right after the punt sailed into space, fans could see the Notre Dame players peeling off to their right with Tim Brown now headed across

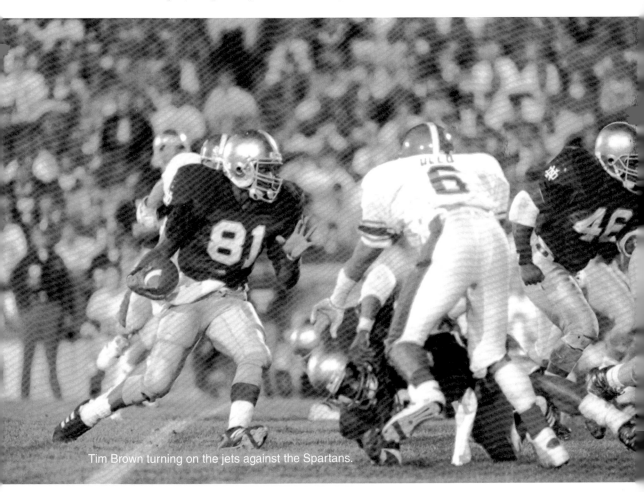

Tim Brown turning on the jets against the Spartans.

the field in that same direction. Once he had reached the wall on his right side, he zipped through a gaggle of failed tacklers and then cut back to his left, with outstanding downfield blocking escorting him as he kept up his sprint, angling to the left. He reached the end zone without a Spartan in the picture. Not long after that explosive punt return, he did it again, still in the game's first quarter. This time, Brown ran back along the left sideline, although the Irish did not go to the bother to set up a wall. Once again, the Spartans showed an underappreciation for Brown's sheer speed. At least two or three players managed to swipe at him as he sped past them, perhaps brushing him with their fingernails. This left the hapless punter. Brown faked to his left, Montgomery took the fake, then Brown sidestepped him to the right. Brown reached the end zone, 66 yards after his journey had begun, joyfully throwing the ball into the air, and received the frenzied congratulations of the Irish fans tucked in that corner of the end zone. In modern football annals, no player had returned two consecutive punts for TDs in the first quarter of a college game.

Not too long after Brown's heroics versus the Michigan State Spartans, Rocket Ismail stunned the other team from Michigan, the Wolverines, with kick returns that left 105,000 Michigan fans in the Big House completely deflated. In three years with the Irish, Ismail scored 15 TDs and averaged an amazing 61 yards on each of those 15 plays—as runner, receiver, or kick returner. Rockne would have loved this level of perfection.

Raghib "Rocket" Ismail crossed the collegiate heavens like a meteor shower from 1988 to 1990 for the Irish. As a freshman he started as a split end on the championship 1988 team and proved immediately to be a nightmare for defenses. Most likely the fastest player on record for the Irish, slightly undersized, he was nevertheless utterly fearless going over the middle, creating serious mismatches for defenses, and could reach top speed in mere steps when going long. His standout performance against Michigan came during his second campaign; one wonders how Bo Schembechler's coaching staff had not yet come to an appreciation of the problems that Ismail presented whenever he stepped on the field. By the end of the 1989 game, however, they would have no doubts as Ismail's heroics gave the No. 1 Irish what they needed for a 24–19 win over No. 2 Michigan.

Rocket's first kickoff TD started the second half of a close game. Holtz had kept the offense pretty much in first gear, especially the passing game (Tony Rice threw only twice the entire game). Using a return tactic that is no longer legal, the Irish had a five-man "wedge" just in front of Ismail as he fielded the ball on his 11-yard line, with another five about ten yards in front of them, with wider spacing. The play called for a middle return. The two outside men of the wedge sealed off Wolverines and Ismail streaked up the middle; Jerome Bettis gave a nudge to the kicker but he tried a lunging tackle, missed it, and Ismail angled to this right toward the sideline, trailed by a much larger Wolverine who realized he was not gaining ground on Ismail so he launched himself at about the 35-yard line, missed his target, and Ismail continued on into the Michigan end zone for the score. In the fourth quarter, following a Michigan score, they had to do it all over again. This time, Rocket fielded the ball at his 8-yard line and ran upfield slightly to his left, encountering the first Wolverine around the 23-yard line. He missed Ismail as yet another Michigan player also failed to tackle him a split second later, although he did spin Ismail around slightly. Rocket then bumped into his own man but his blazing speed kept him going in the right direction. He turned left toward

Raghib (Rocket) Ismail finishing off one of his two long-distance TD kick returns against Michigan.

Part Six

the same sideline he had used in the third quarter, some more Wolverines flailing missed him yet again, and with a good escort he rumbled down the sideline into the Michigan end zone. His escort, Rodney Culver, started pumping his fist at the 25-yard line as the lone Michigan player in the zip code watched helplessly. At least four Michigan players had tried to arrest Ismail's progress and failed.

In 2006, quarterback Brady Quinn was well on his way to establishing a school record for career passing yardage (11,762) and TDs (95). One of his favorite targets was his classmate Jeff Samardzija, a consensus All-American in 2005 with 77 receptions. He caught one more than that, for a total of 78, in 2006 to set the Irish record at the time, and one of those catches was yet another miracle play in an Irish win over UCLA. With a mere 27 seconds left in the game, trailing 17–13, the Irish came to the line of scrimmage in a shotgun formation with four wide receivers, with Samardzija paired up with another receiver to the left. UCLA committed seven men to the pass defense in a cover three (one quarter of the field near the left sideline, half in the middle, one quarter to the right). Quinn received the snap at the UCLA 45-yard line and dropped back several yards, surveying the scene. He had plenty of time as the Irish offensive linemen gave him excellent protection. He made a big pump fake, then quickly moved to his right closer to the line of scrimmage. A UCLA defensive back moved up towards Quinn as the zone defense began to come apart. The pump fake had frozen the other pass defenders and three of them clustered in the middle of the field as Samardzija kept sliding across the defense to his right. Quinn spotted him and fired a pass 16 yards downfield to his big receiver. Samardzija did the rest, catching the ball and outrunning a trailing defender, dodging a tackler who overran the play, almost stumbling at the 15-yard line but keeping his balance, then outrunning two trailing defenders from there to the end zone for the winning score. UCLA had the Irish well-defended at first but the pump fake more or less caused chaos as the Bruins seemed frozen in their tracks even as Irish players were zipping through what was left of the zone defense. For the day, Quinn had passed for 304 yards with 27 completed passes and two TDs (both to Samardzija). For his part, Samardzija caught eight passes for 118 yards and the two scores. The win was an important midseason victory for the Irish as they went on to complete a 10–3 season. The 6-foot-5, 218-pound receiver could have gone to the NFL but chose to play major league baseball, leaving Irish fans with strong memories of his exploits with teammate Brady Quinn.

In 2015, the Irish faced a solid Wake Forest team under the Dome in the last home game of the season. In the second quarter, Wake Forest had the Irish penned in at their 1-yard line. Leading 14–0 at that point, an Irish run picked up a yard.

Jeff Samardzija leaps into the end zone to beat UCLA in 2006 with mere seconds left in the game. *AP Photo/Michael Conroy*

On second down they lined up in an unbalanced line, with two wide receivers split out to the left and a slot man just behind the tight end, also to the left. DeShone Kizer, the quarterback, was about three and a half yards behind the center, with freshman running back Josh Adams another half yard behind him, a tad to Kizer's left, in a modified pistol formation. At the snap, Kizer turned slightly to his left and handed the ball to Adams two yards deep in the end zone. Adams found a nice hole between the linemen on the right side of the formation. A Wake Forest cornerback

Part Six

lunged at him around the 8-yard line but missed. Adams then stiff-armed a safety at the 15 and was on his way, with the two Irish wide receivers now as his blockers.

Notre Dame coach Brian Kelly was kind enough to have Adams and his position coach, Autry Denson, provide their versions of this historic play (the longest run from scrimmage by any freshman in modern college football):

Josh Adams's account of his 98-yard TD run

"It was the second play of the drive and we were backed up in our side of the field. We were just trying to get some space out of our end zone so we ran a safe play; inside zone. Pre-snap I remember the CB being backed off over the tackle and the safety in the middle of the field. We are running to [Mike] McGlinchey's side so there is basically no one on that side that can stop the run. On the snap the corner comes down, I squeeze between the tackle and the guard, and break an arm tackle to get through the line of scrimmage. That's when out of the corner of my eye I see the safety flying downhill, so I hit him with a stiff-arm to try to create some separation. After that I stumbled a bit, but was able to stay on my feet, and all that I saw when I looked up was green grass. So I ran for the sideline and while I am running down the sideline I see Breezy [Chris Brown] sprinting to pick up a block so I know someone is chasing me. As a result, I try to pick up the pace and the next thing I know is Breezy, Will [Fuller], and myself are in the end zone for a 98 yard touchdown."

Coach Autry Denson's account of the run

"The previous week Josh ran for over 100 yards at Pittsburgh because C . J. Prosise left early in the game with a concussion. So fast forward a week later versus Wake Forest, and Josh is the starter that week because C. J. was still in concussion protocol. What I remember most about it is we were backed up and really just trying to get some room to possibly punt if need be. After Josh broke through the line, he hit the Wake Forest safety with a hard stiff-arm and then the race was on. However, as I am watching Josh break into open field I see someone throw off their sideline jacket and running along the sideline with him; it was C. J. Later that year when C. J. won Newcomer of the Year, he shared that one of his most memorable moments of the season was when Josh went 98 yards against Wake Forest, which by the way broke a record C. J. had set earlier that season for a 92 yard run versus Georgia Tech. I was very blessed to coach a group of young men that year, that were not only selfless in regards to putting the team first, but also genuinely loved one another."

And you can bet that Rockne loved it, too … the Perfect Play to set an all-time miracle record for freshmen.

Freshman running back Josh Adams as he starts his record-setting 98-yard TD run against Wake Forest in 2015. *AP Photo/Michael Conroy*

It is important to note that the miracle play is not necessarily the product of an All-American or a Heisman winner. We need only to focus on the last offensive play of the 2017 Irish season (not counting a victory kneeling formation as time ran out)—a play that Irish fans will remember forever—Miles Boykin's 55-yard catch and run to beat LSU in the 2018 Citrus Bowl. It had been an up-and-down season, with Notre Dame reaching the No. 3 spot in the polls in the final quarter of the season, only to have their playoff candle snuffed out by two lopsided losses. They settled for a New Years' bowl game against the LSU Tigers. It turned out to be a defensive struggle, with neither team showing that it could dominate the other offensively. The halftime score had ND in the lead, 3–0, not very comforting. LSU scored their first TD in the third quarter, and the Irish tacked on another field goal, making it a 7–6 contest going into the fourth quarter. LSU kept up the pressure with another TD to take the lead. Coach Brian Kelly had seen enough miscues from starting quarterback Brandon Wimbush and was using Ian Book, the backup, for the second half. Book led the team on a 75-yard march, capped by a 6-yard TD pass to Michael Young and a two-point conversion to tie the game, 14–14. LSU fought back with a field goal to lead 17–14. That's where it stood as the Irish began

Miles Boykin's fantastic catch to beat LSU in the 2018 Citrus Bowl.
AP Photo/John Raoux

what most likely would be their last possession. With the clock showing 1:40 left, Book had the team on the Irish 45-yard line. In a shotgun formation, he had the 6-foot-5, 222-pound Boykin alone to his right, facing a 5-foot-11 corner who was in press coverage; two wide receivers were to Book's left, with the tight end close to the left tackle. Boykin had caught only 11 passes all season and was also, like Book, a sub for much of the campaign. At the snap, Book dropped back a couple of steps, looked to his right, and lofted a high pass towards Boykin. It was almost perfectly placed—too high for the defensive back to bat away. Only Boykin could get a hand on it. And that's exactly what he did. Leaping and stretching, Boykin snagged the ball at the 35-yard line with his right hand, his lanky frame fully extended, as the defender tried to nudge him out of bounds with his shoulder pads. Boykin dodged that feeble attempt and the defensive back ran out of bounds. Just then the strong safety came up to put a hit on Boykin but he missed, too, as the big Irish receiver literally shrugged him off even as the first would-be tackler recovered from his first miss and got back in the action. But he missed again as Boykin sidestepped him and dashed to the end zone for the winning TD. The Irish defense held LSU on their final possession so that Boykin's spectacular, miraculous catch-and-run can live forever in the hearts and minds of Irish fans around the world.

So Knute Rockne's concept of the Perfect Play has been executed numerous times in Irish football history. Every player has to do his job. The countless hours of practices, the innumerable repetitions, even the failed plays all add up to that scintillating moment in a game when the whole operation comes together and an Irish player runs with the ball into the welcoming arms of Notre Dame's football eternity.

A miracle play.

ART VII

MIRACLE MOMENTS:
SECOND EDITION

MIRACLE MOMENTS: Second Edition

In the several seasons since the Irish defeated LSU courtesy of Miles Boykins' stunning one-handed reception of an Ian Book pass in the 2018 Citrus Bowl, national and international events changed the collegiate football landscape in ways that are as yet indeterminate regarding long-term effects.

A short list of these changes would have to include the COVID-19 pandemic, conference realignments, the transfer portal, NIL opportunities for players, and discussions about adding more teams to the college playoff structure. It is a scene that is remarkably unlike the situation that Irish head coach Brian Kelly encountered in his first year at the helm, 2010. Kelly would lead the Irish for twelve seasons, occasionally knocking off top-ranked teams such as Clemson in 2020, and stringing together five consecutive seasons with ten or more wins. He would surpass the immortal Knute Rockne's career win total of 105 victories and he would take the Irish into the final four playoffs twice, although his efforts were not successful, losing both of those contests by double digits. Following his only losing season in 2016, Kelly knew that he had to make some changes to stay competitive with the top tier teams. This led to the string of double-digit season wins, but the team just could not break into the charmed winner's circle, losing twice in disappointing semi-final contests. As Bum Phillips would say, "they were knocking on the door."

Kelly eventually figured out that it would take more than knocking on the door so he took his coaching resumé to LSU after the 2021 season, thus heading up a team that had recently won a national championship. One of his final acts prior to his last season at Notre Dame was to hire the former defensive coordinator from Cincinnati, one Marcus Freeman, a rising star in the coaching ranks.

Marcus Freeman, in his mid-30s when he joined Kelly's staff, had already developed a stellar reputation for creating tough, sophisticated, well-disciplined defensive schemes and defensive players but also for the talents he demonstrated as a recruiter. There was a certain charisma about him; he established strong bonds with his recruits and their parents, as well as players. In short, he was a dynamic, energetic, enthusiastic figure. With the news that Kelly was bound for LSU, Freeman's name was prominently mentioned in the national speculation about the likely successor to the departed head coach. One seeming drawback loomed over the situation: Freeman lacked head coaching experience. Twice before in the modern era Notre Dame had taken the risk of hiring coaches with no experience as head coaches at the collegiate level: Terry Brennan in 1954 and Gerry Faust in 1981. Brennan and Faust had established stunning successes at the high school level, Brennan at Mt. Carmel with three straight championships in Chicago and Faust at Moeller in Cincinnati (with an amazing record of 178–23–2). Brennan had played at Notre Dame under hard driving Frank Leahy, who had himself played for the immortal Rockne. With a pedigree like that, what could go wrong? Faust's incredible success at Moeller, Irish fans enthused, would surely match the national championship years of 1966, 1973, and 1977. Irish fans are not necessarily completely rational in reaching a sober assessment of the Irish's potential. Heart wins every time, but the possibility of a national title miracle was a powerful force in the Irish fan community. A popular groundswell on behalf of Marcus Freeman pretty much foreclosed a broad, time-consuming national search for Kelly's replacement. The Irish were mere weeks away from playing in a much-deserved bowl game. So, for the third time in the modern era the Irish took the plunge and offered the job to Freeman. His introduction to the team was recorded on video—revealing an explosive, wild group of cheering Notre Dame players as they besieged the energized Freeman. The team's captains had recently spoken to the athletic director, Jack Swarbrick, to express the team's sentiments that Freeman was their hands-down choice to be their leader. With that decision, a new era in Notre Dame football started.

New head coach Marcus Freeman leads the team on the field for a 2022 home game.
AP Photo

Part Seven

Then the hard work had to start—prepping for the bowl game against Oklahoma State, assembling a full coaching staff (following some departures), finalizing a successful recruiting effort, meeting media demands, and getting to know the Irish offensive players better. Such tasks are plenty difficult under normal conditions, but this all descended on the new, first-time head coach with a frenzied rush. Somehow, Freeman remained calm and articulate, impressing Irish players, students, the alumni, and the die-hard Subway Alumni. (The Notre Dame Alumni magazine stated in 2022 that the school's alumni body has 151,415 members, but the Subway Alumni number must be in the untold millions). These Irish fans, alumni or not, have very high expectations for the Fighting Irish. Without a national championship since Holtz's 1988 team, and seemingly playing second fiddle talent-wise to the current dominating teams, high hopes abounded, reminiscent of the early months in Gerry Faust's tenure.

Would all of this excitement add up to the latest miracle for Notre Dame?

The Fiesta Bowl game against Oklahoma State started off in the affirmative. The Irish jumped all over the Cowboys in the first half building a 21-point halftime lead, only to see OSU turn the tables in the second half for a 37–35 Fiesta Bowl win. It was a stunning, disappointing loss that took some of the luster off the aura surrounding Freeman's head coaching debut. Irish fans would need to temper their exuberance and fond hopes for an amazing Irish winning streak and a possible national championship. And the scheduled first game of the 2022 season did not make anything easier for the new head coach: top-ranked Ohio State … to be played in Columbus. It was Freeman's *alma mater*. Nothing to see here, right?

As we will see, Marcus Freeman's first full season at Notre Dame ended up with a 9–4 record. It is certainly true that the team was playing its best football after recovering from an expected loss to Ohio State, but also two inexplicable losses to Marshall and Stanford. Predicting the future on a limited data set is risky business in collegiate football. Here are the historic first season results for Irish head coaches:

Freeman	9 wins	Devore	7 wins (1945 as interim head coach; also 1963)
Kelly	8 wins		
Weis	9 wins	Kuharich	5 wins
Willingham	10 wins	Brennan	9 wins
Davie	7 wins	Leahy	8 wins
Holtz	5 wins	Layden	6 wins
Faust	5 wins	Anderson	6 wins
Devine	8 wins	Rockne	3 wins (pandemic-shortened season)
Parseghian	9 wins		

The average for these fifteen first-year Irish coaches is 7.1 wins. The most common outcome is nine wins. Willingham's 10 wins proved to be virtually illusory; he won only 11 games in the next two seasons and was not renewed as head coach after his third season. Rockne's surprising total of three wins is equally illusory. His teams only lost three games in the next six seasons of play, well on his way to his stunning record of 105 wins, 12 losses, and 5 ties. Only Ara Parseghian, Frank Leahy, Dan Devine, and Brian Kelly coached the Irish to stunning heights as might have been indicated in their first season. Lou Holtz is a major exception; his losing first season in 1985 was followed three seasons later with an undefeated national championship. Terry Brennan inherited a team largely molded by the brilliant Frank Leahy. Two seasons later the Irish would only win two games (although Paul Hornung won the Heisman … a testament to Charlie Callahan's extraordinary campaign as Notre Dame's chief sports information figure). In any case, predicting the future based on a first season is a risky venture. It can be said that Freeman's nine wins puts him roughly in the same situation as Parseghian … but also Brennan. Holtz is the one figure whose first season has to be termed an exception to his subsequent successes; he never had another losing season with the Irish. The same can be said for the immortal Rockne (who never had a losing season).

Miracles cannot be predicted. If they could, they wouldn't be miraculous.

Ian Book's TD pass to Miles Boykin in the Irish's 24–17 Citrus Bowl win over LSU was a harbinger of what would eventually become an all-time record for Notre Dame quarterbacks. The catch was miraculous enough, that split second in time when an amazing athlete surpasses himself to make a stunning play. In the case of Ian Book, having started only this one game as a red shirt freshman, he would go on to start the next 34 games as Notre Dame's quarterback, leading the Irish for 35 career wins against only five losses. He would pass for 72 TDs and score another 17 on the ground, for a total of 89 career TDs while racking up nearly 9,000 yards passing. His 35 career wins put him at the top of the list for Irish QBs. His compatriot quarterback predecessors include several Heisman Trophy recipients, All-Americans, College Hall of Fame inductees, national champions, and others who were honored by a variety of accolades. That list includes such luminaries as Gus Dorais, Harry Stuhldreher, Frank Carideo, Angelo Bertelli, Johnny Lujack, Frank Tripucka, Paul Hornung, John Huarte, Terry Hanratty, Joe Theismann, Joe Montana, Tony Rice, Rick Mirer, Steve Beuerlein, and Brady Quinn, among others. Some of these stars had rather short careers under center (World War II a factor, but also injuries, or late-blooming careers). Ian Book's career wins total surpassed the records of all of these famous figures, a testament to his con-

Part Seven

sistency, sheer grit, and quiet leadership skills. One could say with some accuracy that his career from 2017 through 2020 was a slow unfolding of a different kind of miracle, not one that suddenly manifests like a flash of lightning but then disappears. Instead, Book's achievement came about with quiet, steady brilliance over 35 games and four seasons. No one could have predicted it; there was not much flashy about it. That's the point. He went to work, led his team, recovered from mistakes, avoided major injuries, and played his position with the deadly kind of intensity and concentration needed to beat some of the best teams in the country.

The 2018 season started with the Irish ranked just outside of the top 10, at No. 12. They faced the usual collection of fellow powerhouse teams: Michigan, Stanford, USC, Virginia Tech, and Pittsburgh. There were some new teams as well—Ball State and Vanderbilt. After the first three games, the Irish were undefeated but that they had not shown anything that resembled dominance. They seemed content to keep it close as they had uninspiring wins over Michigan 24–17, Ball State 24–16 (they may have either taken them for granted or sleep walked through the game), and Vanderbilt 22–17. They woke up on the road when they lambasted Wake Forest, 56–27. Book had a nearly perfect game against the Demon Deacons, rushing for three TDs and passing for two more. Completing 25 of 34 passes (73.4 percent) on his way to the TD pass trifecta, Book showed great presence and a certain calm as he read his progressions and made good choices.*

Book kept up this pace when No. 8 Notre Dame hosted No. 7 Stanford, firing four TDs to different receivers, including budding WR star Chase Claypool, to lead the Irish to a 38–17 victory over the Cardinal. Book found Boykin with 11 passes for 144 yards and a TD, while RB Dexter Williams blasted Stanford on 21 carries for 164 yards and a TD from 45 yards out. The offense was clicking like a pampered machine, having racked up 94 points in two games. They kept up this torrid scoring pace on another road win when they blasted Virginia Tech in Blacksburg, 45–23. Now ranked No. 6, the Irish decimated No. 24 Virginia Tech with a balanced attack. Dexter Williams surpassed his great Stanford performance by rushing for 178 yards on 17 carries, good for 3 TDs, including a stunning 97-yard scamper. Boykin tacked on two more TDs with his eight receptions. Book played a steady game, hitting 25 of his 35 passes for 271 yards and two TDs. Pitt played its usual tough game against the undefeated Irish, now ranked No. 5. Pitt, with a 3–3 record, managed to lead the Irish until last five minutes left in the game, when Book found Boykin for the game-winning 35-yard TD. Claypool also snagged a

---

* Then Wake Forest quarterback Sam Hartman entered the transfer portal in 2022, and in early 2023 committed to Notre Dame. He will be in contention for the starting QB job for the Irish entering the season.

TD pass and Justin Yoon added two field goals for the nerve-wracking 19–14 final score. A measure of the stout Pitt defense was that Dexter Williams was held to 31 yards with 13 run attempts.

It was a tale of two different halves when the third-ranked Irish met ancient nemesis Navy in San Diego. Notre Dame raced to a 27–0 halftime score, with Dexter Williams racking up three TDs on short sprints to go with Jafar Armstrong's short TD run. The usual triple-option Navy offense managed two short TD runs by their QB after long, patient drives but the Irish added a field goal and a TD pass to Boykin in the third quarter. Navy kept plugging away, scoring on a 32-yard burst and a two-point conversion in the fourth quarter, but Book found an open Boykin for a 22-yard TD and the final 44–22 score.

Back in the Midwest, having somehow slipped to No. 4, the Irish made the short trip to Evanston to meet a 5–3 Northwestern team. The Wildcats managed to hold the Irish to a 7–7 halftime score, both TDs scored on 1-yard plunges. Notre Dame notched two scores in the third quarter with Book TD passes to Boykin (20 yards) and Michael Young, a 47-yard strike. The Wildcats mounted a good comeback in the fourth quarter with a 27-yard TD pass and another 1-yard TD run. The Irish offset those scores with a field goal and a Book TD run of 23 yards for the final 31–21 score.

Back to the No. 3 national ranking, the final home game of the year saw the Irish take on Florida State, a team going through the doldrums from its former winning successes Notre Dame kept the Seminoles feeling the blues with a dominant 42–13 clobbering that moved the season record to 10–0. Ian Book had hurt his back in the win over Northwestern so Brandon Wimbush started at QB. Wimbush wasted little time getting things rolling for the Irish; he hit Boykin with a short TD pass after about 90 seconds of playing time. Then he added another TD with a 6-yard flip to Alize Mack. Justin Yoon rounded out the first quarter scoring with a short field goal. FSU showed some fight to start the second quarter with an 8-yard TD run by Cam Akers. The Irish blocked the PAT though and Julian Love ran it back for a two-point bonus. Dexter Williams exploded for a 58-yard TD run and Mack added another TD reception to close out the scoring for the half, ND leading 32–6. Akers scored again in the third quarter but Yoon hit a field goal and Williams scampered 32 yards for his second score and the final of 42–13. Williams had torched the Seminoles for 202 yards on the ground in his 20 carries.

Book returned from his back injury and the third ranked Irish demolished No. 12 Syracuse in the friendly confines of Yankee Stadium, winning 36–3. It was almost a shutout … Syracuse managed to hit a field goal with 10 seconds left in the game. Book passed for 292 yards with TDs to Williams and Claypool. Williams added another TD with a 32-yard scamper, Jafar Armstrong blasted in from the 9 for another TD, and Justin Yoon tacked on three field goals.

Hoping to complete an undefeated season, the Irish went to LA to meet their nemesis, USC, a team mired in mediocrity but dangerous nevertheless. Book was up to the challenge as he led Notre Dame to a 24–17 come from behind victory, throwing for 352 yards and two TDs, one to Chris Finke and one to Tony Jones, from 51 yards out. Dexter Williams put the Irish in the win column with a 52-yard TD burst and Yoon ended ND's scoring with a field goal.

Irish QB Ian Book escapes the clutches of a Trojan defender, while never losing a home game in 15 career contests. *AP Photo*

A month later, a bitter loss to Clemson in the Cotton Bowl playoff semi-final took off most of the luster of the team's historic season. Clemson prevailed 30–3, dominating all phases of the game. The Tigers would go on to decimate Alabama in the final game of the season to claim the championship. The defeat for the Irish meant going back to the drawing boards to start the process of recruiting top-end talent and then coaching them to the performance level needed to overcome the level of competition found in the top teams. Overall team speed had to be improved, especially in the wide receiver cohort. This process would not be done overnight.

Losing by a landslide to Clemson depressed the media's national ranking to start the 2019 season as the team found themselves ranked No. 9, a rather precarious position but leaving open the possibility of returning to the national playoff if they could duplicate the results from the regular 2018 season—a very tall order. The Irish would open with Louisville on the road and then hold its first home game with New Mexico. These were really prep games for the big third game against No. 3 Georgia. Louisville almost rained on the Irish parade by holding them to a 14–14 first quarter tie, but the Irish D collected itself and held them scoreless until the fourth quarter's Louisville field goal. Meanwhile, Notre Dame added three more TDs for the final 35–17 score. Book passed for nearly 200 yards, with a lone TD throw to TE Tommy Tremble, but he added a short TD run to go with three other rushing TDs to complete the scoring. Former Irish head coach Bob Davie, the Lobos' head coach, had to stay home due to recovery from a heart condition. Missing the game for him might have been a blessing in disguise because his New Mexico team was unable to offer much resistance, succumbing in the Irish home opener 66–14. Freshman safety (and future All-American) Kyle Hamilton opened the scoring in the first quarter with an interception returned 34 yards for a TD, setting the stage for an Irish scoring eruption in the second quarter, 31 points, with four TDs and a field goal. Book did most of the damage with a short TD run followed by passing scores to three different receivers. Four more TDs followed in the second half, three more via the air from Book and another short TD run. Book passed for 360 yards with his 15 completions. The final scoring tally was the most points racked up in many years for Notre Dame.

Ranked No. 7, the Irish went south to meet the No. 3 Georgia Bulldogs, another national test of Notre Dame's overall team quality and execution. They could have used some of the surplus scoring against New Mexico but, lacking that, they could only manage a tough, low scoring defeat to Georgia, 23–17. After a scoreless first quarter, ND scored twice—with a 1-yard TD pass from Book to Cole Kmet, then a Jonathon Doerer field goal, holding a 10–7 lead at halftime. The Bulldogs scored the next four tallies, with three field goals and a 15-yard Jake Fromm TD pass. Book found Claypool for a short TD reception to close out the scoring. The Irish were competitive for the whole game; it was a dramatically better showing than the collapse against Clemson that ended the 2018 campaign. Nevertheless, this Georgia team already had the makings of the team that would dominate everyone in the 2021 and 2022 seasons when they would win national titles. Still, the Irish coaches, players, and fans had to be frustrated with the constant comparisons made with the teams that had led the polls and the important wins in the Nick Saban era.

Overcoming their disappointment, the Irish returned home ranked No. 10 to meet No. 18 Virginia. The Cavaliers jumped out to a 17–14 halftime lead, with Notre Dame scoring via the ground game, Virginia scoring through the air plus a field goal. The Irish registered the next three TDs, with two rushing scores to go with a fumble recovery and return. Virginia tacked on a final field goal, but the Irish were back on the winning track. Book had passed for only 165 yards, but Tony Jones chipped in 131 yards on 18 carries.

Ranked ninth, the Irish met Bowling Green for a home game and sent them packing 52–0. Book got out of the doldrums he faced with Virginia to throw five TD passes before exiting the game with a 35–0 lead. He clicked first with Tremble, then Kmet, then two to Claypool, and one to Javon McKinley, while completing 80 percent of his 20 throws. The Irish subs tacked on one more TD in the second half via airmail, a field goal, and a short run for the final TD and the 52–0 final score.

The surfers from southern California made their biennial journey to northern Indiana (always careful to schedule their games well away from anything as unseemly as snow). The Trojans had been going through a routine of whiplash seasons and the head coach would only make it through half of the next season. Even with rumors lurking in the wings, the Trojans put up a good performance against the ninth-ranked Irish. They started the scoring with a field goal in the first quarter, but Notre Dame responded in the second frame with two TDs and a field goal. Kmet snagged a Book pass for a TD and speedy Braden Lenzy outran the Trojans on a jet sweep for a 51-yard score. Doerer matched the USC field goal for a 17–3 halftime lead. Doerer kicked another field goal in the third quarter while USC added one of its own and a TD via a pass. Doerer later booted his third field goal of the day and Book ran for an 8-yard TD to keep the Trojans at bay as they managed two TDs on a short run and a short pass, but were unable to catch the steady Irish for the 30–27 final score.

Ranked No. 8, the favored Irish were clobbered 45–14 by No. 19 Michigan before nearly 112,000 fans. It was 17–0 before Kmet hauled in a TD pass from Book near the end of the third quarter, but the Wolverines chalked up four unanswered TDs before McKinley caught a TD pass from a sub QB. So much for being the favored team.

Now ranked 16th, Notre Dame may have still been suffering PTSD in the next game, a home affair with Virginia Tech. Book kept very busy hitting 29 of 53 passes for 336 yards and two TDs. He added the last score on a short run to ice the 21–20 win. With 13 carries, he was directly involved in 66 offensive snaps.

Duke was the next opponent. The Irish scored in each frame while holding the Blue Devils to a second quarter TD. Book let her rip for 4 passing TDs, two of them to Chris Finke, to go with a short TD run and a field goal. Book accounted for 320 total yards, 181 through the air and 139 on 12 carries to account for most of the 38–7 result.

The Midshipmen made their journey to the Dome as that rivalry had warmed up after the Irish had spanked them 43 straight times before Navy broke through in 2007. They won three more in the next nine seasons but the Irish were starting another streak in 2017. Navy was one of the few college programs that used a triple option offensive scheme, more or less an advanced version of the original wishbone from the '60s and '70s. The opponents have to play "assignment football" and not chase after decoys. Defensive linemen are not big fans of the kind of blocking they face with this offense. Finally, so few teams operate this scheme that practices cannot focus on it for any extended time. You seldom see anything like this in a season. The Irish, however, played a strong game as they dominated the Middies 52–20. They took advantage of a glaring size and speed differential as Book targeted Claypool for four TD passes, to go with a Lenzy 70-yard TD reception and a fumble recovery score. Even though the halftime score was 38–3, Navy never gave up, slamming in two ground TDs and adding a field goal to win a consolation second half, during which the Irish scored twice to reach their 52 points. Book had 14 completions, half of them to Claypool.

Locked into the No. 16 spot, the Irish closed out their season with three high-scoring wins: beating Boston College 40–7 on senior day, then winning a shootout with Stanford, 45–24, and dispatching Iowa State 33–9 in the Camping World Bowl (which elevated them to No. 12). Book led the way against BC with 26 completions for 236 yards and 3 TDs, and also boosted his team with 66 yards rushing. Against Stanford, Book fired four TD passes with 17 completions good for 255 yards, with Claypool hauling in two of those scores. They added a field goal, a TD on a short run, and a fumble recovery for a TD.

There is a gap of some four weeks between the end of the formal scheduled teams and the assigned date for a bowl game. During this period in 2019 used for extra practices for bowl-bound teams, there were vague rumors floating in the cyberworld about a possible epidemic beginning to manifest in central China. No one then could possibly anticipate the national and worldwide implications of that problem.

Jonathon Doerer bookended the 2019 Camping World bowl game against Iowa State with the first score and the last score, tacking on one in the second quarter and another in the third. Tony Jones had the play of the day—an 84-yard TD rumble. Claypool contributed a TD reception. Book hit 20 of 28 passes for 247 yards on the way to the 33–9 win and a final national ranking of No. 12.

Fans might not have noticed this but the Irish were in the midst of a streak of winning seasons that comes close to previous streaks—Holtz's 1988–91 powerhouses, Leahy's 1946–49 champions, and Rockne's 1919–24, 1929–30 streaks.

The 2020 season was fully scheduled, as usual. Not one of those games was played as scheduled. Rivalry games established nearly 100 years earlier, all across the nation, never materialized in the 2020 season. The ensuing public panic and confusion caused by the pandemic, COVID-19, was reminiscent of the national response in 1918 to the flu that afflicted the world in that year. Sports take on a very different perspective in the midst of large-scale tragedies.

Should the show go on? Can we allow the show to go on? Well, the original "show" (the original schedule) never happened. With the nation and world doing everything possible to survive and defeat COVID-19, ND's first 2020 scheduled game, against Navy in Dublin, Ireland, was a sitting duck for cancellation.

The original Notre Dame football schedule looked like this: Navy, Arkansas, Western Michigan, Wake Forest, Wisconsin, Stanford, Pittsburgh, Duke, Clemson, Georgia Tech, Louisville, USC. Five of these games were rescheduled. The revised schedule kicked off two weeks later, in mid-September. Ten games were played before a grand total of roughly 78,000 fans—a figure the Irish would typically see in one home game. The largest crowd saw the Clemson game played at the Golden Dome—11,011. One game was played indoors with no viewers at all … Boston College. Most such events also involved strict orders about masks and physical spacing, just the tip of the iceberg mandated in response to the pandemic that would eventually kill more than one million Americans and another 5.7 million worldwide. The revised schedule involved ten schools, five of them holdovers from the original plans: Duke, South Florida, Florida State, Louisville, Pittsburgh, Georgia Tech, Clemson, Boston College, North Carolina, and Syracuse. The revised schedule also had Wake Forest as the last game, but that was canceled by ACC officials in order to keep the conference title game intact as originally designed. In sum, despite the hard work to find opponents for the Irish, the faithful would certainly miss the two longtime rivalry games—Navy and USC.

So, after shuffling the national deck, it was Duke that provided the first opposition to the 10th-ranked Irish. Kyren Williams chipped in two TD runs, Book found Avery Davis for a 26-yard TD, and Doerer booted two field goals for a 27–13 victory. Book passed for 263 yards and Williams racked up 112 yards on the ground. The Irish kept it simple in a 52–0 demolition of South Florida. Book passed for 144 yards and eight players contributed 281 yards in the ground attack, accounting for six TDs, to go with a Doerer field goal and a Jordan Botelho fumble recovery and a short TD return. Florida State was the next victim to come north to play the Irish (the first five games of 2020 were played under the Dome). They put up a better fight than USF but succumbed anyway by a 42–26 score. The Seminoles started hot and took a 17–10 first-quarter lead. Michael Mayer snagged an 8-yard TD from Book and Williams zipped 46 yards for the other first quarter Irish score. The Irish brought out a shillelagh to club FSU with three TDs in the second quarter: Williams on a 1-yard burst, Chris Tyree from 45 yards out, and Lenzy with a short pass from Book, who wrapped up the scoring in the third quarter with a short TD run.

Louisville, a team with only one win, put a real scare in the Irish, once again on their home turf. Doerer kicked two field goals for a lead that held until the third quarter but Louisville then marched 83 yards in 13 plays, capping the drive with a 1-yard TD pass. Their defense held the Irish offense at bay, but Doerer struck again with two field goals for the 12–7 win, ugly as it was. Book only moved the ball via passes for 106 yards. Williams made up some of the slack with 25 work horse runs for 127 yards. Other Irish runners added another 105 yards for the 232 yards total.

Notre Dame, now ranked third in the country, finally left its home base for the short trip to Pittsburgh. Whatever doubts that may have haunted the team and the fans following the Louisville escape were dispelled by a convincing 45–3 drubbing of the Panthers. The passing game, invisible in the tough game with Louisville, came back to life when Book found transfer Ben Skowronek for two TDs, a 34-yard play and then a 71-yard bomb. Williams punched in a 2-yard score and Isaiah Foskey snagged a blocked punt in the end zone for a 28–3 halftime cushion. Doerer booted a field goal in the third quarter to go with a 14-yard TD pass to freshman tight end Michael Mayer, aka "Baby Gronk." The Irish tacked on a final short TD run for the 45–3 final tally. Book passed for 312 yards while the running backs contributed another 115 yards.

On the road again, perhaps with an eye peripherally on No. 1 Clemson in two weeks, the No. 3 Irish went to Atlanta to play Georgia Tech. They kept the game under control, in spite of a 93-yard fumble return in the second quarter. Prior to that play, Book spotted an open Joe Wilkins and hit him for an 8-yard TD. Williams smashed in from the 2-yard line and Doerer added a field goal in the second frame. Williams repeated for another short TD for the only TD in the third quarter. The teams traded rushing TDs in the fourth quarter for the 31–13 Irish win. Notre Dame ran for 227 yards and Book added 199 yards passing. The Irish compiled 426 yards of offense to Tech's 238 total yards.

Finally, the Irish get Clemson on their home field, No. 1 Clemson vs. No. 4 ND, both undefeated. COVID became a factor when Clemson's All-American QB, Trevor Lawrence, came down with a case that required him to self-isolate. So, Clemson lost a senior team leader, with a freshman QB to take over that crucial position—D. J. Uiagalelei. All he did was set an all-time record for passing yards by an opponent at an Irish home game: 439 yards with 29 completions in 44 attempts, good for two TDs. The Irish D held Clemson to a mere 34 yards on the ground, muffling Travis Etienne for 28 yards in 18 frustrating runs. Choking the running game forced Uiagalelei to throw the ball. Kyren Williams, in contrast, got the contest off to an explosive start after only 33 seconds in the game when he ran to his left, juked a defender, and hauled the mail 65 yards for the first score. His one run was more than double the yardage on the ground for the entire Clemson backfield.

Kyren Williams celebrates his long TD run to help defeat Clemson in a 2020 ho me win. *AP Photo*

The game turned into an all-time classic thriller, decided in Notre Dame's favor only after two overtime periods. Following Williams's brilliant TD run, Doerer made a field goal for a 10-point first quarter lead, but a Clemson TD pass cut into that lead. In the second quarter, Doerer added two more field goals and linebacker Jeremiah Owusu-Koramoah rumbled into the end zone with a recovered fumble. Clemson added two field goals for the halftime Irish lead, 23–13. Clemson used the third quarter to close the gap by hitting two field goals while keeping the Irish from scoring. Doerer took back the lead with a field goal in the fourth quarter, but Clemson hit one of their own to go with a ground TD. Avery Davis ended a 91-yard drive with a 4-yard TD reception from Book. It was 33–33 at the end of regulation time. The teams traded short TD runs in the first overtime. Williams bookended his opening TD with a 3-yard TD scamper in the second OT. Two sacks of Uiagalelei forced a desperation final play that ended one of the most exciting games when the Tigers failed to score. Notre Dame's offense racked up 518 total yards to Clemson's 473 yards, but 92 percent of that figure came through the air as the Clemson ground game simply never materialized. It was collegiate football at its finest, if not a miracle in itself, given the horrific national conditions taking a huge daily toll on innocent Americans.

The win elevated Notre Dame to No. 2 in the nation. The next game was most likely going to be another barn burner, against the other national Catholic football power, Boston College, led by a former Irish player, QB Phil Jurkovec. The first quarter was a 10–10 affair, the Irish using a Doerer field goal and a 10-yard TD pass from Book to Skowronek. BC managed only two field goals in the second quarter but ND scored three TDs: a short run but two more TD passes to Skowronek—13 yards and 10 yards, both from Book, making the halftime score 31–16. The teams traded TDs in both second-half quarters, with Book running 16 yards or the last Irish score. BC succeeded with a two-point conversion near the end of the game for the 45–31 final tally. Book completed 20 passes for 283 yards and 3 TDs while he also led Irish runners with 85 yards on 10 rushing plays.

Still ranked No. 2, Notre Dame moved a little south to play No. 19 North Carolina. The Irish scored in every frame while holding the Tar Heels scoreless in the second half, propelling the team to a 31–17 final score. The first half was tied 17–17 at the break: with both teams operating efficiently for two TDs each from within the red zone. Williams accounted for those two Irish scores. The teams traded field goals in the second quarter. Notre Dame took charge in the third quarter with a trick play that turned Skowronek into a runner scoring from the

Tar Heels 13-yard line. The fourth quarter saw Williams top off an 89-yard march with a 1-yard TD blast.

In early December Syracuse visited the Dome for the last game of the revised season (the Wake Forest game a week later was canceled by the ACC in order to get on with postseason championship play). Notre Dame beat the Orangemen 45–21, achieving another undefeated "regular" season. Doerer started the festivities with a first quarter field goal but Syracuse scored next in the second quarter with a TD pass before Book took over the game with a 28-yard scoring run, then two scoring passes to Javon McKinley from just outside the red zone. Syracuse scored once in each quarter but Book broke loose again for a 17-yard score, then he spotted McKinley again with a 26-yard TD pass. In the fourth quarter perfect Irish execution blocking let Tyree turn on the jets for a 94-yard TD run. The Irish kindly let a Syracuse runner nearly match that feat with an 80-yard TD and the final score of 45–21 for the Irish.

With a very welcome week off, the team prepped for the ACC title game … Clemson again. This time, Trevor Lawrence had recovered from COVID with no lingering side effects. The No. 2 Irish would have their work cut out for them with No. 4 Clemson. The question lingering in the minds of fans was whether the Irish had matured into the kind of team that could go toe-to-toe in a playoff situation with a historic heavy hitter. Ironically, the statistics for the game showed that this time Clemson shut down the Irish run game for a total of 44 yards while Book did not make up the difference, passing for only 219 yards. In their 34–10 win, Clemson put up 541 total yards, 322 yards from Lawrence's passing. Still, the Irish made it into the national title playoff.

Alabama, the No. 1 seed vs. the Irish at No. 4. The same question remained. Alabama was led by Mac Jones, a QB as good as Clemson's Lawrence, and a host of speedy wide receivers and defenders. The score was 14–0 before Williams earned a 1-yard TD. Alabama added two more TDs and a field goal before Book wrapped up the final 31–14 score with another 1-yard TD late in the game. The Irish managed to put up 375 yards of total offense to Alabama's 437 yards. Book passed for 229 yards but did not find any of his receivers for a touchdown. So, the undefeated "regular" season concluded with two devastating losses to teams that were never really threatened by the Irish.

Sadly, this was Ian Book's last game for the Gold and Blue. With his collegiate career finished he could take some satisfaction in the fact that he had never lost a home game (15 wins) and had set the record for Irish QBs with 30 wins. His on-field career performance was stellar: 728 completions (second all-time for ND) in 1,141 passes, good for 8,948 yards that led to 72 TDs versus only 20 interceptions. He augmented those figures with 361 running plays that produced 1,517 yards and 17 TDs. In sum, his combined offensive yardage reached 10,465 yards that racked up 89 TDs.

The 2021 season found the Irish using a transfer QB for the first time via the new system, the transfer portal, launched in late 2018, one of the most significant NCAA changes in recent memory. Jack Coan came to Notre Dame from Wisconsin. He was originally ticketed for ND to play lacrosse but ended up in Madison anyway for football. So, he was enjoying a homecoming of sorts. He was basically the classic drop back QB, not a speed merchant if he breaks out of the pocket. He had the benefit of a veteran offensive line, an emerging star at tight end, Michael Mayer, and a 1,000-yard running back, Kyren Williams. A stout defense, featuring the All-American safety, Kyle Hamilton, would keep the Irish in most games and was led by a new defensive coordinator—Marcus Freeman.

Ranked 9th nationally, the Irish met unranked FSU at their stadium. Michael Mayer scored the first TD with a 41-yard pass from Coan. FSU tied it up late in the first quarter with an 89 yard run. The 'Noles scored first in the second quarter but the Irish tacked on a 48-yard Doerer field goal and Joe Wilkins snagged a Coan pass to score from the FSU 23 to round out the halftime score, 17–14. FSU took the lead with a 60-yard TD pass early in the third quarter but the Irish dominated the rest of that quarter with Coan TD passes to Kevin Austin and Williams, followed by a 1-yard Tyree scoring run. Leading 38–20 going into the fourth quarter, Notre Dame might have relaxed but FSU didn't, piling up 18 points to tie the game in regulation time. Tied at 38, the Seminoles had the ball first in overtime, gaining 6 yards before they missed a 36-yard field goal try. Notre Dame played it safe and Doerer kicked a 40-yard winner. For his Notre Dame debut Coan passed for 4 TDs and 366 yards, finding Michael Mayer with 9 completions for 120 yards. FSU surprisingly throttled the Irish running game, holding the runners to 65 yards on the ground, while the Seminole backs romped for 264 yards and 3 TDs. Note that this was a team headed for seven losses in the 2021 campaign. Would this bode ill for the unfolding ND season?

The Irish moved up to No. 8 as they prepped to meet Toledo of the Mid-American conference. Such a meeting should result in a blowout, but a similar game with Tulsa a few years earlier had been an eye-opening loss. Sure enough, Toledo pushed the Irish right to the edge, losing a 32–29 thriller. The Rockets posted a halftime 16–14 lead that held into the fourth quarter when ND racked up 18 points to Toledo's 13. Coan played well enough (21 of 33 for 239 yards, 2 TDs, and one interception) but was relieved briefly in the fourth quarter by freshman Tyler Buchner, who promptly fired a 55-yard TD pass to Tyree to help spark the

Part Seven

tcam. The Irish running backs doubled their output over the FSU game. Toledo would end up their season with an underwhelming 7–6 record. The Irish offensive engine was obviously not hitting on all cylinders. The defense was still adjusting to Coach Freeman's new, more aggressive style of play. When would it all come together?

The sports writers were paying attention; they dumped the 8th-ranked Irish to No. 12 the week of the Purdue game, an old but honorable foe. Purdue was undefeated but not ranked. The Irish held them in check for most of the game, allowing only two field goals and a 2-yard TD pass. Meanwhile, Coan looked sharper and Williams was beginning to hit his stride. Coan found Williams and Avery Davis in the open for a 39-yard TD and a 62-yard bomb respectively. Doerer booted two field goals and Williams broke loose for a 51-yard TD sprint to close out the scoring as ND won 27–13.

Jack Coan had plenty of motivation for the next game as his new team, ranked No. 12, would be meeting his old team, Wisconsin, standing at No. 18. It was a Shamrock series game, played at a neutral site (Chicago's Soldier Field). It was tied at 10–10 going into the fourth quarter, but then the Irish unloaded their whole arsenal, scoring 31 points in that frame to Wisconsin's three. Coan played into the third quarter but suffered a leg injury with the teams tied at 10–10. Doerer started ND's scoring with an impressive 51-yard field goal, followed by Kevin Austin's 36-yard TD reception from Coan. The Badgers opened the fourth quarter with a field goal to take the lead 13–10. Thirteen seconds later Chris Tyree crossed the goal line after bolting for a 96-yard kickoff return. Subbing for Coan, Drew Pyne fired a 16-yard TD pass to Kevin Austin. Doerer added his second field goal, and then the Irish defense scored twice within 62 seconds—linebacker Jack Kiser rumbling 66 yards for a TD with an intercepted pass and Drew White added his name to the box score with another interception (the fourth of the day), good for a 45-yard scoring return, putting the exclamation point on a 41–13 Irish victory. This was a total team effort: special teams, a modest offense output, help from key subs, and the defense keeping the Badgers in a hole more often than not.

Number 7 Cincinnati, Marcus Freeman's former team, visited the Dome to test No. 9 Notre Dame. Led by QB Desmond Ridder, a preseason All-American pick, it became obvious that Freeman had left behind a very stout defense for his old team. After a scoreless first quarter, the Bearcats pummeled the Irish for 17 unanswered points, more than enough to win the game right there. Kyren Williams slammed in for a TD in the third quarter and Lenzy scored with a 32-yard pass from Pyne in the fourth quarter. The PAT failed. Ridder scampered in for the final Bearcat TD and they left the stadium with a 24–13 victory. The key was that the Bearcat D throttled the Irish run game, holding them to 84 total yards on the ground in 28 attempts—a 3-yard average. This made it difficult for the Irish to sustain drives; they punted six times. Pyne replaced a struggling Coan and did manage to throw one TD pass.

Back to the drawing board. The Irish would next meet Virginia Tech on the road, usually a tough place for visitors. The Hokies did not disappoint so it was another white knuckle affair, with the Irish prevailing 32–29. It was nip and tuck all the way, with the Irish taking a 14–12 lead at halftime, based on excellent play by Coan's sub, Tyler Buchner, who made a short run for a TD and later made a nice throw to Williams for the second score of the second quarter. The Hokies outscored ND in the third frame with a field goal and an interception of a Buchner pass for a TD. Williams turned on the jets for a 10-yard TD but Tech had a 22–21 lead after three quarters. Kelly had seen enough with his sub QB so sent Coan back into the game. Good move. VT had scored again to widen their lead to 29–22, so Coan's senior leadership late in the game led to a crucial TD pass of 4 yards to Avery Davis, followed by a nifty 2-point conversion pass to Kevin Austin, tying the score at 29–29. The Irish D held steady and the Irish took over as the clock was dwindling. They used 1:34 for seven plays; Doerer hit the game-winning 48-yard field goal with 17 seconds left in the game. With the win the Irish were

All-American Tight End Michael Meyer goes airborne as a defender whiffs. *AP Photo*

5–1 halfway through the season, but three of those wins were by three points each, cliffhangers all.

The next game reinstituted a rivalry lost due to the COVID crisis in 2020, a series that had produced decades of great games: USC, the ultimate rival for the Irish. Notre Dame was the 13th ranked team; USC was unranked and had lost three games so far. The Irish D kept the Trojans in check all the way into the fourth quarter, building a 24–3 lead before SC crossed the goal line early in the final frame. Coan engineered the first TD, a 4-yard pass to Avery Davis late in the first quarter. Doerer booted a field goal in the next quarter and Williams romped for a 5-yard score. He kept up the pressure in the third quarter with a 1-yard blast. SC scored its consolation TDs before freshman QB Tyler Buchner scooted in from the 3-yard line for the 31–16 final score. The Trojans passed for nearly 300 yards and racked up 438 total yards to ND's 383 total yards. The Irish were able to finish off enough drives to build a nice lead before the Trojan offense jelled in the fourth quarter.

Now ranked 11th, the Irish met unranked North Carolina at home. It was beginning to look like ND was maturing into a team that would not be satisfied with three-point wins, as seen earlier in the season. With this new attitude, the Irish would rack up a series of double-digit wins, starting with the Tar Heels. This game would see more than 70 points combined as well as over 1,000 yards of total offense. ND would pull out the win 44–34, thanks largely to a stunning game played by Kyren Williams, who carried the ball 22 times for 199 yards, including the longest run in his ND career, a 91-yard scorcher. Three Irish runners scored TDs: Williams, Coan, and freshman Logan Diggs. Coan added a TD pass as did Buchner. Doerer tacked on a field goal. Like USC, the Tar Heels outgunned the Irish in terms of total yards, only to lose the game by double digits.

The Midshipmen were the next visitors but had to limp back to Annapolis on the short end of a 34–6 score. The teams swapped quarters in terms of scoring, with Navy hitting field goals in the first quarter and third quarter while the Irish matched those scores but also piled on two TDs in the second and fourth quarters. The Irish did most of the damage with three TDs scored on the ground—Williams twice, Diggs once. Kevin Austin plucked a Coan pass out of the air for a 70-yard TD bomb. Coan had a field day, completing 23 of 29 passes for 269 yards to go with 150 yards rushing. Navy managed only 18 yards passing.

Ranked No. 9 the Irish won their ninth game by beating Virginia 28–3. Notre Dame scored in the first three frames and allowed a consolation field goal with less than three minutes left in the game. Coan threw three TD passes: to Mayer, Lenzy, and Austin. Williams added a 22-yard TD.

Creeping up the ranking ladder, the 9–1 Irish hit No. 8. Then they decimated Georgia Tech 55–0 in the final home game of the season. The game-winning score was executed by Doerer when he made a 41-yard field goal after two and a half minutes of play to start the game. For Tech, it was all downhill after that: Kizer, 41-yard TD interception return; Williams a 9-yard TD run; Mayer, a 52-yard TD with a Coan pass; Diggs, back-to-back TD runs; Williams a 1-yard TD run; Doerer another field goal; Myron Tagovailoa-Amosa, a 70-yard fumble recovery for a TD and the final blowout score. The Irish D played their best game of the season, forcing 10 Tech punts.

The 8th ranked Irish concluded the regular 2021 season with a trip west to play Stanford, a team that had been facing some adversity in recent difficult seasons. The Irish pummeled the Cardinal 45–14 to end up with an 11–1 record. Notre Dame posted four first half scores to build a 24–0 halftime lead, then added three more TDs in the second half, while Stanford managed to earn two TDs. Coan did the most damage with 345 yards through the air for 2 TDs, then scored one himself for good measure. Williams chipped in 2 rushing TDs. Overall, the Irish offense racked up 509 total yards while the defense held Stanford to 227 total yards, throttling the Cardinal ground game to a mere 55 yards on 22 carries (2.5 yards per attempt).

With the conclusion of the season, Brian Kelly needed to wrap up some recruiting duties. He and Tommy Rees went to Vancouver, Washington, to meet with the Merriweather family. Their son, Tobias, was one of the highly ranked recruits targeted by the Irish staff. The game with Stanford was played in the late evening of November 27. On November 30, LSU announced that it was hiring Kelly, offering him a ten-year contract good for $95 million. Very few, if any, had the slightest clue that Kelly was thinking of leaving Notre Dame. He had more wins than any Division I head coach and would later claim that he really wanted to have the best possible chance to win a national title.

The spotlight immediately shifted to considering possible replacements. One figure rose to the top of the list almost immediately: Marcus Freeman, the Irish Defensive Coordinator, late of Cincinnati, with a pedigree that included being a starting linebacker for Ohio State. He was a young man whose coaching career was on a rapidly rising trajectory. He was wildly popular with the members of the Notre Dame team. The announcement revealing Freeman's elevation to the head position came on December 3, 2021, mere days after Kelly's departure. He was thirty-five years old, the 30th head coach to lead the team under the Dome.

Fans everywhere were enthusiastic, if not ecstatic, about Freeman's ascendance to the top position. It did not appear that their enthusiasm was tempered by a full awareness of the magnitude of the immediate tasks facing the new head coach. Up front—start preparations for the Fiesta Bowl game with Oklahoma State. Continue recruiting efforts. Fill in gaps in the coaching staff. Get to know all the players better. Make any necessary adjustments in playing personnel (for instance, no Kyren Williams as the starting RB). Deal with the press.

Freeman's first game as the head coach could not have started any better. Notre Dame had averaged 38 points per game in their last seven games of 2021. The Irish looked like that high-scoring No. 5 team in the country as they struck for four first half TDs, all passes from Coan, against the No. 9 Cowboys. They took the kickoff 75 yards in 5 plays in 90 seconds, Lorenzo Styles hauling in the 29-yard TD pass. Tyree snagged another Coan pass for a 53-yard score. The second quarter belonged to the Coan to Mayer TD combo: 16 yards and 7 yards, although OSU struck with seconds before halftime with a short TD pass to Tay Martin. The second half belonged to OSU WR Martin and kicker Tanner Brown: Martin hauled in two short TD passes and Brown tacked on three field goals. Notre Dame scored late in the game when Coan fired his fifth TD pass, this one for 25 yards to Kevin Austin. Thus ended Freeman's first game as a head coach, a 35–37 loss. Coan had a career day: completing 38 of 59 passes for the 5 TDs and a staggering 509 yards, but the Irish run game never materialized—a mere 42 yards on 21 runs. OSU, on the other hand, passed for 374 yards and ran for 234 more, reaching a total of 608 yards. The Irish offense's one-dimensional output was exactly the opposite of Freeman's vision for his Irish offense—run first. Control the line of scrimmage. Limit the other team's control of the clock.

The bloom may have come off the aura around the new head coach. A miracle was not going to happen. Not immediately. The Irish faithful were now in a wait and see posture.

The initial enthusiasm around the change of head coaches lingered through the summer into the first poll ranking. At No. 5, the Irish would meet No. 1 Ohio State in Columbus, the same school that Freeman played for. The Irish scored first with a Blake Grupe field goal on their first possession. Ohio State found the end zone with a 35-yard pass late in the first quarter. In the second quarter, Notre Dame pieced together a 10-play drive covering 87 yards, with Audric Estime slamming his 230 pounds into the end zone from the 1-yard line. That 10–7 lead lasted into the final seconds of the third quarter, but with 17 seconds remaining the Buckeyes took the lead with a 24-yard TD pass. They added another TD on a short run in the fourth quarter and escaped with the 21–10 win. Overall, the Irish were not overmatched in all phases but the running game was not very productive. It was obvious that Michael Mayer, with five receptions, would be the main weapon in the team's passing game moving forward.

While it was not a win, the Irish had acquitted themselves quite well against the top ranked team before a hostile 100,000+ crowd. It was a close game until the very end. Unfortunately, the next game, the home opener for Freeman and the team, seemed to show a retrograde tendency. This first home game was against Marshall, the kind of a team that the Irish would typically turn into roadkill. Not so this time, to the chagrin of all concerned. While the final score, 26–21, seemed close, in fact the Thundering Herd outplayed Notre Dame. The Irish seemed flat and uninspired. Tyler Buchner, who had seen some spot work in 2021, was now the starter at QB and passed for 201 yards while also leading the team in rushing with 44 yards. This latter is an alarming figure; Notre Dame gained only 76 yards on the ground in the Ohio State loss. Now a second team had also stymied the run game. The Irish were now like a boxer using only one hand. Buchner ran for two 1-yard scores and Drew Pyne spotted Mayer in the end zone for a 5-yard TD. Buchner went down with an injured left shoulder and would miss the rest of the regular season following surgery. Pyne would be the guy the rest of the way.

Enthusiasm and excitement now morphed into consternation—or worse. The Irish records indicated that no other head coach has lost his first three games. As it turned out, Freeman is both resilient and intelligent. He practiced self-reflection personally and with the staff. Righting the ship would take quite an effort, but they were up to the task.

An undefeated Cal team was next up. The Irish were no longer ranked. How would this turn out? The first quarter was quiet but Cal posted 10 points in the second quarter while Notre Dame managed only one score—Tyree on a 21-yard pass from Pyne. The teams traded TDs in the third frame but ND still trailed. The Irish pulled away in the fourth quarter by virtue of a Grupe field goal and a Mayer 6-yard TD fling from Pyne for the 24–17 verdict and Freeman's first win as a head coach. Finally. Neither team looked brilliant. The total yards showed underperformance by both offenses: 297 total yards for ND, 296 for Cal. If anything, it was more of a punting duel—six punts for Cal, seven for ND. Further adjustments were in order for Notre Dame.

They next met another undefeated team, North Carolina, on the road. But this time the offense showed signs of resurgence as Pyne clicked on three TD passes while Estime blasted in for two TDs and Tyree chipped in with another. ND put up 24 points in the second quarter to take the halftime lead, with Mayer scoring with a 10-yard dart and Lorenzo Styles from 30 yards out. Logan Diggs hauled in the third TD strike from Pyne, from 29 yards out in the third quarter. Pyne passed for 289 yards, 88 of them going to Mayer, and Estime romped for 134 yards of ND's 287 on the ground. If there was an area for concern it could be found in the Tar Heels' five TD passes. Still, at least the Irish were starting a winning streak and Freeman had his first road victory.

The Shamrock Series found the team in Las Vegas to meet the 16th-ranked BYU team. Pyne had settled in to his role as the starting QB, throwing for three TDs, two to Mayer and one to Jayden Thomas, all towards his 262-yard total. Estime chipped in with 97 yards on 14 carries and Logan Diggs was right behind him with 93 yards rushing. ND's runners toted the ball 45 times for 234 yards. Grupe added two field goals and the D earned a safety to account for ND's 28 points. It looked like things were coming together for Freeman's team.

But Stanford, having a horrible year that would lead to the coach's resignation, put an abrupt halt to any inflated notions of overall team improvement when the Cardinal came to the Dome and left with a 16–14 victory, unlikely though it might seem. Having lost 11 straight games to FBS teams, the Cardinal managed a first quarter TD and then three field goals (one per quarter) while ND languished until the sixth minute of the third quarter before scoring—a 10-yard rumble by Estime. Early in the fourth quarter Pyne threw a 41-yard TD strike to Tobias Meriweather, a promising freshman, forging a 14–13 lead. Stanford managed one final field goal with more than 10 minutes left, plenty of time for Notre Dame to forge the winning points. That did not happen and the final score of 16–14 was a silent rebuttal to fond hopes for a late victory. The Irish would need to restart whatever momentum they had going into this game—in the middle of the season.

The UNLV Rebels were the next visitors to South Bend, sporting one more win than ND had for the season. The Irish had put in a good week of practice and were ready. They jumped out to a 23–7 first quarter lead, based on a 12-yard Estime blast and a Grupe field goal, followed by a 20-yard scoring pass from Pyne to Mayer, and two more Grupe field goals. In the second quarter ND showed a new wrinkle when they blasted TE Mitchell Evans (a high school QB) into the end zone from the 1-yard line to take a 30–7 halftime lead. Tyree and Lenzy added two TDs in the fourth quarter with an 8-yard run and a 4-yard pass, making the final score 44–21. Pyne hit half of his 28 passes for 205 yards, Diggs carried the mail 28 times for 130 yards, and Mayer collected 6 passes for 115 yards. Overall, it was a solid rebound from the Stanford disaster.

No. 16 Syracuse was up next, holding a 6–1 record. It was played in a domed structure but the Irish players did not let that spook them. Indeed, Safety Brandon

Sophomore first team All-American Joe Alt has never allowed a sack. *AP Photo*

Joseph jumped on Syracuse's first play, a pass, and returned it 25 yards for a TD, using seven seconds of the first quarter. Syracuse brought the score to even but ND tacked on two more TDs in the second frame—a 3-yard Diggs run and a 3-yard Thomas reception. Grupe added a field goal in the third quarter but Syracuse hit one also and added a TD. Estime put his stamp on the game with two TDs in the fourth quarter and Grupe added a final field goal to make the final score 41–24. Once again, Freeman's offense emphasized the running game as Pyne only needed to complete nine passes for 116 yards. Meanwhile, the Irish ran the ball 56 times for 246 yards while the defense held Syracuse to 25 runs for 61 yards. Estime carried the main load with 123 yards on 20 carries.

Any progress was happening at the right time as No. 4 Clemson moved north to meet unranked ND on their home turf. The 2020 game between these two had gone into a second overtime. Notre Dame took care of that possibility this time by building an early lead, blanking Clemson for three quarters, then piling on even more TDs in the final quarter, more than offsetting Clemson's futile, all too late response. The first Irish score set the tone for the whole game: A Clemson drive had barely begun before they had to punt deep in their territory but Isaiah Foskey blocked it and linebacker Prince Kollie returned the loose ball 17 yards for the first Irish score. At the end of the second quarter, Pyne shook loose for a 5-yard TD and the 14–0 halftime lead. After a scoreless third quarter ND slammed the lid with three TDs: Estime barged in from the two yard line; freshman All-American Benjamin Morrison reacted to a fluttering Clemson pass, intercepted it, and raced 96 yards for the second tally (to go with his other INT in the game); Mayer topped off the Irish scoring with a 17-yard reception from Pyne. This was a Freeman Special in terms of execution. The Irish scored in all phases of the game—special teams, the offense, the defense. The Irish O line nullified the Clemson D allowing ND's runners to roam loose for 263 yards, with Estime and Diggs both registering 100 yards or more. Pyne passed for a total of 85 yards with nine completions.

All-time Irish sack leader Isaiah Foskey stops a Clemson runner in 2022 home victory.
AP Photo

Up next was Navy, another program that had fallen upon hard times, with only three wins for the season (and the head coach's tenure was nearly over). It was a tale of two halves: ND won the first half; Navy won the second half, although their comeback fell just short. The Irish passing game was featured on four of the team's five TDs: Estime for 30 yards, Lenzy for 38 yards (and the best catch of the year when he plucked the ball off the back of the Navy defender), Tyree with a 5-yard pass, and Jayden Thomas with a 35-yard pass. Pyne scored on his own with an 11-yard run for the halftime score of 35–13. And that was it for the Irish. Navy came back after halftime and mounted a furious defense based on constant full-out blitzes. ND's offensive production dropped like a stone; there was almost no understandable reaction to the constant blitzing. Deer in the headlight comes to mind. Navy kept running its triple option, scoring 19 points in the second half. The Irish escaped with a 35–32 win. It didn't feel like a win though.

It didn't take long for the sour aftertaste of the Navy game to become a motivating factor when No. 18 ND hosted another longtime rival, Boston College, for the final home game. The medicine to take after Navy was to obliterate BC. That is precisely what happened: 44–0. The Irish built a 37–0 halftime lead. It was 10–0 within the first five minutes—a Grupe field goal for starters and a 1-yard burst by Diggs that ended a drive that started on the BC 20. Matt Salerno added a TD with a short pass from Pyne to give ND a 17–0 first quarter lead. Grupe added two more field goals in the second quarter and Estime and Tyree chipped in two TDs to end the scoring in the first half. Estime tacked on another TD in the third quarter for good measure. BC managed only 176 total yards in the game; the Irish D stuffed the BC run game, allowing a total of only 56 yards on the ground. Pyne's 156 yards passing almost matched BC's total output. Irish running backs had a field day against a porous Eagles defense, darting around and over them for 281 yards, with Logan Diggs accounting for 122 yards on 15 carries, including a 51-yard bolt to set up a score.

No. 15 Notre Dame next met their old foe, the No. 6 Trojans of USC in LA. It proved to be a tough loss, 38–27, but Pyne played a magnificent game, completing his first 15 passes for a school record, reaching 318 yards on 23 of 26 attempts. On the other side of the ball was the Trojans' QB who would win the Heisman (Caleb Williams), a Houdini-type escape artist who was trapped by an aggressive Irish rush coming from different angles on several occasions, getting their hands on him, but he managed to twist or dance away to escape sacks. On one play he got away from the initial rush and ran around for about 80 yards behind the line of scrimmage to turn a busted play into a positive. It had to be a frustrating game for the defenders. The Irish offense cranked out 417 total yards, close to USC's 436. The game was just outside their reach, much like the elusive SC QB. Pyne passed for three TDs while USC's Williams ran for three. Mayer caught eight of Pyne's passes for 98 yards and two TDs. Logan Diggs scored his TD on a 5-yard run.

The 8–4 Irish ended up the regular season ranked No. 21. They met No. 19 South Carolina in the Gator Bowl. Unlike the bowl game that started the Freeman era, the Irish found themselves on the short end of the stick in the first quarter, down 21–7. Instead of folding, however, Notre Dame plugged away, scoring in double figures in each of the remaining quarters to cap the season with a 45–38 win, a 9–4 record, and No. 18 final ranking. Buchner returned from his injured shoulder to be the starter, but the Irish had to cover two significant absences when Mayer and Foskey elected not to play. Buchner had a great game, accounting for five Notre Dame TDs, but also two TDs for the Gamecocks that started as interceptions. The teams chalked up 11 TDs. Notre Dame gained the most yards, 556 combined passing and rushing, while the Irish D mangled the South Carolina running game, holding them to 66 yards on the ground. Buchner passed for 273 yards but Dave Sherwood also passed for a 20-yard game on a fake punt that kept a scoring drive alive. Estime ran for 95 yards, Diggs added 88 more and a TD reception, and Buchner pitched in with 61 yards and two TDs. He hit Diggs for a 75-yard score but also Lenzy for 44 yards, and a wide-open Mitchell Evans for a TD. The Irish ended up No. 18 after the bowls were played.

Was the season's cup half full or half empty? Freeman's nine wins put him in good coaching company in the school's history. One loss was by five points and another by two, both winnable games. They were ahead of Ohio State until the fourth quarter. They lost to a Heisman winner who escaped their clutches a few too many times. The glass is at least half full.

The portal giveth and the portal taketh away. The biggest news after the bowl game season came via the transfer portal. ND's Drew Pyne opted to transfer to Arizona State. Wake Forest QB Sam Hartman, on the other hand, transferred to ND. He brings with him 12,967 yards passing, good for 110 TDs against 44 interceptions. In the 2021 and 2022 seasons, Hartman threw 77 TD passes. He was one of five portal transfers headed to ND, including defenders and a wide receiver.

Prophecies are notoriously fickle exercises. Predicting a miracle almost certainly dooms the miracle. Marcus Freeman has shown that he can be a successful college head coach. He is now part of Notre Dame history, which can be exhilarating but also terribly burdensome. The last national championship for the Irish was in 1988 under Lou Holtz. Freeman has stated that a national championship is his goal for Notre Dame. This could be an infectious motivating factor for the team—or it could become an elusive chimera. It would seem, however, that Freeman is building a team that has all the necessary components to challenge for a national title.

And he has the luck of the Irish!

APPENDIX

SELECTED TEAM RECORDS (Current through 2022)

PUNT RETURN YARDS:

Frank Carideo   947   1928–30

STARTING QB WINNING PERCENTAGE:

Johnny Lujack   .932 (20–1–1)   1943, 1946–47

INTERCEPTIONS:

Luther Bradley   17   1973, 1975–77

TACKLES FOR LOSS:

Ross Browner   77   1973, 1975–77

LINEBACKER TACKLES:

Bob Crable   521   1978–81

PUNT RETURNS:

Dave Duerson   103 (869 yards)   1979–82

RUSHING TOUCHDOWNS:

Allen Pinkett   49   1982–85

POINTS SCORED:

Justin Yoon   367   2015–18
(59 FGs; 190 PATs)

RUSHING YARDS:

Autry Denson   4,318   1995–98

ALL-PURPOSE YARDS:

Julius Jones   5,462   1999–2003
(3,108 rushing; 250 receiving; 426 punt returns; 1,678 kickoff returns)

PASS COMPLETIONS:

Brady Quinn   929   2003–06

PASSING YARDAGE:

Brady Quinn   11,762   2003–06

TOUCHDOWN PASSES:

Brady Quinn   95   2003–2006

TOTAL OFFENSE YARDS:

Brady Quinn   11,944   2003–06

TD POINTS RESPONSIBLE FOR:

Brady Quinn   606   2003–06
(6 rushing, 95 passing)

RECEPTIONS:

Michael Floyd   271   2008–11

RECEIVING YARDS:

Michael Floyd   3,686   2008–11

TOUCHDOWN RECEPTIONS:

Michael Floyd   37   2008–11

FIELD GOALS MADE:

Justin Yoon   59   2015–18

KICKOFF RETURN YARDS:

George Atkinson III   2,136 yards   2011–13

Brady Quinn, Notre Dame's all-time leader in passing yardage, TDs, and points responsible for. *AP Photo/Joe Raymond*

About the Author

Michael R. Steele is a distinguished university professor, emeritus, at Pacific University in Forest Grove, Oregon. He has taught there since 1975 and still serves as an adjunct faculty member. The author of *The Notre Dame Football Encyclopedia*, Steele is a 1967 graduate of Notre Dame and resides in Forest Grove, Oregon.